THE SPIRIT VS. THE SOULS

AFRICAN AMERICAN INTELLECTUAL HERITAGE SERIES

Paul Spickard and Patrick Miller
Series Editors

THE *SPIRIT*
VS. THE *SOULS*

**MAX WEBER, W.E.B. DU BOIS,
AND THE POLITICS OF SCHOLARSHIP**

CHRISTOPHER A. McAULEY

University of Notre Dame Press
Notre Dame, Indiana

University of Notre Dame Press
Notre Dame, Indiana 46556
undpress.nd.edu

Copyright © 2019 by the University of Notre Dame

All Rights Reserved

Published in the United States of America

Library of Congress Control Number: 2019021670

ISBN: 978-0-268-10601-0 (Hardback)
ISBN: 978-0-268-10604-1 (WebPDF)
ISBN: 978-0-268-10603-4 (Epub)

∞ *This book is printed on acid-free paper.*

CONTENTS

ACKNOWLEDGMENTS

Having been at this project for so long, I naturally have many people to thank for having been sounding boards, readers, critics, and supporters. Unfortunately, I am bound to forget some of them on the list below and to them I offer my sincerest apologies and assurances that their absence is not meant as a slight in any way. Those whom I have not forgotten are Bipan Ahdi, Sheila Aminmadani, Ingrid Banks, Paul Barba, Stephanie Batiste, Patrick Bellegarde-Smith, Jill Briggs, Manolo Callahan, Michael P. Carter, Nahum Chandler, Rodney Coates, Reg Daniel, Douglass Daniels, Micaela Diaz-Sanchez, Teresa Figueroa, Greg Feitt, John Foran, Aramintha Grant, Cecilia Green, Charles Hale, Tiffany Hale, Mary Hancock, Mark Jay, Gaye Johnson, Terence Keel, Jasmine Kelekay, Savvoula Kolonia, George Lipsitz, Charles H. Long, Ilana Luna, Margaret Matson, Pamela S. McAuley, Rani McLean, Cecilia Mendez-Gastelumendi, Claudine Michel, Katherine Morales, Nicolas Pascal, Natalie Pierre, Mathias Rosenthal, Holly Roose, Elisabeth Schaefer-Wunsche, Paul Spickard, Jeffrey Stewart, Roberto Strongman, Christina Syriani, Kerry Tomlinson, Vilna Bashi Treitler, Carolina Valle, Howard Winant, and Jasmine Yarish.

Slick, this one is dedicated to you, as promised. Chloe has claims on the next one.

Introduction

In a letter to W. E. B. Du Bois dated 30 March 1905, Max Weber praised his American counterpart for his "splendid work," *The Souls of Black Folk*,[1] and insisted that it "ought *to be translated in German*."[2] Weber presumably read the work after having met Du Bois for a "few minutes" at the 1904 St. Louis World's Fair where the German scholar presented a paper on the origins and effects of capitalist agriculture in the eastern and western regions of Germany.[3] It is also likely that in the course of their conversation in St. Louis Du Bois reminded Weber that their paths had already crossed in the early 1890s at the University of Berlin and in the meetings of the Verein für Sozialpolitik (Association of Social Policy) of which they were both members.[4] At the time Weber was lecturing on Roman, German, and commercial law, and Du Bois was a doctoral student in economics. This initial exchange led to Weber's solicitation from Du Bois of an "investigation about the relations between the (so-called) 'race problem' and the (so-called) 'class problem'" in the United States, about which, Weber continued in his letter, "it is impossible to have any conversation with white people of the South without feeling the connection" between the two.[5] Du Bois obliged, and the article, "Die Neger Frage in den Vereinigten Staaten," appeared in the journal that Weber coedited with Werner Sombart, *Archiv für Sozialwissenschaft und Sozialpolitik*, in 1906.[6] Moreover, in the five letters that Weber sent to Du Bois between November 1904 and May 1905,[7] he recorded having found a German publisher (Siebeck) for *The Souls of Black Folk*;[8] his willingness to write an introduction to the translation,[9] his intention to write a "short review of the recent publications about the race problem in America" for which he asked Du Bois for recommendations,[10]

1

and, most striking, his remark that he, too, was "absolutely convinced that the 'colour-line' problem will be the paramount problem of the time to come, here and everywhere in the world."[11] Five years later, Weber lauded Du Bois in the highest terms in an exchange with Dr. Alfred Ploetz on the theme of race and its influence on the social evolution of past and current societies: "I wish to state that the most important socio-logical scholar anywhere in the Southern States in America, with whom no scholar can compare, is a Negro—Burckhardt [*sic*] Du Bois."[12] In short, by all indications, theirs should have been a fruitful scholarly friendship, and one that could have been rich in insights on the events leading up to and immediately after World War I. Such, however, was not the case. After the last letter of their exchange in 1905, their commu-nication abruptly ended. Among a number of goals, I seek in this work to offer some reasons as to why Du Bois and Weber never resumed con-tact after that year.

However, my primary objective in *The Spirit vs. the Souls* is to present a comparative analysis of the scholarly concerns and political positions of Max Weber and W. E. B. Du Bois. I have chosen to compare these two scholars and public intellectuals mainly for two reasons: they present two contrasting perspectives on the rise of European and European American economic development; and as a result of these differences, they took vastly different political positions on both domestic and inter-national issues. With regard to the first theme, whereas Weber mini-mized the role of unfree (i.e., forced, non-wage-earning) black labor in the history and maintenance of Western capitalism, Du Bois saw it as fundamental. And in the second instance, whereas Du Bois was a vo-ciferous opponent of European imperialism and of all other expressions of racial supremacy, Weber was a staunch advocate of German overseas imperialism.

These differences in perspective on the origins and labor regimes of capitalism, and on how to remedy or profit from them, pivoted as much on methodology as conceptualization. While Weber drew his conclu-sions about modern capitalism from comparisons of its ideological and material components primarily with those of the ancient Mediterranean, medieval Europe, and India and China, Du Bois largely drew his, first, from surveys of ancient and medieval Africa and, second, from those of Europe's colonization of the Americas, beginning in the sixteenth cen-

tury, and subsequently other parts of the world, and its sustained invest-
ment in the human trade of Africans until the nineteenth century. These
were certainly not hard and fast lines of social inquiry, for Du Bois was
as comfortable writing about ancient and medieval Europe as Weber was
about American politics in the early twentieth century. Still, their general differences in geographic and demographic concentrations reflected
significant differences regarding, among other matters, the place of
unfree labor in modern capitalism and of religious dictates in determin-
ing which labor regimes would be employed in Europe's overseas colonies. As Du Bois chronicled in a number of works, for the Africans,
Amerindians, and Asians who were incorporated into European empires
(both formal and "informal"), wage-earning labor was not the typical
form of work that they were forced or "encouraged" to perform, contrary
to Weber's (and not his alone) assertion that wage labor was one of the
hallmarks of modern capitalism.[13] Yet, and this is the problem, Weber did
not have non-European workers in mind when he was conceptualizing
the components of modern capitalism.

My sense is that Weber was well aware of the complications that the
inclusion of Europe's overseas colonies would present to his arguments
linking specific religious doctrines to equally specific economic activities
and capitalism to wage labor. This would explain why Weber was at
pains to avoid or to minimize any references to European colonialism in
his religious studies or in his encyclopedic *Economy and Society*.[14] For
example, he asserts in *The Protestant Ethic and the Spirit of Capitalism*
that "colonial booty capitalism" was precisely the kind of economic enterprise that Protestants generally and Puritans in particular morally
shunned and suggests that this was one of the reasons, if not *the* reason,
that the "capitalistic order" was more advanced in New England than in
other British North American colonies. "It is further undoubted," Weber
wrote, "that capitalism remained far less developed in some of the neigh-
boring colonies, the later Southern States of the United States of
America, in spite of the fact that these latter were founded by large capitalists for business motives, while the New England colonies were
founded by preachers and seminary graduates with the help of small
bourgeois craftsmen and yeomen, for religious reasons. In this case the
causal relation is certainly the reverse of that suggested by the materialistic standpoint."[15]

Not exactly, if we both correct and add some of the material or economic details that Weber left out of his synopsis of colonial North American history. What his account fails to mention is that some of the pious men in New England were not content with farming, crafts, or shop keeping, but also had their sights set on "business motives." And one of the few arenas in which they could satisfy their desire for profit was in the carrying trade between their region and the southern colonies and the British Caribbean. Common to both trade networks was New England's supply of slaves, among other commodities, to these southern ports in exchange for tobacco, sugar, and sugar by-products. Thus if capitalism was more developed in New England than in other North American colonies, it was in no small measure thanks to the region's involvement in booty capitalism, contrary to what Weber implies about the particular avenues of Puritan economic enterprise. It was only by ignoring New England's economic links to the large-scale slave societies on the mainland and in the Caribbean that Weber could argue that Puritans uniformly engaged in upstanding commerce.[16]

If Du Bois and Weber had maintained contact after the former's years at the University of Berlin, Du Bois might have convinced Weber to qualify his original assertion about Puritan economic pursuits. In his doctoral dissertation, "The Suppression of the African Slave Trade to the United States of America, 1638–1870," completed just a few years before the publication of the first part of *The Protestant Ethic and the Spirit of Capitalism* and published in 1896, Du Bois had noted how the Puritans of Massachusetts initially opposed "manstealing," except in the cases of warfare, self-pawnship, or purchase by foreign suppliers, only to indulge in it as the prospect grew of the sizable profits that could be made from it: "The temptation of trade slowly forced the colony from this high moral ground. New England ships were early found in the West Indian slave trade, and the more the carrying trade developed, the more did the profits of this branch of it attract Puritan captains. By the beginning of the eighteenth century the slave trade was openly recognized as legitimate commerce."[17]

With the historical facts demonstrating that Puritans became slavers just like other Europeans, irrespective of faith, Du Bois would have been forced to object to what Weber was suggesting about Puritan economic activity on at least three grounds: (1) to have any validity, it requires the jettisoning of the social contexts in which Puritans and other Protestants did not act in ways that conformed to their own tenets and Weber's theory; (2) it attempts to make into a general pattern these selected contexts, thereby obscuring the fact that they were selected; and (3) it privileges wage over unfree labor at a time when the number of unfree workers engaged in commercial agriculture and mining was many times greater than the number of wage earners engaged in commodity production.[18] Taken together, Du Bois would probably have concluded that Weber's theory of Protestant economic action applied primarily to certain intra-European relationships, not to those between Protestants and Africans, Amerindians, and Asians.

I suspect that Du Bois would have agreed with the line of reasoning that I attribute to him if for no other reason than the fact that the collective black experience demanded it. However much Du Bois may have early subscribed to romantic pairings of specific populations with specific modes of thought and conduct as he expressed them in, for example, his address, "The Conservation of Races," he knew that the very achievements for which he praised certain European peoples did not include their treatment of people of African descent either at home or abroad. If the "English nation stood for constitutional liberty and commercial freedom; the German nation for science and philosophy; [and] the Romance nations stood for literature and art,"[19] these were not the institutions and practices that they exported to the colonies or extended to colonized peoples. The people who counted as people in all European colonial territories and in the settler republics that emerged from them, such as the United States, were legally free white men (and, to a lesser extent, people of European descent generally), certainly not the bulk of the indigenous or imported unfree populations. Unlike Weber, Du Bois could not simply disregard these populations because they challenged a questionable theory but instead proposed a theory of capitalism with imperialism, unfree labor, and racism as its mainsprings.

From this perspective, I believe that Du Bois would have ultimately agreed with Kieran Allen that Weber was a "sociologist of empire," not only for his advocacy of German imperialism, but for his silence on the subject in his discussions of the development of capitalism in Europe and in his studies of India and China. Remarking on the content of Weber's *Religion of India*, Allen notes that the "most glaring omission from a book which discusses the lack of capitalist development is the impact of colonialism. Nowhere does Weber examine how the colonization of India by Britain might have retarded India's development."[20] Rather than reflect scholarly neutrality on the subject, let alone objectivity, Du Bois would have read Weber's skirting of the imperial dimensions of capitalism and, by extension, the role of unfree labor in its inception and maintenance as scholarly bias pure and simple. On these grounds, Du Bois would have had no choice but to interpret *The Protestant Ethic and the Spirit of Capitalism*, as well as its companion studies, *The Religion of China* and *The Religion of India*, as primarily explorations in ideal types and only marginally as works of historical sociology.

For these reasons and a number of others that I discuss in the pages that follow, I take issue with those scholars who suggest that the exchange between Weber and Du Bois is an indication that they agreed on many of the issues of the day, both academic and political, which presumably only distance and their respective scholarly and public commitments foreshortened. Foremost among these is Aldon Morris, who emphatically makes this case in his pathbreaking *The Scholar Denied: W. E. B. Du Bois and the Birth of Modern Sociology*.[21] While I am certainly inclined to agree with him that Du Bois probably gave Weber more food for thought on social stratification than vice versa, contrary to the direction in which their exchange of ideas is typically presented, I do not take Du Bois's influence on Weber to consider the cultural rather than biological bases of race membership to mean that Weber became any less Eurocentric or racist as a result. As we will have occasion to review in chapter 3, many of Weber's characterizations of the Chinese were as patently baseless and racist as his racial-cultural descriptions of Poles, as was his insistence, despite Du Bois's provision of evidence to the contrary in "Die Neger Frage in den Vereinigten Staten," that black people could not operate machinery because they suffered from some vague neurotic condition.[22] I cannot see how Du Bois could have taken these slights, both intellectual and political, as indicative of his inclusion in Weber's "fraternity of sociologists." With this sort of hazing, Du Bois would have declined pledging.

I have similar misgivings about Lawrence Scaff's presentation of the Weber–Du Bois relationship in his justly acclaimed *Max Weber in America*. Certainly, as Scaff underscores, thanks to the year and a half that Du Bois spent at the University of Berlin, he and Weber studied with many of the same luminaries, shared "connected interests in comparative agrarian economies, the dynamics of industrialization and urbanization, exacting methods of social research, and the prospects for structural reform,"[23] and were both members of the policy-oriented think tank, the Verein für Sozialpolitik. However, their common scholarly interests and methodological approaches should not blind us to the significant differences in intellectual perspectives and political stances between them. Foremost among these were their respective social standpoints and target audiences. Except perhaps in those cases in which he was commissioned to undertake a study, the subjects and audience of Du Bois's writings were primarily black Americans, a racial minority less than two generations removed from slavery at the turn of the twentieth century and whose fitness to be citizens was questioned by the vast majority of white Americans as a matter of course. By contrast, Weber wrote from the vantage point of a socioeconomically and culturally secure German Protestant, who felt free to write on an impressive range of subjects for an audience of fellow German academics from a similar social milieu.

A related concern is that some have been or will be tempted to "use" the Du Bois–Weber exchange to suggest that Weber was far less Eurocentric or racist than others have charged. This temptation is understandable if one subscribes to the view that how a person treats another individual from a different population is a reliable indication of how that first person views the group with which the second person identifies or is identified. However, this assumption is frequently challenged by those instances in which individuals, like our first person, embrace individuals like our second one, less as members of distinct populations and more as exceptional ones who have assimilated their cultural norms. I suspect that Weber had feelings of this sort toward Du Bois in particular and about black people generally: Du Bois was an impressively credentialed Germanophile whose mixed ancestry made him that much more remarkable. From this vantage point, as noteworthy or even extraordinary as were Weber's solicitation and publication of Du Bois's article on black America in his journal, his letter exchange with Du Bois, and his praise of Du Bois as a scholar, these gestures do not outweigh his fundamental biases against, in this instance, black people. Furthermore, I cannot imagine that these biases did not affect his scholarly treatment of themes in which black people and other populations of color figured prominently in the modern era.

Another reason that I take issue with uncritical presentations of the Weber–Du Bois dialogue is what they consciously or unconsciously suggest about the reasons for its ending—that Du Bois bears the greater responsibility for its finality as he was the one whose increasing political and intellectual radicalization led him to leave the academy some four years after their last correspondence. While I largely believe that there is some truth to this interpretation the evidence for which I present in the second and third chapters of this study, I take issue with what this line of reasoning assumes about the relationship between public and "pure" intellectuals, "detached" and engaged scholarship, and scholarship and "propaganda," and its assumption that the termination of the Du Bois–Weber exchange was the result of largely later political differences rather than of scholarly ones at the time. Instead, I take the counterposition that an examination of Weber's and Du Bois's scholarship, no less than their political orientations at the time of their reconnection, reveals significant differences of which, I maintain, they were both aware, despite the tone and even content of their letters. This is not to deny that Du Bois became more antiracist and anticapitalist in the years immediately following their last exchange, a stance that would have put him increasingly at odds with Weber's latent and manifest Eurocentric and racist assumptions, but it is to say that the roots of their future parting of the ways were present while they were in contact. From this perspective, the Russian Revolution of 1905 and the Niagara movement to which Weber and Du Bois, respectively, turned their attention, provided them with convenient excuses to end their dialogue without addressing their disagreements.

In the first chapter I explore these differences in an unorthodox way, by imagining how Du Bois and Weber "honestly" read the work(s) of the other with which they were or would have been familiar, *The Souls of Black Folk* and *The Protestant Ethic and the Spirit of Capitalism*. The difficulty of this approach is that I take it without the help of either scholar's notes or detailed reviews of the other's writings, for as far as we know they do not exist. In fact, we have no proof that Du Bois ever read Weber's most popular work, although it is hard to imagine that Weber would not have sent Du Bois some past and present issues of the *Archiv für Sozialwissenschaft and Sozialpolitik*, in which the original version of *The Protestant Ethic and the Spirit of Capitalism* appeared in 1904 and 1905, along with the issue in which his article appeared on the socioeconomic conditions of black Americans in 1906.[24] Moreover, even if Du Bois had not read Weber's most popular work, he was certainly familiar with some adulterated version of the argument. Therefore, despite the evidentiary limits of the exercise, I still contend that we know enough about these two men to advance what were or would have been their likely reactions to the content of the other's work. My interpretation suggests that there was as much contention as admiration in their reciprocal readings.

In the second chapter I explore the influence of the German historical school on Du Bois's and Weber's early sociological work and compare their agrarian studies as Weber presented his at the 1904 Congress of Arts and Sciences, where he and Du Bois reconnected, and as Du Bois presented his in "Die Neger Frage in den Vereinigten Staaten." In addition to addressing the different policy measures that each proposed, I discuss the reasons that Du Bois pioneered participant observation fieldwork in the course of his agricultural studies, no less than in his groundbreaking urban study, *The Philadelphia Negro*. I also address here the intellectual challenges both scholars faced as pioneers in sociology in an age when nationalism, racism, imperialism, and romanticism were rampant.

In the third chapter I trace Weber's and Du Bois's perspectives on Western economic development. Here I underscore, among other matters, the means by which Weber sought to minimize the returns from unfree labor and imperialism in what we may call Protestant capitalism and to attribute to Jews, Chinese, Indians, and other religious or national populations, engagement in "adventurer's" or other forms of "political capitalism," which he deemed irrational. I show that Du Bois, in contrast, never tired of reiterating the contributions that unfree black labor made to the development of Western capitalism. In short, whereas Du Bois suggested the multiplier effects of and linkages between imperialism and slavery and key sectors of western and central European economies, Weber declared them inconsequential, except to those individuals or firms who owned specific mines or plantations.

I devote the fourth chapter to a discussion of Weber's and Du Bois's divergent political views and positions. In the main, I chronicle here the unforeseen and unconscious consequences of Weber's brand of national-ism that called for Germany's overseas expansion for the economic and political gains that could be derived from it. As for Du Bois, I trace his opposing black/pan-African nationalism and socialism to his applica-tion of a Marxist-inspired analysis of western European society in the years before World War I, which he put forward in his remarkable essay, "The African Roots of War."[25] To illustrate their political differences, I compare the two scholars' writings on Russia, a country about which both wrote extensively, albeit in two different eras and from markedly different perspectives.

In the fifth and final chapter, I explore how the most influential Du Bois and Weber scholars have handled and interpreted their positions on capitalism, social science methodology, and politics. Thus far I have found that both men have been protected by their admirers—Weber from criticism of his Eurocentrism, Du Bois from the charge of elitism—and slighted or dismissed by their detractors—Weber for the reason just named, Du Bois for having engaged in more advocacy or propaganda than "objective" research. I argue here that what is needed is a more bal-anced approach to both scholars: one that recognizes their strengths and weaknesses without romanticization or demonization and that does not seek to separate artificially their political positions and scholarship.

CHAPTER ONE

The Free vs. the Bound

In light of their fruitful meeting in St. Louis in 1904, how do we explain the short duration of Du Bois and Weber's contact thereafter? One easy answer is that they had other immediate preoccupations: for Du Bois, it was political activity in the Niagara movement, a mobilization that aimed as much to contest North American racism as Booker T. Washington's response to it; for Weber, it was interest in the Russian Revolution of 1905, for which he learned Russian in just three months. These are possible and plausible explanations of the brevity of their contact, but I do not think that they were the primary reasons. Rather, I believe that its roots can be traced to the works that both scholars produced at the time of the break and with which the other was familiar, either directly or indirectly.[1] In Du Bois's case, this was obviously *The Souls of Black Folk* and, to a lesser degree, his article "Die Negerfrage in den Vereinigten Staaten" (The Black Question in the United States); and in Weber's, the two essays that he published in the *Archiv für Sozialwissenschaft und Sozialpolitik* in 1904 and 1905 (which he reworked in early 1920) that constitute *The Protestant Ethic and the Spirit of Capitalism*. Although, as I stated in the introduction, I cannot "prove" my argument by means of conventional evidence, what I propose as a substitute is to read these works as I imagine each man would have read the other's. Despite the unavoidably hypothetical nature of this exercise, I believe it is one that sheds light on why their amiable contact was so short-lived.

THE TRIALS OF THE SOULS

If we assume that what most appealed to Weber about *The Souls of Black Folk* were those elements of it that he explored in his own work, it is not difficult to determine what they are. For one, it displays an intellectual versatility—drawing as much on history and sociology as on psychology and politics—that was in line with Weber's own scholarly predilections. In the anthology, Du Bois sought to chronicle and analyze the "social revolution" that was the emancipation of enslaved black Americans and the response of white American society to black "freedom" in the four decades after the Civil War. In more general terms, Du Bois mapped the continuities and changes in social interaction between these two racial groups in this period by paying particular attention to the specific policies and practices that aimed to facilitate or hinder the recognition of blacks as free people. In this endeavor Weber undoubtedly recognized Du Bois's adoption of what the former would later label the *verstehen* approach to social phenomena. By *verstehen*, or sympathetic understanding, Weber meant the need for the scholar to attempt to comprehend the world such as it was or is lived by the population in question by assuming that their attitudes and actions made or make sense to them, without judgment. Weber, like many other readers of *The Souls of Black Folk*, was probably unaware of Du Bois's pioneering, *verstehen*-inspired sociological studies of the rural South and *The Philadelphia Negro*, in which he combined the study of primary and secondary documents, the distribution and collection of questionnaires and testimonies, and residence among and daily interaction with the black southerners whose lives he was investigating. Still, even if Weber was oblivious to the methodological innovations that Du Bois employed in these studies that preceded and provided the material for *The Souls of Black Folk*, we can well imagine that even someone like Weber who was knowledgeable about so much of the world both past and present learned a few things about human relations and political economy in Du Bois's pages. Take, for example, the following passage on the economic plight of black sharecroppers in Dougherty County, Georgia.

> The underlying causes of this situation are complicated but discernible. And one of the chief, outside the carelessness of the nation in letting the slave start with nothing, is the widespread opinion among the merchants and employers of the Black Belt that only by the slavery of debt can the Negro be kept at work. Without doubt, some pressure was necessary at the beginning of the free-labor system to keep the listless and lazy at work; and even to-day the mass of the Negro laborers need stricter guardianship than most Northern laborers. Behind this honest and widespread opinion dishonesty and cheating of the ignorant laborers have a good chance to take refuge. And to all this must be added the obvious fact that a slave ancestry and a system of unrequited toil has not improved the efficiency or temper of the mass of black laborers. Nor is this peculiar to Sambo; it has in history been just as true of John and Hans, of Jacques and Pat, of all ground-down peasantries. Such is the situation of the mass of the Negroes in the Black Belt to-day; and they are thinking about it.[2]

A number of the components of this passage would have been familiar to Weber. First is the reference to the coercive measures that capitalists the world over have had to employ in order to transform peasants or former slaves into reliable wage workers. Weber himself would address this theme in a number of places, including *The Protestant Ethic and the Spirit of Capitalism*. Second is Du Bois's related objective to demonstrate the general or universal principles at work in southern social phenomena independent of the racial membership of the actor(s) in question. Primary among these is that unrewarded and underrewarded labor of any kind does not make for inspired workers. And third is Du Bois's recognition of the fact that an "objective" scholarly or even lay understanding of social relationships requires the adoption of the vantage points of the different parties whose interaction is under scrutiny. In this instance, Du Bois voiced simultaneously the plaints of capital and labor so as to present a balanced picture of the post–Civil War South. Here was impartiality and identification with the underdog.

Weber undoubtedly found Du Bois's fair-mindedness and his passion for social justice without bias in presentation not only praiseworthy but also in conformity with his own prescription of "value-neutral" scholarship. On perhaps no other methodological point did Weber insist as much as he did on this one. In his view, the place for partisan pronouncements is at political rallies and churches, in editorials and clubs, not in lecture halls or academic publications.[3] Weber must have been struck, then, by Du Bois's implicit adherence to this prescription in his evenhanded treatment of even the people and institutions he held dear in *The Souls of Black Folk*. One of these was the Freedmen's Bureau, about whose shortcomings Du Bois had this to say:

> The most perplexing and least successful part of the Bureau's work lay in the exercise of its judicial functions. The regular Bureau court consisted of one representative of the employer, one of the Negro, and one of the Bureau. If the Bureau could have maintained a perfectly judicial attitude, this arrangement would have been ideal, and must in time have gained confidence; but the nature of its other activities and the character of its *personnel* prejudiced the Bureau in favor of the black litigants, and led without doubt to much injustice and annoyance. . . . Bureau courts tended to become centres simply for punishing whites, while the regular civil courts tended to become solely institutions for perpetuating the slavery of blacks. Almost every law and method ingenuity could devise was employed by the legislatures to reduce the Negroes to serfdom,—to make them the slaves of the State, if not of individual owners; while the Bureau officials too often were found striving to put the "bottom rail on top," and give the freedmen a power and independence which they could not yet use. (30)

There may not be a better example of Du Bois's scholarly impartiality in *The Souls of Black Folk*. Here he demonstrates his ability to be as critical of an institution that he otherwise commended as he is willing to defend the interests of those who, some would contend, had forfeited their rights to cry injustice. As Weber would well have understood, it would have been all too easy for Du Bois to justify the Freedmen's Bureau courts' treatment of former Confederates and slaveholders as restitution for past crimes. But this type of reasoning was contrary to Du Bois's conviction that injustice cannot be rectified through vengeance. If anything, acts of vengeance only provoke counterresponses that serve to exacerbate, not transform, already volatile social relations. More to the point, vengeance would not move members of either racial group to rid themselves of the stultifying personality traits cultivated in the slave regime: delusions of racial superiority in one, discouragement of ambition in the other. Throughout *The Souls of Black Folk* Du Bois never tires of exhorting both racial camps to make changes, as he does here:

> It is not enough for the Negroes to declare that color prejudice is the sole cause of their social condition, nor for the white South to reply that their social condition is the main cause of prejudice. They both act as reciprocal cause and effect, and a change in neither alone will bring the desired effect. Both must change, or neither can improve to any great extent. (136)

There were dangers, however, to such a presentation of the facts, the dangers of which Weber was well aware, as we know from his political writings. Above all, it minimized the differences in power, in this instance, between blacks and whites in Jim Crow America. In equalizing the responsibility for the struggles of black Americans, Du Bois rendered equal, in effect, their ability to change their collective lot and the desire of their white counterparts to no longer discriminate against them. However, in light of the fact that black Americans had the law only partially on their side but certainly not law enforcement, to speak of equal responsibility for the relatively poorer performance of blacks was to deny the discrepancies in power between themselves and white Americans. Or it was to speak like a classic liberal in an illiberal society where two of liberalism's central tenets—equality before the law and equality of opportunity—were not guaranteed. For by the logic he expressed in this passage, Du Bois revealed his expectation of his fellow black Americans to collectively will themselves to socioeconomic success despite the political and economic constraints of Jim Crow America. In light of his own emphasis on power relations between social actors, we can imagine Weber musing that Du Bois had perhaps erred too much on the side of the antiblack South. Yet as a liberal (in the nineteenth-century meaning of the term), we can also imagine Weber's agreement with Du Bois on the primacy of individual actions and obligations, however extraordinary the particular sociopolitical circumstances.

Taken to its logical conclusion, nevertheless, the celebration of the individual, particularly by gifted men, lends itself to the cultivation of elitism, in many respects the opposite of liberalism. Common to both Weber and Du Bois was the belief that only a select few can lead the masses to new levels of consciousness and courses of action. To these "elect" Du Bois would give the name "Talented Tenth," whereas Weber, believing them to be even smaller in number, called them charismatic or prophetic leaders. That Weber and Du Bois included themselves in this select group we have ample reason to suspect. For such reasons, Weber could have only nodded in approval with Du Bois's criticisms of the colleges and universities founded for black people in the aftermath of the Civil War.

> But these builders did make a mistake in . . . lowering the standard of knowing, until they had scattered haphazard through the South some dozen poorly equipped high schools and miscalled them universities. They forgot, too, just as their successors are forgetting, the rule of inequality:—that of the million black youth, some were fitted to know and some to dig; that some had talent and capacity of university men, and some the talent and capacity of blacksmiths; and that true training meant neither that all should be college men nor all artisans, but that the one should be made a missionary of culture to an untaught people, and the other a free workman among serfs. And to seek to make the blacksmith a scholar is almost as silly as the more modern scheme of making the scholar a blacksmith; almost, but not quite. (65)

A more forthright expression of liberal elitism one is hard pressed to find in *The Souls of Black Folk*, and Du Bois provides many examples from which to choose. Throughout the work Du Bois laments the "ig-

norance" (of "life itself," he claims at one point) of former slaves and
their descendants.

On this point, we have evidence that Weber shared Du Bois's opinions but with a pointed racial edge. During the southern portion of his
nearly three-month sojourn in the United States in 1904, Weber wrote
a letter home in which he contrasted the, we assume, fairer-skinned and
better-dressed students of Tuskegee Institute to the "semi-apes one en-
counters on the plantations and in the Negro huts of the 'Cotton Belt.'"[4]
On some matters, Weber could be an unremarkably ordinary man of his
time, contrary to what some of his boosters would have us believe. However, in fairness to him we should recognize that some of Du Bois's remarks would only have fueled, not tempered, Weber's characterization of
poor, rural blacks. Later in this study I address the degree to which beliefs such as these shaped Weber's treatment of matters bearing directly
or indirectly on people of African descent in the modern world.

Finally, I cannot end this hypothetical Weberian reading of *The
Souls of Black Folk* without mentioning Du Bois's brief portrait of the religion of black America. In fact, apart from addressing one of Weber's
primary intellectual pursuits, Du Bois, like his German counterpart, recognized religion's integral relationship to virtually all other social and
psychological phenomena. Weber probably also recognized in Du Bois's
treatment of black American religion one of his own strengths: the
ability to condense complex historical developments into manageable
and sensible reconstructions.

First, there is Du Bois's description of the anthropological and sociohistorical transformation of the African's religious experience through
the processes of captivity and enslavement. "His religion," Du Bois
begins, "was nature-worship, with profound belief in invisible surrounding influences, good and bad, and his worship was through incantation
and sacrifice. The first rude change in this life was the slave ship and the
West Indian sugar-fields. The plantation organization replaced the clan
and the tribe, and the white master replaced the chief with far greater
and more despotic powers" (141). Yet, despite the "terrific social revolution" that this wrenching experience necessarily was,

> some traces were retained of the former group life, and the chief
> remaining institution was the Chief or Medicine-man. He early

appeared on the plantation and found his function as the healer of the sick, the interpreter of the Unknown, the comforter of the sorrowing, the supernatural avenger of wrong, and the one who rudely but picturesquely expressed the longing, disappointment, and resentment of a stolen and oppressed people. Thus . . . within the narrow limits allowed by the slave system, rose the Negro preacher, and under him the first Afro-American institution, the Negro church. (141–42)

With the passage of a few generations, the spiritual eclecticism of the enslaved themselves, combined with the deliberate actions taken by masters and missionaries, facilitated Christianity's eventual assimilation of African-derived beliefs and practices, particularly in its Baptist form.

In this synopsis of the development of black American religion, Du Bois illustrated the dynamic nature of spiritual belief. In agreement with Weber, he recognized that religious outlook, like other social phenomena, not only has its own independent power strong enough to shape social action, but is itself subject to change through the workings of variables such as time, context, and intention. In another passage, Du Bois took this point a step further and suggested that the social regimes under which black Americans live shape their religious orientations and, in turn, their different political stances.

Feeling that his rights and dearest ideals are being trampled upon, that the public conscience is ever more deaf to his righteous appeal, and that all the reactionary forces of prejudice, greed, and revenge are daily gaining new strength and fresh allies, the Negro faces no enviable dilemma. Conscious of his impotence, and pessimistic, he often becomes bitter and vindictive; and his religion, instead of worship, is a complaint and a curse, a wail rather than a hope, a sneer rather than a faith. On the other hand, another type of mind, shrewder and keener and more tortuous too, sees in the very strength of the anti-Negro movement its patent weaknesses, and with Jesuitic casuistry is deterred by no ethical considerations in the endeavor to turn this weakness to the black man's strength. Thus we have two great and hardly reconcilable strivings; the danger of the one lies in anarchy, that of the other in hypocrisy. The one type of Negro stands almost

ready to curse God and die, and the other is too often found a trai-
tor to right and a coward before force. (146–47)

Du Bois goes on to add that the first personality type is representative of
the northern black, who "tend[s] toward radicalism," whereas the second
is typical of her southern counterpart, who tends toward "hypocritical
compromise" (147)

In this socioreligious explanation of the roots of the ideological
divide that separated northern and southern blacks, Du Bois hardly dis-
guises who he thought were the archetypal figures of both categories:
himself or William Monroe Trotter and Booker T. Washington. Even if
these references were initially lost on Weber, he would certainly have
applauded Du Bois's demonstration of the interplay of social status, religion, and psychology in the lives of black Americans.

Yet, as much as Weber found *The Souls of Black Folk* worthy of praise
and even a German translation, he must have found certain aspects of it
questionable, if not displeasing. From what we know of his personality,
few intellects earned his unqualified praise. In light of his scholarly explorations before, during, and after the time when he presumably read
Du Bois's work, Weber probably found objectionable three of the black
American scholar's contentions: his claim that the "problem of the twentieth century is the problem of the color line" (see below), despite Weber's
professed agreement with Du Bois's contention; his notion of double
consciousness and the veil; and his list of specifically black contributions
to American society.

In the opening of the second chapter of *The Souls of Black Folk*, titled
"Of the Dawn of Freedom," Du Bois provided a complete explanation of
what he meant by his now-famous slogan: "The problem of the twentieth century is the problem of the color line,—the relation of the darker
to the lighter races of men in Asia and Africa, in America and the is-
lands of the sea" (16). However, it should be fairly obvious that Du Bois
did not intend to limit his remark to the twentieth century; after all, that
century had only just begun when the work was published. Rather, his
prediction was based on events and processes that began in the early
sixteenth century, namely, the European colonization of the Americas
and the institutionalization of racial enslavement. From other references
in the work, it is also clear that Du Bois had in mind a number of

specifically mid- to late nineteenth-century developments: the legacy of slavery in the emancipation era, Otto von Bismarck's coordination of the "scramble for Africa" at the Berlin Conference of 1884, and the formal entry of the United States into overseas imperialism in the Spanish-American War. With great but perhaps not extraordinary foresight, Du Bois reasoned that it would not be long before colonized people would demand fundamental changes in the colonial relationship. History would prove him right.

For his part, Weber surely thought that Du Bois's "problem of the twentieth century" was too centered on black Americans, despite his claim to the contrary; it was the application to world events of experiences drawn from, at most, a secondary if not tertiary part of it. Far more important to him were the effects of what Europeans were imparting to the rest of the world: rational calculation. In place of superstition, tradition, and constraining religious mandates, the West was spreading the gospel of technical efficiency, market response, and cost-benefit analysis. That this process entailed grave social losses, particularly in the way that people thought and how they defined themselves and others, Weber was acutely aware and lamented them in *The Protestant Ethic and the Spirit of Capitalism* and elsewhere. However, these concerns did not stop him from being a staunch advocate of German overseas imperialism. Moreover, Weber must have realized on some level that, part and parcel of the European imperial project in Africa and Asia, the objectives of nineteenth-century imperialism were the extension of the color line and, of necessity, the belief in European racial superiority over non-Europeans. In fact, he said as much in his remark to Du Bois about the color line fast becoming the "paramount problem" worldwide without admitting how his very position on German imperialism contributed to it. Nor was Weber able to foresee how Germany's imperial pursuits could rekindle imperial rivalries (dormant for almost a century) similar to those that plagued Europe between the sixteenth and eighteenth centuries—only this time on a far deadlier scale. Nor would he have been able to imagine that a regime in his own country would one day seek to impose an imperial and racial order on Europe based on beliefs similar to those that guided European actions in their overseas colonies.

In the case of Du Bois's formulation that black Americans live behind the veil of their blackness and gain from it a "second sight" or "double consciousness"—"this sense of always looking at one's self through the eyes of others" (8)—the metaphor might well have reminded Weber of Plato's parable of the cave in *The Republic*.[5] In this story chained captives in the depths of a cave are positioned to face a curtain or veil onto which are projected, by the light of a fire behind the veil, the shadows of people and objects moving in front of the entrance of the cave above and opposite them. One of Plato's objectives in the parable is to suggest that, like the prisoners, we often mistake the projection for the real; or, to use Plato's characters, what the prisoners see on the screen is, at best, an inaccurate representation of the actual movements (even less the intentions) of those who are moving past the entrance of the cave. In Du Bois's substitution of Plato's screen with the veil of double consciousness, black, not white, Americans are the ones who are both moving past the entrance of the cave and the prisoners who have been able to free themselves from their chains, ascend the cave's entrance, grow accustomed to sunlight, and then reenter the cave to share with their white counterparts what they have seen. Thus, in his use of the veil metaphor, Du Bois suggests that, despite the obvious disadvantages that come with living behind it, the American racial system ironically offers blacks another optic through which to view the social world that it discourages whites from either using or imagining.[6] In this domain, then, if not in others, the very subordination of the black American allows her to enjoy a perceptual superiority over her white counterparts.

It is hard to imagine that Weber would have agreed with Du Bois on this point. Not, of course, because he could not follow Du Bois's argument but rather because Du Bois's assertion suggests that black Americans or any supposedly subordinate population can perceive more of the social world than white Americans or any supposedly superior population. For according to this logic, German Poles, who occupied arguably the lowest rung of the Prussian social hierarchy at the end of the nineteenth century and whose very presence aroused Weber's ire, had a broader understanding of the German social context than other Germans, in particular, broader than privileged German Protestants like himself. I believe that this would have been too great a stretch for Weber. After all, as noted earlier, despite calling into question both the biology of race and its use as an explanatory variable in social investigation,

Weber continued to subscribe to biological understandings of racial identity. All this is to say that if Weber expressed doubts about blacks' psychological stability, we cannot imagine that his assessment of their intellectual capacities (Du Bois excepted, of course) would have been any better than and certainly not equal to those of the majority of whites.

Similar sentiments would arguably have moved Weber to reject Du Bois's list of contributions that blacks have made to American society in particular and, by extension, to Western civilization in general. If reject is too strong, then we can be sure that, at the very least, Weber would have thought that Du Bois's contentions were in need of serious qualification. Take, for example, Du Bois's early claim in *The Souls of Black Folk* that "there is no true American music but the wild sweet melodies of the Negro slave" (14). If in 1904 Weber already held the opinions on music that he would express at the end of his life, then he would have included even black Americans in his remark that the "musical ear of other peoples has probably been even more sensitively developed than our own, certainly not less so."[7] However, he would have been quick to add that the only true American music must be European derived on the grounds that the United States is primarily an offshoot of European civilization, the only one to have produced "rational harmonious music."[8]

Du Bois's closing remarks in *The Souls of Black Folk* would have elicited an even stronger negative response from Weber. It reads in part:

> Your country? How came it yours? Before the Pilgrims landed we were here. Here we have brought our three gifts and mingled them with yours: a gift of story and song—soft, stirring melody in an ill-harmonized and unmelodious land; the gift of sweat and brawn to beat back the wilderness, conquer the soil, and lay the foundations of this vast economic empire two hundred years earlier than your weak hands could have done it; the third, a gift of the Spirit. . . . Would America have been America without her Negro people? (189)

"Yes," Weber would have undoubtedly responded to this last question, and he would have gone on to add that the economic impact of enslaved black and wage-earning labor was largely regional and modest[9] and that if any "spirit" shaped American culture it was the Protestant spirit and not some derivative of it refashioned in the slave quarters. As harsh and even unfair as this may read, these imagined reactions on Weber's part are consistent with the assertions he made in a number of his writings, including, as we shall see shortly, *The Protestant Ethic and the Spirit of Capitalism*. In short, despite his enthusiastic letter to Du Bois on *The Souls of Black Folk*, Weber fundamentally disagreed with Du Bois on a number of essential points.

At this juncture, let us now turn to how Du Bois presumably read *The Protestant Ethic and the Spirit of Capitalism*.

THE CALL OF THE SPIRIT

As a Protestant son of a small New England town, Du Bois would have been familiar with many aspects of Weber's most popular work. Indeed, the very observation that prompted Weber to write the essay—"the fact that business leaders and owners of capital, as well as the higher grades of skilled labor, and even more the higher technically and commercially trained personnel of modern enterprises, are overwhelmingly Protestant" in turn-of-the-century Germany[10]—was one that Du Bois obliquely highlighted in his autobiographical writings. In a number of these he noted that whereas German and Irish Catholic immigrants constituted the bulk of Great Barrington, Massachusetts's working class, the mill owners were of Protestant stock. In his youth, Du Bois admits that he was content to explain this class division as nothing more than the "result of work and saving." "The rich," he continued, "rightly inherited the earth. The poor, on the whole, were to be blamed. They were lazy or unfortunate and, if unfortunate, their fortunes could be easily mended by thrift and sacrifice."[11] If we juxtapose Du Bois's recollection of his hometown division of labor to how he then rationalized it, we can see how he was almost naturally inclined to agree with Weber that this coincidence of class and religion was anything but accidental. Rather it was the result of a particular ethic, or as Weber defined it, "an obligation which the individual is supposed to feel and does feel toward the content of his [professional] activity, no matter in what it consists."[12]

That Du Bois was raised in a milieu in which a certain ethic governed social behavior is as clear from the course of his own life as it is from the passage cited above. All of its main components were there: work and saving, thrift and sacrifice, and contempt for laziness and wasted talents. However, despite his intimate familiarity with that ethos, Du Bois had probably not given much thought to the relationship between Protestantism and capitalism beyond some commonsense considerations (e.g., the formula wealth = work + saving) before reading or hearing about Weber's thesis. Du Bois would have found similarly appealing not only the breadth and depth of Weber's knowledge of various religious doctrines but also his very methodical approach to their relationships to economic action in general and to capitalism in particular. More than this, *The Protestant Ethic and the Spirit of Capitalism* would have moved Du Bois to reflect on the ways in which Protestantism shaped his own thought.

For example, Weber would have reminded Du Bois that all those raised in the Christian faith are forced to grapple with three spiritual uncertainties: how their behavior will affect the ultimate judgment of their souls, the impossibility of truly knowing God's will, and whether their interpretations of the Bible are correct. Generally speaking, slight or major differences of belief on any one of these questions have resulted in as many Christian denominations. The Catholic Church has historically responded to these spiritual conundrums with the prescription, for the laity, of participation in and receipt of the holy sacraments; and for some priests, monasticism, or their physical removal from the useless distractions of the daily world in order to be more receptive to God's revelation. The Calvinist counter to Catholicism's requirements was twofold: the shattering of the promise of the sacraments with the finality of predestination or the immutability of the state of one's soul; and the "substitut[ion] [of] the spiritual aristocracy of monks outside and above the world [with] the spiritual aristocracy of the predestined saints of God within the world" (74–75). Although there is little or nothing here with which Du Bois would not have been familiar, in reading Weber's synopsis of the main currents of Christianity, Du Bois might well have considered the degree to which a variation of Calvinist thought operated in his own life. He may well have thought that despite the apparent similarities between the "ivory tower" of the university and the monastery, his devotion to social scientific investigation was not for the purpose of advancing knowledge for knowledge's sake but for that of putting his findings to use in the material world.[13] Unbeknownst even to him at this juncture, in less than five years he would take this "worldly asceticism" a step further and leave academia for more than twenty-five years and become one of the founders of the National Association for the Advancement of Colored People (NAACP).

All this was to come. For the moment, Du Bois would have found the methodology that Weber employed in *The Protestant Ethic and the Spirit of Capitalism* particularly compelling. Here, Weber isolated, as best he could, the variable of religious belief from Europe's precapitalist economic systems in order to estimate the degree to which the former acted as the independent variable in the rise of the "spirit of capitalism" or "rational conduct on the basis of the idea of the calling" (122). As a pioneer of the social sciences, Weber sought to apply the scientific method—observation, hypothesis, experimentation (or comparison), and theorization—to the question of the relationship between religious convictions and economic action to the extent that it is possible. As intimated earlier, Weber settled on the Christian preoccupation with salvation as the ideological point of departure of his investigation because that promise is "common to all the denominations." Of course, not all denominations responded to this challenge in like manner. Therefore, in order to render equal these variations in paths to salvation, Weber introduced one of the concepts for which he is best known: the ideal type, or the "artificial simpli[fication]" of explanatory concepts, variables, or outcomes into their "most consistent and logical forms" in order to compare them to other concepts, variables, or outcomes (56). Weber consequently treats Catholicism, Lutheranism, and Calvinism and their offshoots as conceptual models derived mainly from how they were supposed to operate in theory and only secondarily from how they operated in practice. Finally, Weber had to demonstrate how certain religious ideal types, through a process that we can liken to internal combustion, lent themselves to new orientations of human activity in the material world that their promoters did not intend. On this last point Weber noted, "We shall have to admit that the cultural consequences of the Reformation were to a great extent . . . unforeseen and even unwished for results of the labours of the reformers. They were often far removed from or even in contradiction to all that they themselves thought to attain" (48). What, then, can we imagine that Du Bois drew from Weber about the evolution of these unintended metaphysical turned material movements?

On this question, as on so many others, Weber's mastery of the relevant literature and his novel ways of interpreting otherwise disparate or even contradictory data could not but have impressed Du Bois, as they have countless others. Beginning naturally with Luther, Weber reconstructs the steps that led the father of the Reformation to rethink the meaning of activity in the material world. "At first," writes Weber, "quite in harmony with the prevailing tradition of the Middle Ages . . . [Luther] thought of activity in the world as a thing of the flesh, even though willed by God. It is the indispensable natural condition of a life of faith, but in itself, like eating and drinking, morally neutral" (40). With prayer, study of the Bible, and reflection on contemporary events, Luther began to reconsider worldly activity as a moral and divine duty, and rejected monasticism's "renunciation of the duties of this world as the product of selfishness, [a] withdrawing from temporal obligations" (41). As Weber noted, this reformulation of the meaning of work was momentous, for it "inevitably gave everyday worldly activity a religious significance, and first created the conception of a calling in this sense" (40). With this we can only imagine that Du Bois would have nodded in agreement. He would also have agreed with Weber that the response to one's calling runs the risk of leading to fatalism or the belief that the "individual should remain once and for all in the station and calling in which God had placed him, and should restrain his worldly activity within the limits imposed by his established station in life" (44). Du Bois had not only seen proof of this in the religious orientation of many southerners, both black and white, but also knew how this religious philosophy could rationalize a secular social order based on race, power, gender, and class distinctions.

Even harsher ("inhuman" is how Weber describes it at one point) than a strict or literal interpretation of the calling is Calvin's doctrine of predestination. Permitting the attainment of salvation neither "through the Church and the sacraments" nor by modeling one's behavior after those whom one believes to be among God's "elect," because they "differ externally in this life in no way from the damned," Calvinism offered its adherents no external crutches for spiritual consolation (61, 65). However fatalistic these dictates, to question this ordering of humanity was the height of human presumptuousness, Calvin argued, because the ways of God are beyond the comprehension of the mortal mind. For his followers, who, unlike Calvin himself, were uncertain of the fate of their souls, the weight of his teachings proved unbearable; they needed signs that they were among either the elect or the damned. In response to their congregations' irrepressible and impatient desire to know the fate of their souls, Calvinist ministers, Weber maintains, engaged in what Calvin himself would have considered moral cheating: they taught their flocks that it is "an absolute duty to consider oneself chosen" and that they should model their behavior after those who were unquestionably among God's elect, the Hebrew patriarchs of the Old Testament (66, 69). Neither practice, of course, offered the certainty of God's grace, but both offered the hope of salvation in an otherwise hopeless doctrine. But their most important contribution was to promote the "idea of the necessity of proving one's faith in worldly activity" (74–75). Of all the forms of "worldly activity," the highest is diligent work in a calling, and the ultimate sign of one's faith is the "rational planning of one's whole life in accordance with God's will" (100). Consequently, Calvinists, and the denominations that they inspired, ceased to shun wealth creation and capital accumulation on the grounds that they lent themselves to moral laxity and indulgence in luxury and instead saw in them paths to the fulfillment of God's commandments. With such results apparently emerging from concerns over salvation, we can understand Weber's contention that "religious forces . . . are the decisive influences in the formation of national character" (102).

Du Bois certainly understood this claim as well, although he might have insisted, as he did in his 1897 address, "The Conservation of Races," that nationality (or racial membership, as the two coincided, according to Du Bois), more than religion, determines the most distinctive characteristics of particular populations.[14] Still, in his presocialist years, Du Bois would have appreciated Weber's resistance to the appeal of economic determinism that maintains that religion is merely an epiphenomenon of class forces. Instead, Weber sought to take religion on its own terms without recourse to economic inputs. In this respect, the Protestant ethic was Weber's answer to Marx's "primitive accumulation."

There were limits, however, to Du Bois's enthusiasm for Weber's "faith-based" approach to the rise of the spirit of capitalism. Despite his disclaimer at the end of *The Protestant Ethic and the Spirit of Capitalism* that "it is, of course, not my aim to substitute for a one-sided materialistic an equally one-sided spiritualistic causal interpretation of culture and history," in some areas he did just that (125). This alone is not what would have troubled Du Bois, as he would have understood in Weber's presentation of his argument the scholarly tendency to overstate one's alternative formulation when writing against a dominant one. Rather, what would have chafed Du Bois was Weber's apparent exaggeration in his essay of the role of religious forces in economic action whenever he indirectly makes reference to black labor. One such example is Weber's suggestion that the "remarkable circumstance that so many of the greatest capitalistic entrepreneurs—down to Cecil Rhodes—have come from clergymen's families might be explained as . . . an extraordinary capitalistic business sense . . . combined in the same persons and groups with the most intensive forms of piety which penetrates and dominates their whole lives" (9). Another example is Weber's claim that capitalism took root more rapidly and profoundly in New England than it did in the American South, which I noted at the outset of this study. There are other examples, but they are even more oblique than these.[15] Put in more explicit terms, Weber's mention of Cecil Rhodes and the American South invokes respectively the European colonization of Africa in the late nineteenth century and the European and European American slave regimes spanning roughly the sixteenth through nineteenth centuries.

Perhaps more than problematic, Du Bois would have found Weber's two claims puzzling, if not contradictory. If, as Weber insists, capitalism and its spirit should not be equated with "absolute unscrupulousness in the pursuit of selfish interests by the making of money," which, he continues, "has been a specific characteristic of precisely those countries whose bourgeois capitalistic development, measured according to Occidental standards, has remained backward," how is he able to call Cecil Rhodes one of the "greatest capitalistic entrepreneurs" when his activities in southern Africa were literally guided by the *auri sacra fames*, or greed for gold (and diamonds), like other "unscrupulous" adventurers (21)? And if Weber could categorize Rhodes as an exemplary capitalist, by what criteria can he maintain that southern planters were any less successful capitalists than he or New England entrepreneurs were? And even if one agrees that capitalism was more developed in New England than in the southern mainland colonies, where enslaved labor dominated commercial agricultural production, one must also recognize that some portion (if not a pivotal one) of New (and "Old") England capitalism grew around the shipment of slaves and slave-cultivated crops to and from British North America and the Caribbean, the processing of some of those same crops, and the supply of New England exports to the South and the Caribbean.[16]

For Du Bois these considerations were more than debaters' points on esoteric concerns; they were indications of his profound differences with Weber and other scholars of his ilk on the pressing matter of the rise of the modern world and of capitalism, differences that some contemporary scholars have either avoided or minimized in their presentations of the intersections of Du Bois's and Weber's lives and interests. Whereas Du Bois underscored in *The Souls of Black Folk* and in countless other publications before and after its appearance the pivotal role that African and African American labor played in the capitalist transformation of the Western economy, Weber, as the passages cited above suggest, consistently minimized or flatly denied that contribution on the questionable grounds that its economic impact was limited both in the number of people who benefited from it and in the number of business and institutional innovations it engendered. For Du Bois, a position like Weber's would have been an untenable one, which relies as much on a narrow understanding of the economics of empire and unfree labor as it does a selective history: by and large, it removed Protestants from both enterprises.

And what was also ironic about Weber's limited view of the economic benefits of empire and unfree labor was its timing and contradiction of his own political positions: he expressed this at the height of European overseas imperialism of which he was a vocal supporter. Taken together, Weber's circumvention of imperialism had to be more than a mere oversight. As a general rule, when a scholar whose mind is nothing short of "encyclopedic," as Weber's was,[17] consistently chooses to avoid an otherwise obvious theme, this avoidance is rarely a matter of insufficient thought about the theme in question but a refusal to alter his worldview to the extent that the subject requires. To borrow a concept from Marshall Hodgson, the formidable American scholar of Islam and the Muslim world, Weber's evasion of modern imperialism was part of his "scholarly precommitments" or his "unconscious and hence unanalyzed . . . commitment to partisan viewpoints."[18]

Whether Du Bois knew of or even considered Weber's determined omission of modern imperialism in his work we cannot say with any certainty. What we do know, nevertheless, is that contra Weber and almost the entire western European and European American professorate, Du Bois devoted most of his scholarly work to the reinscription of black labor and black movements for social justice in the making of the Western world, capitalist and all. Therefore, even if he never mentioned Weber by name in any of his scholarly or popular work, or ever read *The Protestant Ethic and the Spirit of Capitalism*, Du Bois spent most of his academic and public career challenging the Eurocentric logic that guided Weber's and other European and European American scholars' work on capitalism and modernity generally.

It is similarly plausible that Weber's steadfast insistence on the uniqueness of Western social development was partially motivated by Du Bois's challenges to it in *The Souls of Black Folk*; in "Die Neger Frage in den Vereinigten Staaten," his article for Weber's journal; and in his Harvard dissertation, "The Suppression of the African Slave-Trade to the United States of America, 1638–1870," to which Weber referred in his lectures at the University of Munich in 1919.[19] This contention is less improbable when we bear in mind that Du Bois was the only scholar of color with whom Weber had some sort of relationship, however brief. Consequently, it is quite possible that Du Bois's thoughts about the "rise of the West" may have carried, consciously or unconsciously, a special significance, greater perhaps than if they had been formulated by a fellow European or Euro-American. For to whom else but Du Bois did Weber direct his remark, "In the period from the 16th to the 18th century, slavery signified as little for the economic organization of Europe as it did much for the accumulation of wealth in Europe,"[20] in response to Du Bois's claim that the "contemporary industrial development of America is based on the blood and sweat of unpaid Negro labor in the seventeenth, eighteenth, and nineteenth centuries"?[21] Thus, despite the necessarily speculative nature of our exercise, it is not far-fetched to imagine that, given their contact and renown, Weber and Du Bois long influenced each other's ideas.

ALTHOUGH *The Protestant Ethic and the Spirit of Capitalism* and *The Souls of Black Folk* are vastly different works about equally different people and experiences, they are united by history: the century that saw the Reformation also witnessed the large-scale transport of African captives to the Americas. In the combination of these events, some Africans became Protestants, and some Protestants became slavers and slave owners. Although neither Du Bois nor Weber centered his analyses on these points, they would ultimately become sticking points in their conceptions of capitalism, and the role of black and unfree labor in the capitalist world economy. Until then, both scholars shared a willingness to make broad claims about the supposedly common worldviews of specific groups while remaining attentive to the variety of perspectives within these shared identities. This was no doubt what drew Weber to Du Bois, in addition to his balanced treatment of the competing forces in the postemancipation South. For Du Bois, the appeal of *The Protestant Ethic and the Spirit of Capitalism* would have been its confirmation and explanation of the doctrine on which he had been reared and had not entirely dismissed. That time would come, however, not long after this, their second encounter.

CHAPTER TWO

Fields of Study

There can be no doubt that Du Bois's chance breakfast with Weber at the St. Louis World's Fair made him nostalgic for the nearly two magical years that he spent in Europe, primarily in Germany. Those years were magical because it was there and then that he experienced what life could be like for a black person without being defined by the adjective, as he was in the United States, but recognized as the substantive;[1] magical because it was there and then that he had the opportunity to study with some of the most esteemed minds of the Western world and to take in the culture of what westerners considered the pinnacle of world culture; magical because it was there and then that, on the occasion of his twenty-fifth birthday, he would record the following famous words in his diary, with the aid of "candles, Greek wine, oil, and song and prayer."

> Night—grand and wonderful. I am glad I am living. I rejoice as a strong man to win a race, and I am strong—is it egotism—is it assurance—or is it the silent call of the world spirit that makes me feel that I am royal and that beneath my scepter a world of kings shall bow. The hot dark blood of a forefather is beating at my heart, and I know that I am either a genius or a fool. . . . I do not know—

perhaps I shall never know: But this I do know: be the Truth what it may I will seek it on the pure assumption that it is worth seeking—and Heaven nor Hell, God nor Devil shall turn me from my purpose till I die. I will in this second quarter century of my life, enter the dark forest of the unknown world for which I have so many years served my apprenticeship—in the chart and compass which the world furnishes me I have little faith—yet I have nothing better—I will seek till I find—and die. There is a grandeur in the very hopelessness of such a life. I therefore take the world that the Unknown lay in my hands and work for the rise of the Negro people, taking for granted that their best development means the best development of the world.[2]

And fulfill this pledge he did.

Leaving aside his indulgence in youthful self-confidence, we wonder if Du Bois would have or even could have experienced those same feelings and visions in the United States for much the same reasons that Weber would not have experienced a significant release from his nervous torment if he had not made his trip to the United States: distance from the source of frustration allows the mind to relax and recall what it needs to sustain itself. Yet, Du Bois had not gone to Germany for the unanticipated benefits of living free of racist ire, however much good that did his person and intellect, but to further his academic training from the likes of Gustav Schmoller and Adolph Wagner. However, just exactly what Du Bois took away from the lecture halls and seminars at the University of Berlin no less than from the meetings of the Verein für Sozialpolitik has been the subject of an implicit dispute among Weber scholars, with North Americans largely downplaying the significance of Du Bois's German years and Germanists, foremost among them Kenneth Barkin,[3] presenting a convincing case for the degree to which German history, culture, and thought entered into and remained in Du Bois's consciousness even before his stay in the country. While I am inclined to agree with the Germanists for reasons that will become clearer in the coming pages, I caution against weighting any one influence on Du Bois more than a host of others, given just how eclectic and fiercely independent his thinking was. Moreover, as he stated in *Dusk of Dawn* in a passage that I believe is relevant to this discussion, the demands of blackness, both intellectual and emotional, tempered even the magic of his German years.

> Had it not been for the race problem early thrust upon me and enveloping me, I should have probably been an unquestioning worshiper at the shrine of the social order and economic development into which I was born. But just that part of that order which seemed to most of my fellows nearest perfection, seemed to me most inequitable and wrong, and starting from that critique, I gradually, as the years went by, found other things to question in my environment.[4]

Du Bois would subject Germany to that questioning as well.

THE GERMAN HISTORICAL SCHOOL

If, as Jurgen Herbst named them, the common elements of the renowned German historical school were the "concept of the social organism, the rejection of speculative theories, the reliance on empirical data, the practice of the higher criticism, the search for limited generalizations, [and] the use of the comparative method,"[5] then Weber and Du Bois, like the founding members of the Verein für Sozialpolitik, Gustav Schmoller and Adolph Wagner, all subscribed to that mix. For "an association of scholars, government officials, and other specialists interested in investigating current social problems and promoting reforms through legislation,"[6] the elements of the German historical school furnished the tools by which to collect and assess social data, which could then be used to formulate policy proposals. However, general agreement on the overarching methods and motives of social investigation did not mean that there was unanimity among Verein members, particularly in an organization that was straddling scholarship and social engineering. Some, like Weber, were troubled by the temptation of academic members of the Verein to compromise scholarly impartiality to advance their own policy agendas.[7] Others, like Schmoller, were steadfastly against comparisons that led scholars to isolate social variables hypothetically and to calculate probabilities from the supposed interaction of those variables, irrespec-

tive of place, time, and context, much as the Manchester school practiced, according to Schmoller and other German critics.[8] Still others,
like Adolph Wagner, wanted statistics applied to "all phenomena" so as
to facilitate the discovery of "behavior patterns . . . which in the large
numbers of cases possess a regular character determined by the constant
causes."[9]

Still, no one engaged in these debates contemplated a return to the
sort of historical writing that privileged great men, great states, and
power politics as the elemental stuff of history à la Gibbon or Ranke,
however much history and related fields owed them for their exemplary
use of primary sources and their insistence that the historian reconstruct
the past on the basis of what really happened as opposed to what is supposed to have happened. Fledgling sociologists, like Weber and Du Bois
and a host of other social scientists who drew from historical works, took
these prescriptions very seriously for a number of good reasons. Foremost was probably the desire to prove to historians, perhaps above all,
that the distinct field of sociology was indeed necessary. This challenge
was especially pressing given that "much of the work done by historians
was sociological."[10] However, sociology's value was helped in this by the
very social developments that called it into being, which were of a markedly different sort from those that existed in the recent or distant past.
Among these were the contest over the distribution of land between
large landowners and family farmers; the unprecedented scale of domestic and international migration; the steady overtaking of artisanal
production by machine output; the corresponding rise of increasingly
organized working classes; the relentless swelling of cities and the en-
trenchment of residential segregation by class, ethnicity, and race; the
emergence of a variety of reform movements to address issues as varied
as poverty, alcoholism, and women's rights; and the increasing seculariza-
tion of the common understanding of the world's workings, despite
regular church attendance on the part of many. Even historians had to
agree that these developments demanded chronicling and analyses even
at the risk of devolving into journalism, a possibility that was not considered beneath scholarly research as it is today.[11]

What historians did object to was the use of their studies to uncover
patterns of social action that were then applied to societies and contexts

outside of the ones from which they were drawn. As Du Bois himself put it, the "attempt to reduce human action" into empirically manageable (if not always quantifiable) categories for the purpose of formulating "law[s], rule[s], and rhythm[s]" about it[12] struck many as an imposition of questionable projections of future human conduct based on equally problematic formulations drawn from past and present human behavior. As Hegel and other idealists warned those who aimed to raise any field that engages with human behavior to the status of a science, they "must not be beguiled by the false analogy of physics or mathematics, which looking for the widest obtainable, least varying, common characteristics, deliberately ignores what specifically belongs to only one time and one place, seeking to be as general, as abstract, as formal as possible."[13] What idealists feared in the works that would later come to be known as social scientific generally and sociological specifically was that they would deny their subject—us—the very characteristic that makes us human and presumably different from most of the animal world: the ability to make, at any moment, choices different from what is expected of us.[14] In short, the principal desire of some of sociology's detractors was to retain humankind's endless possibilities and the uniqueness of individual action, even if it could be shown that many of us make similar choices under similar circumstances. Without the entertainment of these possibilities, they reasoned, we risked losing our own humanity.

As subscribers to the German historical school, sociologists on both sides of the Atlantic had to contend with the objections of their respective nationalists who thought that this new field threatened to dismember the social body, once again, into competing constituencies. The timing of sociology's rise did not help to allay these fears or give it a warm reception, coming as it did in the wake of unification and reunion, which were still causes for celebration in Germany and the United States. However sympathetic sociologists may have been with these nationalistic concerns given that many of them shared them, the majority could not help but consider these sentiments little more than blaming the messenger, for who could deny that modern societies were divided by class, religion, ethnicity, interests, and power, to name just a few of the elements that separated members of the same body politic? If anything, the challenge for sociologists no less than for political scientists, politicians, and contemplative people in these societies generally was to determine the form of the social glue that held these societies together. Nevertheless, this question was no more compelling to the majority of sociologists than the intellectual obligation to record and analyze the social world as free from projected illusions as possible, particularly those of the social harmony variety that romantic nationalists stressed.

Weber's and Du Bois's immediate responses to the intellectual challenges to their adopted discipline came in the form of their sociological studies themselves rather than in theoretical reflections on the nature of the field; these last would appear some years later, with Weber supplying a far larger number than Du Bois. For the comparative purposes of this study and, in particular, to privilege their respective work with which the other was familiar, I will limit my direct remarks to Weber's address to the 1904 Congress of Arts and Science in St. Louis, the portions of Du Bois's article on "Die Neger Frage in den Vereinigten Staaten" devoted to blacks in southern agriculture, and Weber's 1893 address on the results of the Verein für Sozialpolitik's study of agricultural conditions in eastern Germany, "Developmental Tendencies in the Situation of East Elbian Rural Labourers," which Du Bois heard in Berlin.[15] Of course, in light of the fact that these presentations were drawn from larger studies, I refer to that research when appropriate.

THE EASTERN QUESTION

As is typical of practically every subject he covered, the content of Weber's St. Louis address was far broader and deeper than its modest title suggested. For it is, at once, a comprehensive, yet accessible, survey of European agrarian history since the fourteenth century, replete with telling details and useful regional comparisons. In the main, Weber's lecture is structured around a series of contrasts: European versus North American agrarian patterns; customary versus capitalist social relations; and western versus eastern European agricultural development. Let us begin with the last of these dichotomies and discuss the others in reverse order.

Midway in his St. Louis address, Weber informs his American listeners that the key to understanding often misunderstood German politics and middle-class culture can be found in the agrarian history of eastern Germany and the ways in which that history differs from that of the country's west. However, as Weber notes, through the fourteenth century, rather than divergence there was "comparative uniformity" between the two regions, with the "greater part of the lord's income depend[ing] on the taxes the peasants contributed."[16] What changed in subsequent centuries, according to Weber, was the eastern peasantry's ability to maintain the level of revenue to which eastern landlords-cum-Junkers had become accustomed. Weber attributed this decline in eastern peasant contributions to mainly two factors: the absence of local urban markets for agrarian produce and the redundancy of crops due to the unvaried topography of the eastern plains. Of the two, Weber asserted that the urban factor was decisive for peasant production.

> But nothing could and nothing can be substituted for that educating influence which is exerted upon the peasant by an intensive formation of urban communities, by well-developed local communication, by opportunity and inducement to sell rural products in the nearest possible local markets. . . . Where these influences of culture, which cannot be replaced even by the best labor and best will, were lacking, the peasant frequently lacked the possibility and always the incentive to raise the yield of his land beyond the traditional measure of his own needs. (378, 380)

Unable "as in the west" to draw sufficient incomes from the "peasants' taxes, tolls, tithes, and rents," eastern landlords had to supervise production themselves and become "operating landlord[s]" (378, 380). As Weber underscores, this was their last desire, just as it would have been for any aristocracy to assume such plebian tasks, but management was, "under the historically established conditions, the only possible economic means of obtaining a higher income" (380). However, rather than result in the freeing of the eastern peasantry from the land and the creation of a wage-earning agricultural population, this form of agrarian capitalism on the contrary "bound" the peasantry "more and more to the soil" and reduced him to a "serf with the duty of giving his children to the lord as menials, as furnishing his horses and wagons for husbandry, his own labor power for all sorts of work during the entire year, while his own land was considered more and more a mere reward for his labor" (380).

Although he did not state it explicitly, the Junkers' assumption of estate management was, in Weber's estimation, the first step in the capitalist transformation of eastern Germany, more important apparently than even the employment of wage workers, as he insisted on elsewhere. Still, the fact that the Junkers were not yet asking themselves the modern capitalist question—"From this given piece of land how can I produce as many as crops as possible for the market with as few men as possible?"— indicated to Weber that they were not yet modern capitalists (367).

Weber did not speculate in his address on whether the Junkers would have increasingly opted to employ seasonal wage labor in the course of the nineteenth century without the advent of the French Revolution and its successors in the sociopolitical upheavals of 1848 throughout Europe. However, as it happened, those events forced the Junkers to make considerable concessions to their former serfs by midcentury, which probably led many of them to reconsider the older, aristocratic attitude of giving the "greatest number of men . . . work and sustenance" on one's holdings (367). These concessions included "a cottage, land[,] . . . the right of pasturage for their cows," and a "certain portion of grain" in exchange for working the Junkers' estates (382). Elsewhere Weber labeled this arrangement patriarchal capitalism to capture the twin facts that it still privileged the landlord's economic interests and that his interests were also those of the cottagers for the obvious fact that they both gained or lost from the harvest yield. Hence, Weber's reference to the "community of interests" that characterized patriarchal capitalism, despite the landlord's unquestioned authority over his tenants.

This apparently harmonious agrarian compromise was short-lived, however. Beginning in the last quarter of the nineteenth century, the Junkers initiated the dispossession of the cottagers because of the "rising valuation of the land; their lord withheld pasture and land, kept his grain, and paid them wages instead" (382). By these measures, the "old community of interests was dissolved, and the farm hands became proletarians. The operation of agriculture became a seasonal operation, restricted to a few months. The lord[s] hired migratory laborers since the maintenance of idle hands throughout the year would be too heavy a burden"

(382). However, even more destabilizing, for Weber, than the dissolution of the patriarchal system and its replacement of the "community of interests" between landlord and cottager with the conflict of interests between landlord and seasonal hand was the ethnicity of these agricultural wage workers: Polish. Although the language that he used to describe Poles in his St. Louis address was far less inflammatory and derogatory than that which he employed in his Freiberg lecture a few years earlier, it was still only a matter of degree: "frugal" and "untutored" had now euphemistically replaced "inferior." And Weber still felt it his duty to issue a warning to his North American listeners that if the "enormous immigration of untutored elements from Eastern Europe grows, a rural population might soon arise here which could not be assimilated by the historically transmitted culture of this country. This population would decisively change the standard of the United States and would gradually form a community of a quite different type from the great creation of the Anglo-Saxon spirit" (384).

Some in the audience must have found Weber's singling out of Slavic immigrants curious when, in their minds, other European immigrant populations posed similar threats to the cultural integrity of the United States. Others, like Du Bois, who were familiar with Germany from having either studied there or visited, understood the context of Weber's concern, even if they did not share his alarm. His other warning, however, of the socioeconomic and sociopolitical consequences of the end of continental North American expansion probably struck a chord in all his listeners, even if the tune was ultimately the same.

As Weber saw it, in an ironic twist, the "winning of the west" would inevitably lead to the establishment of a landed aristocracy such as that which presided over Europe at the time and the defeat of the European settler-farmer. With the Pacific Ocean now serving as a boundary rather than as the limit of the frontier, the growth of the North American population would, over the intermediate and long terms, increase land prices, decrease agricultural revenue and wages, demote the entrepreneurial small farmer to the ranks of wage laborer either in the countryside or in urban industry, reduce the size of inherited landholdings, and make it unfeasible for the average farmer "to gain a possible fortune by agriculture," as it was then the case throughout Europe (366). Furthermore, under the pressure of these forces, in addition to those created by moneyed industrialists and commercial titans who purchased land for prestige rather than for income, and by agribusiness's perennial hunt for cheap hands, the small farmer's "struggle for existence often becomes an economic selection in favor of the most frugal, which means, of those most lacking in culture" (368). How Weber came to equate a group's cultural level with its material requirements need not detain us here, however fascinating that might prove. Rather, the important element to note is that in subscribing to this belief he had cause to condemn the workers themselves no less than the rural capitalists who hired them.

In the final analysis, even if Weber's predictions of the political-economic future of the United States drew too heavily on European experiences and consequently failed to take into adequate account the roles of corporate land purchases and economic downturns in the concentration of landownership and the decline in family-owned farms instead of population density, his linking of capitalism's labor requirements with the subversion of national character undoubtedly confirmed what many had already concluded and gave others pause.

THE SOUTHERN QUESTION

From his reading on German agriculture at the University of Berlin, his own observations of rural Germany while a student there, and his then ongoing studies in the rural South, Du Bois would have taken great interest in Weber's entire St. Louis lecture. Still, two of Weber's assertions, which touched directly or indirectly on black southerners, would have been of particular importance to Du Bois. The first of these was Weber's contention that the "present difficult social problems of the South in the rural districts . . . are essentially ethnic and not economic" (364); and the second, that the "number of Negro farms is growing, as is the migration from the country into the cities" (384), although it is unclear whether Weber was referring here to the urban migration of blacks. In his article for Weber's journal, "Die Neger Frage in Vereinigten Staaten," Du Bois responded directly to both of Weber's statements.

First, he had to disabuse his readers of the idea that slavery had indeed ended in the United States in the wake of its Civil War. Thus, early in his article Du Bois states without qualification that "[s]lavery continued in the Southern states in two forms and under different names: as peonage and as convict slavery."[17] Both were predictable outgrowths of the sharecropping system or the compromise agricultural arrangement between the recently emancipated and former slaveholders or new landlords to accustom both parties to contractual agreements. In his thick description of the sharecropping system in "Die Neger Frage in Vereinigten Staaten," Du Bois also explained to his German readers the reasons why and how sharecroppers could scarcely avoid long-term indebtedness by the system's design.

The most frequent kind of the sharecropping system consisted in giving a piece of land to the freed family—usually 40 to 80 acres—and taking part of the yield as rent. The size of this part depended on what the worker himself supplied. If he supplied nothing but his own labor and that of his family members, while the owner provided the tools, the draft animals, and the provisions, then the latter received two-thirds of the harvest; if the worker supplied his own provisions, the owner received half of the harvest. If the worker also supplied tools and animals, then the owner received one-quarter to one-third of the harvest. . . . [I]f the worker was lucky and industrious, the total rent of the land was eventually set at this or that much cotton or money, and then the true tenant or renter [Pachter] replaced the sharecropper [Halbpachter]. . . .

This system proved to be very unsatisfactory. The end of the season usually found the freedman without surplus or in debt; furthermore, under the mild laws concerning debt collection current at the time, the merchant[,] . . . caught between the landlord and the worker, was in constant danger of losing everything. Because the freedman was the real producer of the harvest, it was obviously in the merchant's interest to enter into a direct relationship with him, if he [the merchant] could only acquire some kind of legal claim on him [the freedman]. On the other hand, the freedman, who readily attempted to escape from a relation that was hardly better than the old slavery, gladly applied directly to the merchant. . . . Thus the economic situation changed between the years 1870–80 as follows. [The landlord] provided the land, lodging, and animals. The rent amounted to either a precisely delineated part of the harvest, a

certain number of pounds of cotton per acre, or a specific cash sum.
[The freedman] bought his supply of food, clothes, etc. directly
from [the merchant] on credit. New laws that gradually emerged
favored [the merchant] who could insure himself through a promis-
sory note that represented a second mortgage on [the freedman's]
ripening crop, the rent to be paid to [the landlord] being the first.
(290, 291–92)

In a word, the vast majority of recently freed people left the shackles
of slavery only to be rebound by the chains of variable rent and interest,
with their creditors sharing a common interest in their indebtedness. Yet
was this not the design of denying freed people any compensation in the
form of land or money for unpaid work as part of the emancipation
package? How much, then, did the status of the former southern slave
differ from that of the former Prussian serf, Du Bois must have thought
as he recounted the economic constraints on black freedom in "Die
Neger Frage in Vereinigten Staaten": in the place of a "community of
interests" linking Prussian cottager and landlord in the harvest yield,
there was a conflict of interests over the yield between the southern
sharecropper and landlord, no less than between the sharecropper and
the merchant. Instead of enjoying certain rights and privileges free of
charge as cottagers did in the patriarchal system, sharecroppers had to
pay for all of their needs in money or in kind with interest; and instead
of being an intermediate stage between forced and wage labor as the
cottager's was, landlords and merchants could prolong indefinitely sharecropping and its intended outcome, debt peonage, by creative bookkeep-
ing and exorbitant interest. Moreover, once in debt, the sharecropper
family was legally obligated to fulfill the terms of its abusive contract, for
it was a contract. And if the family fled, it ran the great risk of being
caught and returned to the landlord for whom it worked, or worse, of
serving prison time and working for other masters. For given the prevailing belief of the white South, that black people would not work regularly
unless reduced to a condition approaching slavery, coupled with the
clause of the supposedly slavery ending Thirteenth Amendment, that
"involuntary servitude" is a "punishment for a crime whereof the party
shall have been duly convicted," and rampant antivagrancy or, more aptly
termed, anti–freedom of movement laws, with which black people

exclusively were charged, few if any southern courts would rule in favor of a sharecropping family fleeing abuse. Rather, southern states took advantage of the economic, political, and social vulnerabilities of the recently emancipated to convict them in staggering numbers (Du Bois reports that "about 70 percent of all prisoners in the South are black," presumably in 1905) for the purpose of leasing them to private, corporate, and public entities in a variety of industries and infrastructural projects (300). This convict lease system, as it was coined, was nothing other than a "new slavery" to Du Bois, with the state now taking the place of the planter. Thus, "the state," remarked Du Bois, "became a merchant in crime and profited so much by this trade that it had a yearly net income from its prisoners; those who used convict labor also made a great profit. In these conditions, it was almost impossible to free the state from this corrupt system" (300). In brief, the former Confederacy had ensured that the abolition of slavery would not mean freedom to the recently emancipated and their descendants.

Du Bois was sure to state in his article that the "occasional visitor to the South" would have missed these features of the region: "Instead he notices the increasingly frequent occurrence of black faces during the journey southwards, but otherwise the days glide peacefully by, the sun laughs and this small world seems as happy and content as other worlds that he has visited" (322). To such a visitor, as Weber was, it could indeed seem that the rural South's "present difficult social problems . . . are essentially ethnic and not economic." But to a resident and researcher of the region, such as Du Bois was, the "occasional visitor's" understanding of the South's inner workings inverted reality. In two pointed remarks in "Die Neger Frage in den Vereinigten Staaten," Du Bois directly addressed Weber's misconceptions. In the first instance, he noted that "in the [southern] countryside . . . almost all serious collisions between the two races in the last decade originated as conflicts between landlords and workers" (296). And in the second, he noted that the "Negro question is only one indication of the increasing class and racial privileges [in the United States generally] and not, as many optimistically believe, its cause" (326). On the other hand, Du Bois did confirm Weber's statement that the "number of Negro farms is growing," reporting that "40 years after emancipation 25.2 percent or one-quarter of all Negro farmers had become property owners" (304).

Finally, like Weber, Du Bois ended his article with a series of warnings to the United States. However, what is most striking about Du Bois's warnings are how they directly challenged the core of Weber's warnings. In the place of supposedly uncivilized and unruly immigrants posing the greatest cultural threat to a nation, Du Bois substituted class polarization, of which racism was but a cruel expression. In two highly illustrative passages on American society in the early twentieth century, Du Bois drew the links between the two.

> Americans begin to show not only open contempt for the "bastard races," but also a growing respect for snobbism and they gladly began to forget the color of their grandfathers' fingernails. (325)

And:

> Class hierarchy grows today in America, in the land that was founded as a mighty protest against this folly that rules the world. It grows almost undisturbed, for its victims today are mostly blacks. But the Americans should not for that reason let themselves be lulled into a false security! The Negro question is only one indication of the increasing class and racial privileges and not, as many optimistically believe, its cause. (326)

Taking these statements together, Du Bois was proposing here a Marxist view of racism long before his identification with that political-economic outlook; that is, that class polarization necessitates racism, but racism only redirects but does not reduce class polarization. Immigrants were no more to blame for this state of affairs than black people, and on this point as well, Du Bois seems to direct his words at Weber. Although he was not yet at the point of advocating capitalism's abolition, he was certainly asserting here that it was the culture of capitalism that warranted greater condemnation than the supposed cultural shortcomings of blacks and European immigrants. Otherwise, he would have been sure to include in his warnings the manner in which the exclusion of blacks from the democratic process and institutions affects their operation everywhere, in much the same way that the devaluation of black labor correspondingly degrades white labor.

IN THE FIELDS

Another less apparent difference between Weber's and Du Bois's agrarian studies was the way in which they collected personal data on the populations under study: through "an amazingly wide range of research methods, such as participant observation, survey research, archival research, ethnographic research, and statistical analysis,"[18] in Du Bois's case; through questionnaires and consultation with local records and regional histories in Weber's.[19] In fairness to Weber, I must point out that he did not determine the methodological strategy of the Verein's study of eastern German agricultural conditions, and he did recognize the limitations of its findings.[20] Still, what would prove telling about his participation in a study whose basis was not direct contact between researcher and population was that, unlike Du Bois, Weber would never engage in fieldwork, despite having opportunities to do so. We can point to a number of reasons for this, reasons of which Weber's class position, political beliefs, time constraints, and mental health are all factors. However, if we consider the ways in which Du Bois's background and early life experiences contrasted with Weber's, we gain an understanding of why Du Bois was a pioneer of fieldwork and Weber was not.

That Du Bois should have been the one to introduce fieldwork to American sociology makes perfect sense if one reflects on his personal history, his intellectual predilections, and his social position as a black man in a white-identifying North America. About the first influence we will recall that Du Bois's "black" experience was an atypical one: he was the son of small-town New England, in his particular case, Great Barrington, Massachusetts, where his extended family accounted for a large portion of the black presence there. In practical terms, this meant that Du Bois's background was of limited help to his studies of black life in the rural South and Philadelphia.[21] Yet there were benefits to Du Bois's unlikely rearing: although he arrived in the communities he studied as an outsider who could assume very little about the practices and meanings of life there, as a black person he considered himself and was presumably considered by the members of these black communities a racial insider who recognized their basic humanity.[22] In other words, Du Bois was uniquely positioned to provide both the observations and sensitivity

required of a sound community study and the awareness of the historico-
structural position of black people both locally and nationally.

There was another dimension to Du Bois's youth in Great Barrington that influenced his decision to live in the communities whose
lives he was investigating: his early journalistic experience. While in his
teens, Du Bois began writing articles for the *New York Globe* and the
New York Freeman.[23] For these dispatches, Du Bois visited various
churches and civic organizations in Great Barrington and its environs
(he became a member of some of them) and attended numerous public
events and celebrations. Despite his frequent use of his articles as a
means to counsel townsfolk, especially black ones, on how they should
spend their money and leisure time, his reporting gave him invaluable
experience in participant observation and the art of interviewing.

Du Bois carried this twin pursuit of chronicling and counseling to a
rural community of Tennessee where he taught basic education for two
summers while attending Fisk University in Nashville. This was an instance of Du Bois making something out of a choice that was not his
own: it was the decision of Du Bois's Great Barrington benefactors that
he attend a historically black university in the South before seeking admission to his first choice, Harvard, from which he would later receive a
BA and a PhD. Du Bois maintained that, unlike his relatives who were
deeply disturbed by and disappointed in the decision to send him South
to college, he recognized in it an opportunity to "touch" the "former land
of slavery." Fisk's students, generally "five to ten years older" than Du
Bois, "could paint from their own experience a wide and vivid picture of
the postwar South and its black millions. There were men and women
who had faced mobs and seen lynchings; who knew every phase of insult
and repression; and too there were sons, daughters, and clients of every
class of white Southerner."[24] However, Du Bois wanted more than other
people's stories about southern black life; he wanted to know it by ex-
periencing it personally, especially its rural dimension, which was its
foundation. Hence his decision to teach summer school in Nashville's
countryside.

> I was not content to take the South entirely by hearsay; and while I
> had no funds to travel widely, I did, somewhat to the consternation
> of both my teachers and fellow-students, determine to go out into

the country and teach summer school. I was only 18 and knew nothing of the South at first hand, save what little I had seen in Nashville from the protected vantage ground of a college campus. I had not seen anything of the small Southern town and the countryside, which are the real South. If I could not explore Darkest Mississippi, at least I could see East Tennessee, which was not more than 50 miles from the college. I determined to know something of the Negro in the country districts; to go out and teach during the summer vacation. I was not compelled to do this, for my scholarship was sufficient to support me, but that was not the point. I had heard about the country in the South as the real seat of slavery. I wanted to know it.[25]

And true to his resolution, Du Bois would know the South intimately.

Another reason for Du Bois's desire to engage in fieldwork when and where possible was to delineate the class distinctions within black communities. His motives for this, I would argue, were as much academic as political, as were his intended audiences. The first was to declare to fellow scholars and to a white reading public that, contrary to what their racial assumptions dictated in the absence of contact and investigation, black people were not some indistinct and poverty-stricken mass but a varied population as measured by occupation, education, income, property ownership, and so on. Only stubborn bigotry or willful ignorance could maintain otherwise, but racism relies on reductionism because it cannot handle variation. And as for the second, it was to remind the black elite of these communities of its social obligation to its less fortunate members, with the exception, it seems, of the "submerged tenth" as Du Bois labeled the "lowest class of criminals and prostitutes":[26] to help these last acquire the moral and material foundations of middle-class life. With regard to the first objective, Du Bois ended his study of Farmville, Virginia, with this reflection:

A study of a community like Farmville brings to light facts favorable and unfavorable, and conditions good, bad, and indifferent. Just how the whole should be interpreted is perhaps doubtful. One thing, however, is clear, and that is the growing differentiation of classes among Negroes, even in small communities. This most natural and encouraging result of 30 years' development has not yet been sufficiently impressed upon general students of the subject, and leads to endless contradiction and confusion.[27]

Although Du Bois did not underscore his second objective in his agrarian studies, he did so in *The Philadelphia Negro*, the larger, yet complementary urban study that he was completing at the time that he conducted fieldwork in Farmville.

> Nothing more exasperates the better class of Negroes than this tendency to ignore utterly their existence. The law-abiding, hard-working inhabitants of the Thirteenth Ward are aroused to righteous indignation when they see that the word Negro carries most Philadelphians' minds to the alleys of the Fifth Ward or the police courts. . . . So far they are justified; but they make their mistake in failing to recognize that, however laudable an ambition to rise may be, the first duty of an upper class is to serve the lowest classes. The aristocracies of all peoples have been slow in learning this and perhaps the Negro is no slower than the rest, but his peculiar situation demands that in his case this lesson be learned sooner.[28]

Irrespective of the motivations and politics involved in his pursuit of demonstrating class distinctions in black communities, both rural and urban, the impetus contributed to Du Bois's pioneering work in sociology.

By contrast, there was nothing in Weber's biography that was comparable to Du Bois's that would have nudged Weber to engage in the type of direct social investigation that Du Bois did early in his academic career. This is no judgment but a matter of fact. Proudly middle class, nominally Protestant in a Protestant-identifying country, and a member of an internationally renowned professorate, Weber belonged to Germany's bourgeois establishment. His place in it was secured by the commercial success and political activities of his paternal grandfather and father: Karl August Weber was a successful linen merchant who provided his grandson with a model of the Protestant businessman for *The Protestant Ethic and the Spirit of Capitalism*; and Max Weber Sr. spent nearly thirty years in the Prussian House of Deputies and a dozen in the Reichstag. With these biographical highlights, I do not mean to suggest that Weber's background determined his outlook on all issues but that on the matters of ethnicity, class, and nation, to name but these three, his perspectives were mainly derived from his privileged social position, which was little interested in the direct viewpoints of Germany's ethnic and religious minorities or its working class. In my view, this is why Weber felt comfortable making certain grand claims about German Poles, Catholics, Jews, and workers generally (just as he later would about Chinese and Indians) without discussions with members of those groups. Of course, Weber was not alone in this, and Du Bois himself indulged in making unsubstantiated claims about certain segments of the black poor even when his fieldwork gave him the opportunity to interview members of that population.

WHAT IS TO BE DONE?

As their agrarian studies had been solicited by governmental offices or semigovernmental organizations (as in the Verein's case), Weber and Du Bois were expected to make policy recommendations on their findings. In Du Bois's case, however, it is more appropriate to refer to policy principles rather than to specific policies given that, at this juncture, Du Bois was foremost interested in the bedrock beliefs that shaped the formulation and implementation of social policies. Still, what is striking about Weber's and Du Bois's policy visions are their diametric opposition: where the former was calling for the expulsion of a conquered and colonized people from eastern Germany no less than from their ancestral lands, the latter was calling for the admission into the American body politic of a formerly enslaved people. Apparently, on matters of race and nation Du Bois and Weber were at the opposite ends of the political spectrum. Yet Weber's solicitation from Du Bois of an article on black life in the United States suggests that Weber was at least sympathetic to the black American quest for full citizenship. How, then, do we make sense of Weber's ostensibly contradictory positions on racial and ethnic inclusion in the United States and Germany?

The simple answers to these questions are, one, that despite his warnings about the cultural consequences of a large influx of Slavs into the United States, Weber thought that ethnic and racial pluralism was foundational to that country and would continue to be so; and two, that contrary to what a sizable number of white Americans believed, black Americans did not pose a greater social threat to American society than Slavs, despite the congenital nervous condition and occasional simian appearance of blacks that Weber alleged. Thus, Du Bois's concluding pronouncement in his *Archiv* article might have found a receptive ear in Weber.

> In the struggle for his human rights the American Negro relies above all on the feeling of justice in the civilized world. We are no barbarians or heathen, we are educable and our education is increasing; our economic abilities have proven themselves. We too want to have our chance in life. Whoever wants to get acquainted with our living conditions, be welcome; we demand nothing other than that one gets acquainted with us honestly and face to face, and does not judge us according to hearsay or according to the verdict of our despisers.
>
> And above all consider one thing: the day of the colored races dawns. It is insanity to delay this development; it is wisdom to promote what it promises us in light and hope for the future.[29]

What Weber did not mention in his own parting words in his St. Louis address were the policy measures he had advocated against the Polish presence in eastern Germany just a few years earlier. This reticence was hardly necessary in light of the fact that it was common North American practice to restrict the immigration of specific European populations.[30] Yet what might have been surprising to even a gathering of transatlantic WASP professors was the call for the expulsion of Poles in eastern Germany and their replacement with Germans from the west of the country. For in the Americas, at least, such policies were typically applied to Amerindian, African, and Asian populations, not to fellow European ones. Even in Europe itself, these measures to "forcibly expel thousands of recent nonnaturalized Russian and Galician Polish immigrants, [were] a then-unprecedented act in peacetime."[31] Moreover, as Weber himself could have predicted from the findings of the eastern German agricultural study, the Prussian Settlement Commission's efforts to re-Germanize the East with farmers from Germany's west would not offset the countermovement of eastern German farmers heading west: in the twenty years after the founding of the commission in 1886, it was able to convince only 130,000 western Germans to settle in the east as against nearly one million easterners who departed for the west.[32] Germans, like Poles, sought their own definitions of freedom, not those that the German government offered, however enticing the terms.

STRANGE SILENCES

A remarkable aspect of the Weber–Du Bois exchange was each man's decision either to withhold comment from or to not include in his own academic work or autobiographical reflections the other's research findings or policy recommendations. Two of the most glaring are Du Bois's silence on Weber's anti-Polish remarks and Weber's dismissal of Du Bois's reflections on the origins and maintenance of racism in the American South.

If, as Nahum Chandler convincingly argues, Du Bois was in attendance for Weber's 1893 lecture before the Verein, "Developmental Tendencies in the Situation of East Elbian Rural Labourers,"[33] then Weber's St. Louis address was the second time that he heard Weber lecture, and the second time that he heard the German scholar make unflattering remarks about Poles. Of course, in fairness to Weber, we cannot single him out for having sentiments that were common to academics, politicians, and laypeople alike.[34] Yet it is precisely the pervasiveness of anti-Polish expression in the years that Du Bois was in Germany that makes his silence on the subject so puzzling. For if German scholars, like Weber, were comfortable making public pronouncements on the deficiencies of Poles, we can only imagine the type of comments they made in more informal settings, such as pubs or even seminars. This silence is all the more striking for its selectivity; Du Bois made sure to mention both his visit to Poland and the anti-Polish policies of Russian-administered Poland in at least three of his autobiographies: "A Pageant in Seven Decades," *Dusk of Dawn*, and *The Autobiography of W. E. B. Du Bois*.[35] In *The Autobiography*, where Du Bois provides the most expansive retelling of the circumstances of his visit to Poland, it began with his friendship with a Polish student, Stanislaus von Estreicher, at the University of Berlin who questioned the uniqueness of American racism and invited Du Bois to Cracow to see for himself. Du Bois recorded in his travelogue:

> Finally I came to Krakow and my friend. It was an interesting visit and an old tale. Tyranny in school and work: insult in home and on the street. Of course here, in contrast to America, there were the privileged Poles who escaped personal insult; there was the aristocracy who had some recognized rights. The whole mass of the oppressed were not reduced to one level; nevertheless the degradation was only too familiar.[36]

No such recollections from Berlin, however. To what can we attribute Du Bois's uncharacteristic silence on a subject of such importance to him? My colleague Jeffrey Stewart has provided possibly the most convincing explanation: the difficulty Du Bois had criticizing the people and places that treated him kindly.[37] This was perhaps one of the reasons he could not bring himself to seriously critique Stalin's Soviet Union, as I discuss in chapter 4.

Whatever his reasons for not calling attention to German anti-Slavism generally and Weber's especially, Du Bois missed an opportunity to call both into question. I say this not out of some naive belief that Du Bois's words or those of any other person could have changed the course of history, as subscribers to the great men theory of history would assert, but rather to suggest that if, as a black American who had studied in Germany and who was furthermore a deep admirer of its history and people, Du Bois had publicly drawn parallels between antiblack policies and practices in the United States and anti-Polish ones in Germany, he could have put his German hosts on the defensive. Similarly, if he had challenged Weber directly on his anti-Polish sentiments, he could have forced Weber to respond to the charge presumably less crudely than he had prior to this hypothetical point, which, among other results, would have also forced Weber scholars to meet the issue head-on rather than clumsily avoid it. Still, this is a lot to retrospectively ask of anyone, let alone a young scholar in a foreign land.

Although Weber's silence about Du Bois's expertise in particularly southern race relations was not as politically consequential as Du Bois's silence about Weber's anti-Polish views, it was troubling nonetheless. It was also ironic in light of what Weber had gone on record to say about Du Bois's scholarship years earlier. Still, we can point to instances where Weber implicitly called into question the very points that Du Bois highlighted in "Die Neger Frage in Vereinigten Staaten." One of these was Du Bois's description of the "rural police force" during slavery.

> The need to provide ordered conditions and surveillance of the slaves effected a cautious common procedure among the masters. The South was never rid of the fear of an insurrection and the fateful attempts of Cato, Gabriel, Vesey, Turner and Toussaint transformed this fear into an ever-present specter. Thus, a rural police force was developed that was at its post primarily at night and whose task it was to prevent nightly wanderings and meetings of slaves. This organization was usually very effective and held the slaves in fear. All whites belonged to it and had to fulfill their precisely defined service in specific intervals.[38]

Contrast this now with Weber's explanation of why poor rather than elite whites were the "actual" purveyors of racial animus in the South during slavery.

> The sense of ethnic honor is a specific honor of the masses (*Massenehre*), for it is accessible to anybody who belongs to the subjectively believed community of descent. The 'poor white trash,' i.e., the propertyless and, in the absence of job opportunities, very often destitute white inhabitants of the southern states of the United States of America in the period of slavery, were the actual bearers of racial antipathy, which was quite foreign to the planters. This was so because the social honor of the 'poor white' was dependent upon the *declassement* of the Negroes.[39]

There is a lot that could be said in response to this juxtaposition of Du Bois's and Weber's differences over the sources of racial sentiments in the white population in the slave era. However, one point is readily apparent: Weber's proposition required the disregard of Du Bois's explanation of the racial sentiments held by non-slaveholding whites in the

South. It also required the avoidance of the material reasons that so many southern whites were propertyless and unable to secure viable employment, however obvious these may have been to Weber. These, too, Du Bois supplied in "Die Neger Frage in den Vereinigten Staaten," where he noted that slave owners constituted "only five or six percent of the white population" and typically "possessed 20 to 200 slaves and several hundred acres of land" and that artisans comprised some portion of the enslaved population in the South.[40] Therefore, if poor whites clung to a "sense of ethnic honor," as Weber termed it, it was due not only to the fact that their skin color protected them from enslavement but also to the simultaneous fact that the system of racial slavery impoverished them while enriching their property-owning (of land and slaves) kin. To Du Bois, any sociological understanding, worthy of the name, of the slave-era South and afterward would have to take such class sentiments into account. But to claim, as Weber did, that southern slaveholders did not exhibit "racial antipathy" is both a perversion of the historical record and an inversion of the material and ideological sources of racial identity formation.

However, far more significant, in my opinion, than their disagreement over which class was the greater promoter of racial antagonism in the slave South is the fact that Weber neither named nor referenced Du Bois in the section of *Economy and Society* where the passage cited above appears. To interpret this as a slight seems entirely reasonable given that in the academic world the primary gesture of scholarly respect is citation, even if in disagreement. That Weber chose not to extend this courtesy says far more than his claim that Du Bois was the "most important sociological scholar anywhere in the Southern States in America, with whom no scholar can compare."

DU BOIS'S INSPIRATIONS

At this juncture, it seems appropriate to return to a question that I raised at the beginning of this chapter: if the German scholars whom Du Bois encountered at the University of Berlin and in the Verein provided him with models and methods of conducting sociological research in the

United States. In Du Bois's telling, they did neither. Fairly typical of his indirect comments on the twin themes are those he made in his important essay, "My Evolving Program for Negro Freedom," in which he states that he had undertaken *The Philadelphia Negro* with "no research methods" but then goes on to remark that he compiled schedules, "went through the Philadelphia libraries for data[,] . . . [and] mapped the district [Philadelphia's Seventh Ward], classifying it by condition."[41] Yet were not some of these research techniques the very ones that German scholars either in the University of Berlin or in the Verein employed in their case studies, among which was Weber's own *The Conditions of East Elban Agricultural Workers*? If so, why, then, the omission by Du Bois of the exemplary role German scholars played in his intellectual and professional formation? I can imagine at least a couple of reasons: to highlight the ethnographic methods that he pioneered without the help of either the University of Berlin or the Verein; and to assert obliquely that social investigation "by proxy" rather than in person is suspect. Still, whatever one's feelings about Du Bois's minimization of the German influences on his thought and scholarship, this slight seems hardly justifiable in the areas of scholarship and reform and scholarship and activism. For what a number of German social scientists combined in their professional and private lives, far more than their North American counterparts, were teaching, research, and state service. More than simply a reflection of the fact that they were state employees, the German professorate largely looked to the state to maintain sociocultural continuity, however defined and envisioned, and therefore sought to work with it for what its members saw as the greater national good amid significant social transformation. In this regard, the founding of the Verein was part of a much longer German tradition. That Du Bois sought to adopt and adapt the Verein's research and reform agenda (albeit for more progressive ends) is suggested by his consistent pursuit of these twin aims in all of the organizations that he either cofounded or of which he was a member. I do not mean to imply with this line of argumentation that there were not North American models from which Du Bois could have drawn inspiration that had research and reform agendas (he does name the Tuskegee and Hampton Conferences in "My Evolving Program for Negro Freedom") but that the combination was certainly reinforced by what he witnessed in Berlin. It seems to me that Du Bois could have acknowledged this influence despite his disappointment with the political path that Germany had taken in the first half of the twentieth century.

THE TENSIONS OF CULTURE

Despite the substantial differences in the policy conclusions that they drew from their agrarian studies, Du Bois and Weber continued to put stock in notions that seemed to defy the very discipline that they were advancing. I am referring here to spirits and souls, but the list could also include ideals, ethics, and even races. Of course, Weber and Du Bois were not alone in their invocation of these amorphous and immeasurable concepts, for many in the mid- to late nineteenth century in particular had recourse to them much as their predecessors had a century or more earlier in response to what they perceived to be the Enlightenment's "shallow" and "utilitarian" project of revealing the "laws" of social behavior for all of humankind.[42] However, Du Bois and Weber were very much men of the Enlightenment who, while recognizing the singularity of specific phenomena, peoples, and individuals, were also in pursuit of patterns and tendencies across societies and eras. Hence the irony in the fact that their references to souls and spirits should have occurred at precisely the time when they both took pains to demonstrate the empirical foundations of sociological data gathering, classification, and analysis into which they could only awkwardly, at best, situate the former. For if one of the goals of sociology is to demystify the terms of social interaction, then recourse to souls, spirits, and other literally immaterial phenomena seems like a return to or residue of pre-Enlightenment thought.

To this charge, both of our protagonists (Weber more emphatically) countered that they were simply trying to make sense of the same issues with which Enlightenment thinkers grappled: namely, the variety of cultural practices that have existed in roughly similar material environments. This was certainly the case for black Americans, who, despite having been legally reduced to the lowest economic unit for two hundred years, at minimum, in the Atlantic arena, managed to forge cultural practices and norms that not only defied their socioeconomic condition, but were also distinct from those of their white neighbors. And in the European world, cultural variations, of which religious beliefs and rituals are among the clearest expressions, have been as numerous as Europe's official and regional languages. With these and countless other examples in mind, Weber and Du Bois sought to give the cultural or "spiritual" dimension of human existence the freedom to act on and in the material world, unlike those who argue that matters of the spirit merely conform to human interests. As Weber once remarked on this subject, "Religious rationalization has its own dynamics, which economic conditions merely channel."[43]

However, a social scientist's invocation of spirits and other cultural phenomena has its own hazards. First and most obvious is the risk of essentializing a population, a system, or an era.[44] Culture-invoking or culture-centered approaches to social phenomena demand that virtually every member of a particular group or child of a specific epoch behave in a way that corresponds to how the formulators have characterized or stereotyped that population: blacks are supposed to act like this, Protestants in this way, and Jews in yet another way. (How black Protestants are supposed to conduct themselves is open to debate.) In this sense, cultural arguments are totalizing and static in that they prescribe the range of choices that any one of us is permitted to make; they reduce the variety of potential ways of being for an entire population. As a result of the limits they impose on the individual's behavior, cultural theories of social action lend themselves to overuse or to just plain abuse. Weber provides a glaring example of this temptation. In *Economy and Society*, he elaborates on a claim that he earlier made in *The Protestant Ethic and the Spirit of Capitalism.*

> The Jews were relatively or altogether absent from the new and distinctive forms of modern capitalism, the rational organization of labor, especially production in an industrial enterprise of the factory type. The Jews evinced the ancient and medieval business temper which had been and remained typical of all genuine traders, whether small businessmen or large-scale moneylenders, in Antiquity, the Far East, India, the Mediterranean littoral area, and the Occident of the Middle Ages: the will and wit to employ mercilessly every chance for profit, 'for the sake of profit to ride through Hell even if it singes the sails.'[45]

To account for Jewish representation in Germany's textile, electric, metal, machine-making, and processing industries, Weber qualified his earlier claims about Jewish absence in industry by remarking in his final lectures that the "Jewish manufacturer . . . is a modern phenomenon."[46] Presumably, by the mid- to late nineteenth century, German Jews had been sufficiently possessed by the capitalist spirit and had become sufficiently convinced of the correctness of the Protestant ethic. Could there be any other explanation from a culturalist perspective for such a marked departure in the behavior of some segment of a people?

A related problem with cultural approaches to social interaction is that they are highly teleological, or preconception driven, particularly on the matter of how a group adopts a cultural stance or practice. Such a tendency is admittedly unavoidable to some extent: researchers, laypeople, and detectives normally set out to explain a phenomenon or event by working "backward" from the event itself. However, in that commonsense process, those investigators have already assumed that the main clues of the event's causes lie somewhere in the event itself and not in other, indirect or circumstantial factors that are just as likely to have resulted in a similar or the same phenomenon. Du Bois provides an example that illustrates the point. In his 1897 address to the American Negro Academy, which he would later head, Du Bois asserted that, thanks to "their race identity and common blood . . . and more important, a common history, common laws and religion, similar habits of thought and conscious striving together for certain ideals of life . . . [t]he English nation stood for constitutional liberty and commercial freedom; the German nation for science and philosophy; the Romance nations . . . for literature and art, and the other race groups are striving, each in its own way, to develop for civilization its particular message, its particular ideal."[47]

Apart from the fact that such a pat formulation is short on the details of, to take one example, England's historical predisposition to excel in certain types of political and economic programs, it still suggests that Germany's or any other country's historical trajectory discouraged those same developments because of something in its people's blood and background. This denial of alternative possibilities, of the plasticity of otherwise malleable variables, is the risk that cultural arguments run in their explanations of social phenomenon. On this matter Marshall Hodgson

remarked, "Rather than being an ideally fixed pattern . . . supplying a determinant body of ideas and practices, a cultural heritage forms a relatively passive setting for action. Within that setting, any given juncture
may bring a fresh turn of orientation; or at least its outcome will be relatively unpredictable, for the same setting will allow for varying sorts of
actions according as circumstances, temperaments, and problems vary."[48]
Ironically, in the attempt to free humanity from the straitjackets into
which materialist theories had put it, culturalists had, in many respects,
merely substituted materialist theories with their own.

   Finally, culture-centered approaches to social phenomena are difference obsessed. Despite the attention that Weber drew to the similarities
of some aspects of different religious systems and Du Bois's claim that
"there is no reason why, in the same country and on the same street, two
or three great national ideals might not thrive and develop, that men of
different races might not strive together for their race ideals as well,
perhaps even better, than in isolation,"[49] the fact is that culture-privileging
approaches to social phenomena put a premium on how one group is
categorically different from another. For if neither common historical
movements nor common social variables nor political evolution is the ultimate source of one's culture, then no two cultures are similar beyond
the fact that they are cultures. Each culture is distinct, discrete, and at a
distance from fellow ones. Sidelined or minimized in this orientation are
the possibilities of common phases, stages, or influences between populations. Consequently, cultures largely stand in opposition to one another. As benign as they initially may seem, cultures are in a constant
state of conflict, with, at times, surprisingly deadly consequences.[50]

A FORK IN THE ROAD

In the years subsequent to the publication of *The Souls of Black Folk* and
The Protestant Ethic and the Spirit of Capitalism, Du Bois and Weber followed divergent paths in the area of culture and social action.[51] Weber
continued to make the interaction between the two one of the centerpieces of his sociological work. In the decade before his death, he completed three other religious-cum-cultural studies—*The Religion of China*,
The Religion of India, and *Ancient Judaism*—which he intended to serve

as companions to and as bases of comparison with *The Protestant Ethic and the Spirit of Capitalism*. Central to these studies and substantial parts of his compendium, *Economy and Society*, is what Weber termed the ideal type or the hypothetical imagining of "what course a given type of human action would take if it were strictly rational, unaffected by errors or emotional factors and if, furthermore, it were completely and un-equivocally directed to a single end."[52] An everyday example, which par-tially captures the meaning of the ideal type, is the construction, "If I had known, I would have . . . ." And this is precisely what he sought to highlight in the ideal type—that it is a common cognitive practice of academics no less than laypeople once they have perceived in others or themselves specific aims and the means of achieving them.

However, it is precisely the implicitness or unstated use of the ideal type that makes it problematic. For the risk that the employer of the ideal type runs is conflating the factual and the projected, or the real and the ideal. This, I believe, is the pitfall of *The Protestant Ethic and the Spirit of Capitalism*. Curiously, Weber's denunciations of scholarly bias did not include the abuse of the ideal type. Rather, foremost on his list of infractions was a scholar's unannounced interjection of personal opin-ion into his studies.[53]

For Du Bois's part, he ceased subsequently to employ culturalist lan-guage to explain social phenomena, save for a couple of instances, and there he did not refer to black people but the "souls of white folk."[54] I return shortly to what he said about them. Rather than the partial reality that the study of a particular group's culture provided, Du Bois wanted to comprehend the "far mightier social environment—the surrounding world of custom, wish, whim, and thought which envelops [a] group and powerfully influences its social development."[55] In the terminology of his former philosophy professor, William James, Du Bois felt that too much social scholarship departed from "first things" or "principles, 'categories,' or supposed necessities" rather than from "last things" or "fruits, conse-quences, facts."[56] Rationality was presumably one of those "first things" that drove Du Bois in the early twentieth century to "desert Schmoller and Weber" and to "f[a]ll back upon . . . Royce and James."[57] Rather than hypothetically suspend or dispense with the irrational and unpredictable as the ideal and other rationality-based types propose, Du Bois sought to restore them to their rightful place in the domain of the factual.

Facts, in social science, I realized were elusive things: emotions, loves, hates, were facts; and they were facts in the souls and minds of the scientific student, as well as in the persons studied. Their measurement, then, was doubly difficult and intricate. If I could see and feel this in East St. Louis, where I investigated a bloody race riot, I knew all the more definitely, that in the cold, bare facts of history, so much was omitted from the complete picture that it could only be recovered as complete scientific knowledge if we could read back into the past enough to piece out the reality. I knew also that even in the ugly picture which I actually saw, there was so much of decisive truth missing that any story I told would be woefully incomplete.[58]

Although Du Bois mentions the East St. Louis race riot of 1917 in the above passage, his interest in Chance, or the "inexplicable," as he apparently interpreted the social unrest in the midwestern city, began much earlier, certainly as early as the Congress of Arts and Science where he met Weber, which prompted him to right one of the few theoretical pieces he ever wrote, "Sociology Hesitant." In that essay, Du Bois proposed a means of reconciling the opposition between the natural and social sciences by asserting that "in time and space, Law covers the major part of the universe, but . . . the area left in that world to Chance is of tremendous import."[59] Defining Chance as those "actions undetermined by and independent of actions gone before,"[60] Du Bois counseled sociologists to "assum[e] the data of physics and [to] study within these that realm where determinate force is acted on by human wills of indeterminate force."[61] However, what Du Bois left unclear is whether sociologists should categorize racial stratification as an expression of social "law" or chance.

THE BREAK

In the various versions of the essay that ultimately became "The Souls of White Folk" in *Darkwater*,[62] Du Bois implies that the belief in white superiority in virtually all areas and by all measures is a recent chance phenomenon: "a nineteenth and twentieth century matter, indeed."[63] Yet, with his wide knowledge of human history, Du Bois would have readily admitted that the means and ends of white supremacy—"by emphasis and omission" to convince all involved that "of all the hues of God whiteness alone is inherently and obviously better than brownness or tan"[64]— have been employed by all self-declared superiors who aim to justify their dominant social position. Still, what is more striking about this essay than where Du Bois situated sociologically white supremacy is his ultimate retreat from cultural explanations of social phenomena altogether.[65] In a passage at once both sarcastic and serious, Du Bois mocks white supremacist thought: "In fine, that if from the world were dropped everything that could not fairly be attributed to White Folk, the world would, if anything, be even greater, truer, better than now. And if all this be a lie, is it not a lie in a great cause."[66] No, responded Du Bois, because instead of racial and cultural fictions, he sought human facts, and the most pressing of these at the time were World War I and the degree to which it reflected the state of European "civilization."

> In the awful cataclysm of World War, where from beating, slandering, and murdering us the white world turned temporarily aside to kill each other, we of the Darker Peoples looked on in mild amaze. . . .
>
> As we saw the dead dimly through rifts of battle-smoke and heard faintly the cursings and accusations of blood brothers, we darker men said: This is not Europe gone mad; this is not aberration nor insanity; this is Europe; this seeming Terrible is the real soul of white culture—back of all culture,—stripped and visible today. This is where the world has arrived,—these dark and awful depths and not the shining and ineffable heights of which it boasted. Here is whither the might and energy of modern humanity has really gone.[67]

To state the obvious, this was a damning indictment of European culture (only slightly softened by his generous melding of European culture and the cultures of the world) and one that Du Bois first expressed only a few years after his correspondence with Weber. Yet by 1910 and certainly by 1917 Du Bois was outraged not only by what people of European descent had done and continued to do to black Americans,

Africans, and Asians, but no less by what they were doing to each other in World War I, inspired, he would argue, by the same racist and ethnocentric logic that they cultivated in overseas empire building. Thus, absent in "The Souls of White Folk" is any reference to or praise of English governance, German philosophy, or Romance artistry, for as far as Du Bois was concerned these elements of European civilization did not outweigh murder of genocidal proportions for which European "civilization" was responsible in the colonies and in Europe itself. This was a double challenge to one, at least, of Weber's main contentions—that European- or Protestant-ushered modernity is rational—for profit-driven imperialism and its repercussions were unreason to the core. As discussed in the next chapter, even if Weber had not died just after the war, it is unlikely that he would have addressed the war's causes. But in an indirect response to Du Bois and others who had seen in World War I a clear indication of European barbarism, Weber reasserted, in his general introduction to his comparative studies of religion, his belief in European superiority in a variety of domains and fields, from the natural sciences to government, from philosophy to musical composition.[68] Apparently expecting these sorts of claims in the aftermath of World War I, precisely because of the ways in which it called into question Western civilization, Du Bois offered in his "anticipatory reply" to Weber, as Nahum Chandler aptly put it,[69] an alternative explanation of European achievements.

> Why, then, is Europe great? Because of the foundations which the mighty past have furnished her to build upon: the iron trade of ancient, black Africa, the religion and empire-building of yellow Asia, the art and science of the 'dago' Mediterranean shore, east, south, and west, as well as north. And where she has builded securely upon this great past and learned from it she has gone forward to greater and more splendid human triumph; but where she has ignored this past and forgotten and sneered at it, she has shown the cloven hoof of poor, crucified humanity,—she has played, like other empires gone, the world fool.[70]

As imperfect and questionable the items on the list and the circumstances under which they were transferred, we follow Du Bois's point:

Europe's successes have been, to a greater or lesser extent, syntheses of the world's contributions, not of Europe's alone, as Weber would have it, wherever he and like-minded commentators marked Europe's boundaries. Needless to say, by the time of Weber's death in 1920, he and Du Bois were at odds over a number of issues.

WHEN WEBER AND DU BOIS met over breakfast in St. Louis at the 1904 Congress of Arts and Science, it was more than just the reconnection of two acquaintances; it was the meeting of two founders of the field of sociology in their respective countries. At the time of their reunion they had already undertaken major rural and urban studies and were primed to do more. Little wonder that Weber solicited from Du Bois an article on the state of black America, offered to have *The Souls of Black Folk* published in German, and encouraged Du Bois to spend a sabbatical in Germany. However, within two years of this positive and promising exchange, their contact ended, not to be resumed. One plausible answer to this puzzle is that in the time that Du Bois had taken to submit his article to Weber, which included reflecting on Weber's address in St. Louis, he realized that he disagreed strongly with Weber on a number of substantive issues. These included the place of unfree labor and race in capitalism, no less than on the subject of imperialism. Du Bois's love affair with imperial Germany had ended, and his relationship with Weber was one of the casualties.

CHAPTER THREE

The Fruits of Merchant's Capital

In light of the theme on which I ended the previous chapter, one could justifiably argue that German idealism and romanticism initially had the greatest intellectual impacts on Weber and Du Bois. Despite the empirical foundations of their sociological and historical work, they were still prone to refer to certain populations, institutions, and systems as possessing fixed attributes that were impervious to changes in the social contexts in which they lived or operated. Nonetheless, despite these idealist leanings, I maintain that the honors for the person who exercised the most profound intellectual impact, directly and indirectly, on Weber and Du Bois should go to Karl Marx, whom Isaiah Berlin named the "true father of . . . modern sociology."[1] For proof of this we only have to consider whether Weber or Du Bois or a host of other social commentators of the late nineteenth and twentieth century could have written some of their most important work, academic and popular, without Marx's insights into and emphasis on the economic or material determinants of society. To review, these are that the material bases of any society are located in its division of labor, the main (two) classes that that division creates,[2] and the means of production that its laboring classes employ to provide their social superiors with the products they demand.

The hallmark of capitalist societies is the emergence of and relationship between the bourgeoisie (today's CEOs and majority shareholders), or the owners of the means of production, and the proletariat, or those former peasants and small farmers who were dispossessed by money-driven landlords of their landholdings and who had to consequently offer their labor to the bourgeoisie in order to earn a livelihood. In its vulgar or polemical version, Marxist thought posits that all of the apparent noneconomic ideas and institutions of a given society reflect and reproduce its class structure. In practical terms this means that a society's educational, legal, political, and cultural systems are but projections of and insurance measures for the maintenance of the economic interests of the class that lives off the labor of the subordinate one. The ensemble of a society's division of labor, the dominant instruments of production, and the prevailing ideology that informs that society's primary social institutions Marx called mode of production. In his early writings Marx identified four modes of production throughout history: Asiatic, ancient, feudal, and bourgeois or capitalist.[3]

MARX AND MAX

For his part, Weber took little issue with either Marx's description of the structure of capitalist society or the assertion that the dominant beliefs of a given society are normally those of its privileged classes. What troubled him was the potentially reductionist uses of Marxist thought to render powerless noneconomic, or cultural, forces (to the degree that these operate independently of economic ones) in both the noncapitalist and capitalist eras. This was critical for Weber. For as I suggested earlier, what Weber objected to and challenged was the tendency by economic determinists of both the Marxist and liberal varieties to ascribe to past actors the economic motivations and preoccupations of the capitalist societies within which the latter currently live(d). Thus, quite apart from the merits of his findings, one of Weber's many contributions to the social sciences generally and to the ongoing debate of capitalism's rise in particular was to raise the question of how religious or cultural precepts can (semi-)independently shape material or economic action. Moreover, in order to explore this question, Weber had to perform two difficult

intellectual operations that were also contributions to social scientific inquiry: he could not assume that the actions of noncapitalist agents who
followed specific religious norms were driven by the profit motive, for
that would be to ascribe anachronistic capitalist motives to them; and,
accordingly, he had to imagine that the economic impacts of their actions were not their intentions.

However, these observations of Weber's dialogue with Marxism
mainly apply to his treatment of noncapitalist societies; in his political
writings on modern capitalism he exhibits a noticeable appreciation for
Marxist perspectives on what lies at the heart of capitalist society against
which they rail. In fact, on occasion the force and emotion behind some
of his remarks on capitalism could not have been more passionately expressed by a Marxist himself or herself. In his 1916 "open letter" to the
editor of *Die Frau*, Weber had this to say:

> Anyone who has even a penny of investment income which others
> have to pay directly or indirectly, anyone who owns any durable
> goods or consumes any commodity produced not by his own sweat
> but by that of others, lives off the operation of that loveless and un-
> pitying economic struggle for existence which bourgeois phrase-
> ology designates as 'peaceful cultural work.' This is just another
> form of man's struggle with man, one in which not millions but
> hundreds of millions of people, year after year, waste away in body
> or soul, sink without a trace, or lead an existence truly . . . bereft of
> any recognizable 'meaning.'[4]

This is Max, not Marx! And this was neither the first nor the last time
that Weber expressed the workings of capitalism in ways that we associate more with Marx than with him. In line with this understanding
of capitalism, Weber also thought it natural and logical that different
social classes should have different political-economic interests that are
generally conflictual. This is simply the normal state of capitalist society.
Cross-class causes (such as nationalism) can attenuate but can never entirely eliminate this basic feature of capitalism.

Alienation and class conflict were not, however, the only concepts
that Weber borrowed from Marx's inventory of capitalism; two others
are equally important in themselves and for our purposes: wage payment

is the quintessentially capitalist form of labor remuneration; and merchant's capital is unable to transform one mode of production into another. Each of these contentions requires some elaboration.

The Faux Fruits of Merchant's Capital

Like Marx, Weber maintained that wage labor is one of the requirements of modern, industrial capitalism.[5] Its cost-effectiveness was as clear to them as it has been to capitalists themselves. Wage labor obviates an initial outlay of capital to secure a labor force (as in slavery) and its maintenance when the demand for its use evaporates (again, in contrast to slavery). In these last instances, firm owners simply lay off that unneeded portion of their workforce. This ever present threat "is an important incentive to the maximization of production," Weber argued. Moreover, this threat along with wage labor dependence more generally enable employers to "select the labor force according to ability and willingness to work."[6]

For Marx, wage labor suits capitalism perfectly because, like the latter, it is theft masquerading as fairness: it creates the illusion that the capitalist pays his employee the full value of her labor in a given day when, in fact, he cheats her of some portion of it by having her work beyond the time for which he actually pays her. With wage payment, "surplus-labor and necessary labor glide one into the other"[7] is how, in one instance, Marx expressed its shortchanging of the worker. In another, he remarked that the "value of labor-power, and the value which that labor-power creates in the labor-process, are two entirely different magnitudes; and this difference of the two values was what the capitalist had in view, when he was purchasing the labor-power."[8] Thus, where Weber saw proof of rational accounting and calculation in wage labor, Marx saw capitalist theft pure and simple. Weber may have decried the alienation that is both cause and effect of modern capitalism, but he thought the rationality that it expressed far more commendable than lamentable.

If Marx and Weber agreed that the wage earner is a prerequisite of modern capitalism, they also had cause to disparage those forms of economic activity that failed to advance its emergence and expansion. Such was their assessment of merchant's capital, of which they recognized two principal types: usury, or the interest charged on borrowed money; and long-distance trade. Weber categorized this last form of merchant's capital, along with tax farming, war profiteering, and colonialism, as political capitalism because the opportunity to engage in these economic activities is typically granted by political actors, either domestic or foreign.[9] They were thus politically determined rather than competitively won monopolies. Consequently, the recipients of these privileges have cause to be both politically and economically conservative: politically, because their livelihoods depend on the continued rule of the power holders who had awarded them their monopolies in the first place; and economically, because they have been shielded from competition, which normally acts as a catalyst of technological and organizational innovation. One of those innovations was the adoption of wage labor.

Marx's economic criticism of merchant's capital went further than this. To him, the great weakness of merchant's capital was not so much that it was monopolistic but that its members were generally uninterested in the production techniques employed by those whose goods they moved to other markets. Merchants are generally concerned solely with exchange, not production. In figurative language, Marx described merchant's capital's limits in the following manner, with "extremes" referring to the means or methods of production and "premises" to a society's social development or the extent of its division of labor: "Merchant's capital is originally merely the intervening movement between extremes which it does not control, and between premises which it does not create."[10]

Merchant's capital's acceptance of the prevailing methods of production contrasts sharply with industrial capital's preoccupation with managing them. In light of Marx's emphasis on work and production as quintessential human activities, we are not surprised by his ranking of industrial capital above merchant's capital. From this assessment of these two forms of capital, Marx drew four conclusions. First, whereas "in the pre-capitalist stages of society commerce ruled industry, . . . [i]n modern society the reverse is true" (325). Second, "wherever merchant's capital still predominates, we find backward conditions [of production] . . . whose lack of development [is] the basis of its existence" (322, 324). Third, "as soon as capital has established its sway over production and imparted to it a wholly changed and specific form—merchant's capital . . . becomes the servant of industrial production" (321, 331). And fourth, merchant's capital "cannot by itself contribute to the overthrow of [an] old mode of production, but tends rather to preserve and retain it as its precondition" (329). In the following passage, Marx elaborates on this point.

> To what extent [merchant's capital] brings about a dissolution of the old mode of production depends on its solidity and internal structure. And whither this process of dissolution will lead, in other words, what new mode of production will replace the old, does not depend on commerce, but on the character of the old mode of production itself. In the ancient world the effect of commerce and the development of merchant's capital always resulted in a slave economy. . . . However, in the modern world, it results in the capitalist mode of production. It follows therefrom that these results spring in themselves from circumstances other than the development of merchant's capital. (326–27)

Here was Marx's proof that merchant's capital is unable, by itself, to transform one mode of production into another: its failure to carry through the supercession of the ancient by the feudal but its success in facilitating the transition from the feudal to the capitalist suggests that other, more decisive variables dictate that process. When we read this passage and compare it to Weber's assessment of the economic impact of colonial trade on western Europe below, we cannot help but be struck by the conceptual parallels between the two, despite the differences in emphasis.

> Th[e] accumulation of wealth brought about through colonial trade has been of little significance for the development of modern capitalism. . . . It is true that the colonial trade made possible the accumulation of wealth to an enormous extent, but this did not further the specifically occidental form of the organization of labor, since colonial trade itself rested on the principle of exploitation and not that of securing an income through market operations. . . . It follows that the markets for domestic industry furnished by the colonies under the conditions of the time were relatively unimportant, and that the main profit was derived from the transport business.[11]

No less than Marx, Weber argued that merchant's capital merely conformed to, rather than transformed, the existing mode of production.

Weber and Sombart

This view of merchant's capital, however, put Weber at odds with fellow political economist and coeditor of the *Archiv für Sozialwissenschaft und Sozialpolitik*, Werner Sombart. This difference of opinion is noteworthy in light of the fact that some of Weber's most important studies arguably owe their conception and execution to Sombart's contributions. For example, Weber began the essays that would comprise *The Protestant Ethic and the Spirit of Capitalism* a mere two years after the publication of the first edition of Sombart's encyclopedic *Der Moderne Kapitalismus.*[12] A decade later a second exchange between Sombart and Weber took place: shortly after the appearance of Sombart's *The Jews and Modern Capitalism,*[13] Weber devoted one of his studies on religion and economic action to ancient Judaism.[14] Sombart had the final word with the publication of the second and double-in-size edition of *Der Moderne Kapitalismus,*[15] in which he more emphatically argued than in the first that Jews were the people whose culture most embodied and whose activities most advanced the spirit of capitalism.[16]

For our purposes, more important than either the answer or the question itself of whether Jews or Protestants were the vessels of the capitalist spirit are two other points, one on which Sombart and Weber agreed, another on which they differed. To begin with their obvious point of agreement, it was Weber's and Sombart's shared belief that like people and places, eras and epochs, every social system and structure has its spirit or culture that characterizes its expression and evolution, hence the "spirit of capitalism" and the debate over which group embodies that spirit. For Weber, the acknowledgment of such an ethos was consistent with his belief that noneconomic culture can shape social organization as, if not more, powerfully as strictly economic logic, however broadly defined. For Sombart, recourse to spirits or culture as explanatory categories of observable social phenomena was clearly a significant reversal of how Marx ordered social matters, with material "reality" governing collective consciousness and hence culture.[17] Ironically, Sombart proved more of an idealist than even Weber in one important respect: whereas

Weber recognized doctrinal differences within Protestantism, Sombart's Jews are monolithic and unaffected by theological disputes.

However, despite Sombart's essentialist portrait of Jewry, he did not stereotype them, as Weber did, as quintessential merchant capitalists to the exclusion of any involvement in industry. The reason for this was simple: unlike Weber, Sombart did not subscribe to a definition of modern capitalism that separated its merchant's forms from its industrial forms; they were both capitalism to him. Therefore, he expected to find, and found, Jews actively involved in industrial enterprises. "As soon as modern capitalism differentiated between the technical and commercial aspects of all economic processes," Sombart remarked, "so soon was the Jew engaged in both. It is true that commerce attracted him more, but already in the early capitalistic period Jews were among the first undertakers in one industry or another."[18] This trend continued into the early twentieth century, where Sombart found that Jews made up "almost a seventh part of all directorships, and nearly a quarter of all the boards of directors" of the most important German industries, despite "form[ing] exactly only a hundredth part of the entire population of the German Empire."[19]

The Personal Is Economic

Weber's insistence on the conceptual separation of merchant's and industrial capitals and the minimization of the importance of the former in relation to the latter may well have had "personal" sources, and this was neither the first nor the last time that a social scientist transformed a personal experience into a universal one. The first of these was that the rise of Germany's *economic* might seem to owe nothing to merchant's capital in the form of an overseas empire, as was the case for England or France. Rather than with the fruits of merchant's capital as in those cases, the story of German industrialization begins with the customs union, or *Zollverein*, the introduction of and improvement on British machinery, the railroad, and active state support for manufacturing. These were the economic components of national integration that preceded the formal founding of the German state by more than a generation. In fact, one could argue that the railways, above all, facilitated German political unity as much as Bismarck's wars against Austria,

Denmark, and France. Their many multiplier effects and the backward and forward linkages that they supplied or engendered were instrumental to German industrialization.

> New firms of contractors and a new labor force sprang up to lay tracks and to build bridges and stations. New engineering firms supplied locomotives and rolling-stock and provided facilities for maintenance and repairs. Iron-foundries were inundated with orders for nails and wheels. At first some railway equipment was imported—particularly from England and Belgium—but Germany soon depended less and less upon foreign supplies. Borsig of Berlin, Henschel of Cassel, Hartmann of Chemnitz, Klett of Nurnberg and Maffei of Munich were some of the engineering firms that specialized in the construction of locomotives and the manufacture of railway equipment.[20]

Thanks mainly to the rapid development of the railway industry, German iron and steel production also fed the country's shipping, armaments, and machine industries before larger firms entered into the production of consumer goods such as sewing machines and automobiles. Thus, quite unlike the industrialization process in other countries where the transition from the mechanization of the textile industry to that of machine making itself occurred over the course of decades, the German version moved quickly from the textile phase to the heavy industry phase of industrialization in less than a generation.

From most appearances, then, German industrial capitalism was based primarily on the creation and supply of a large domestic market. Interregional specialization was crucial to this process: whereas Prussia's Junkers, or large-scale landowners, supplied the country with its daily bread, Rhineland industrialists provided it with manufactured goods. From this course of events, it is easy to understand how Weber and others could believe that German industrial capitalism was mainly a domestic affair and how its example "proved" that industrialization and economic diversification generally are endogenous developments. Furthermore, it probably seemed to Weber, as it has to others, that the German case proved that overseas commerce was unnecessary for industrialization, although it could help to maintain and expand the markets for manufactured goods.

Another possible reason for Weber's insistence on the economic un-importance of merchant's capital may well have been due to its role as one of the causes of World War I. By this, I want to raise the possibility that either from discomfort with or even embarrassment about this factor in the war's lead-up, Weber chose to not address it. Weber himself suggested as much in his puzzling remark in "The Profession and Voca-tion of Politics," that only "old women" were interested in the question of who or what was responsible for the outbreak of World War I.[21] To say the least, this is not the kind of quip that we would expect to hear from a scholar on a subject as momentous as the causes of World War I, if only to be able to avoid a similar one in the future. However, in light of the fact that Weber was a vocal advocate of an aggressive German im-perialism from the time that he became a public figure in the mid-1890s until midway through World War I, any recognition of how this overseas land grab stoked intense rivalries between the Great Powers would have implicated him and like-minded public figures in the war's buildup. This was perhaps reason enough to not pursue the question.

However, it was precisely in these imperial conflicts in Africa that Du Bois traced the origins of World War I, a question that interested him as much as Weber's "old women." In his justly famous article, "The African Roots of War," which he penned in the Great War's second year, Du Bois interpreted the "holocaust" (his word) as the confluence of three more or less mutual and simultaneous forces: western European labor's militancy and demand for a larger share of corporate profits drove Euro-pean capital to seek out compensatory sources of returns in primarily African resources and labor. Africa also happened to be one of the con-tinents where Germany aimed to satisfy its imperial ambitions after uni-fication. It was a delicate balancing act, and one that ultimately proved unsustainable.

The present world war is, then, the result of the jealousies engen-dered by the recent rise of armed national associations of labor and capital whose aim is the exploitation of the wealth of the world mainly outside the European circle of nations. These associations, grown jealous and suspicious at the division of the spoils of trade-empire, are fighting to enlarge their respective shares; they look for expansion, not in Europe but in Asia, and particularly in Africa.[22]

We have no record of Weber having read or responded to Du Bois's assertions, which pointedly implicated the former, given his strong encouragement of German imperialism. Still, I see in Weber's "old women" remark some discomfort with where the pursuit of empire left Germany in the course and aftermath of World War I, which left him inclined to dismiss the relationship between, in this case, merchant's capital and war even as a topic of scholarly inquiry.

Similarly, Weber may have had a familial reason for understating the economic import of merchant's capital: his mother's side of the family (the Souchays) owed its wealth to it. Unlike his proto-industrialist uncle, Karl David Weber, who served as a model of the spirit of capitalism for having been one of those exemplary "young m[e]n from one of the putting-out families [who] went into the country, carefully chose weavers for his employ, greatly increased the rigor of his supervision of their work, and thus, turned them from peasants into laborers,"[23] Weber's maternal great-grandfather, Carl Cornelius Souchay (1768–1838), did not make the bulk of his money from actual commodity production. Rather, he was a merchant's capitalist par excellence.

> Together with a close network of relatives, friends, and associates, Souchay ran an import-export firm, traded in futures, and acted as discount banker, bill broker, commission and shipping agent, and industrial investor, primarily in Frankfurt, London, and Manchester. His operations extended to the Near East, the Far East, and Russia. He was (in Weber's terms) an 'adventure capitalist' in the tumultuous years of the French Revolution, the Napoleonic Wars, and the Continental Blockade (1806–1813), a successful smuggler of English goods, a great wartime profiteer, a lucky speculator, and one of the few entrepreneurs who managed to perpetuate his gains in the postwar decades. In the 1830s, his firm, Schunck, Souchay & Co., was the richest merchant house in Britain.[24]

Souchay also had business ties to the Caribbean, given that "until 1821 [his] Frankfurt firm dealt in 'overseas foods' (such as tea, coffee, [and] cocoa),"[25] the principal producers of which (save for tea) were Europe's Caribbean colonies. It was perhaps on Carl's advice that another Souchay, Corneille (1784–1837), established a coffee and sugar plantation on some nineteen hundred acres in Cuba.[26]

Had the Souchays been Jews, they would have been a typical example of all that was wanting in merchant's capital. However, they were Protestants, which complicated matters, as did the fact that some portion of the fortune that Carl left his family afforded Weber a comfortable middle-class lifestyle when he was no longer able to earn a living as an academic. Here was yet another reason for Weber to not explore fully the economic ramifications of merchant's capital.

However, Weber's tendency to omit or downplay the facts that did not conform to his prediction of the economic behavior of particular populations extended beyond specific religious communities and encompassed whole nations. Such was his ambivalent and short treatment of the Dutch, whose economic behavior was contrary both to what he supposed appropriate for Calvinists, in particular, and to the neat division of capitalism into its commercial and industrial, political and market variants. However, there may have been another reason for Weber's uncharacteristic curtness on the Dutch Republic's economic achievements in its "golden" seventeenth century, one that had little to do with the Dutch themselves. Rather, Weber's reticence about the Dutch commercial empire no less than their finishing and service industries may have had more to do, in the final analysis, with what they suggested about England's path from commercial rival of the Dutch to the "first industrial nation."

The Dutch Conundrum

Weber was of two minds about the Dutch. On the one hand, he slighted them for being among those who exhibited "absolute unscrupulousness in the pursuit of selfish interests by the making of money[,] [which] . . . has been a specific characteristic of precisely those countries whose bourgeois-capitalistic development, measured according to Occidental standards, has remained backward."[27] And as if to make certain that he included the Dutch in this damning portrait of moneygrubbing, Weber hastened to add, "But we shall see that those who submitted to it without reserve as an uncontrolled impulse, such as the Dutch sea captain who 'would go through hell for gain, even though he scorched his sails,' were by no means the representatives of that attitude of mind from which the specifically modern capitalistic spirit as a mass phenomenon is derived, and that is what matters."[28]

Elsewhere, however, Weber attributed the Dutch Republic's "capitalistic development" to its Calvinist culture. And if by capitalistic development Weber meant the criteria that he enumerated in the lectures that became *General Economic History*—"appropriation of the physical means of production by the entrepreneur, freedom of the market, rational technology, rational law, free labor, and finally the commercialization of economic life"[29]—then the republic was indeed capitalist, despite the relatively small number of wage earners; but which country had any more in the seventeenth century? How, then, do we make sense of Weber's conflicted assessment of the Dutch spirit and practice of capitalism?

The short answer is that while Weber recognized Dutch commercial achievements, he implicitly faulted the republic for not having industrialized like England. In this criticism of the Dutch, Weber was not the first, nor would he be the last. However, the fact that the Dutch did not industrialize before the English does not mean that the country was bereft of industries in the seventeenth and eighteenth centuries; its woolens industry, centered on but not limited to Leiden, was renowned in Europe; and its equally dispersed shipyards, of which the "flyboat" was literally its flagship, put out a larger number of vessels at cheaper costs than its European rivals. The Dutch had also established a number of industries that were directly related to their overseas trade either to process or imitate the American and Asian goods that were unloaded on their docks: sugar, tobacco, porcelains, cottons, and silks.[30] And we must be sure to note, as Weber did indirectly, that the Dutch were able to purchase, in the first place, these last mentioned Asian commodities thanks to their access to Amerindian-cum-Spanish precious metals.[31] Perhaps Weber had this and the Dutch in mind when he wrote in *General Economic History* that the "stream of precious metals flowed through Spain, scarcely touching it, and fertilized other countries, which in the 15th century were already undergoing a process of transformation in labor relations which was favorable to capitalism."[32]

That Weber was aware of those Dutch industries that owed their existence to Spanish bullion and Dutch shipping we cannot say with any certainty. On the whole, Weber's references to the Dutch economy are limited to remarks on its international trade. In themselves these silences are not remarkable but for the fact that one of them—the manufacture of cotton prints based on Indian originals—was the first to be mechanized and, for that reason, is considered by a number of scholars one of the sources of the Industrial Revolution. However, from the following passage about the development of the English cotton industry, we gain the impression that Weber knew something about the Dutch precedent.

> The decisive factor, however, in the triumph of the mechanization and rationalization of work was the fate of cotton manufacture. This industry was transplanted from the continent to England in the 17th century and there immediately began a struggle against the old national industry established since the 15th century, namely, wool, a struggle as intense as that in which wool had previously been involved against linen. The power of the wool producers was so great that they secured restrictions and prohibitions on the production of half-linen, which was not restored until the Manchester Act of 1736.[33]

The Dutch are not the only ones absent by name from Weber's account; missing also are the English East India Company whose trade with the Mughal Empire brought Indian cottons into England; the Indian artisans whose designs spurred the "craze for calicos" in many European countries, which resulted in, first, the successful lobbying activities by English woolens' manufacturers to prohibit calicos from the British market and, later, the imitation of them by English entrepreneurs; and the overseas markets that kept the industry alive when the British market was declared off-limits, including Atlantic Africa where Indian cottons and then English imitations were the principal items in the exchange for African captives. In other words, if Weber had mentioned both the Dutch and their cotton printing industry by name in his brief and fragmentary account of England's path to the mechanization of the cotton industry, he would also have been compelled to mention not only the links between commercial and industrial capitals but also those between Europeans, Africans, Amerindians, and Asians in the making of English industrialization. Moreover, such a discussion would arguably have required Weber to qualify his characterization of the mercantilist policies that the British government adopted in the seventeenth and eighteenth centuries. This point warrants further comment.

The Method to Mercantilism

Mercantilism, to which Weber devoted a few pages in *General Economic History*, is the name that political economists have given to the panoply of mainly English and French policies that aimed to centralize political power at home and organize trade for maximum domestic economic benefits. The Dutch, once again, served as the model of the second of these objectives, if not also of the first, for they were the principal carriers of the most coveted cultivated and crafted commodities in Europe's seventeenth-century trading world. Despite the understandable logic of mercantilism, Weber designated it as irrational because it relied on and promoted "fiscal and colonial privileges and public monopolies," whereas rational economic activity is that which is "oriented . . . to market opportunities which were developed from within by business interests themselves on the basis of saleable services."[34] Refraining from any commentary on the ambiguity of the precise boundaries of "within" and the naturalization of "market opportunities," my problem with such a division of economic activities into the categories "rational" and "irrational" is the same as that which I highlighted in the merchant's capitalism / industrial capitalism dichotomy: the failure to take into account the many instances of overlap between the two. I have already noted how merchant's capital can stimulate finishing enterprises, or, to paraphrase Paul Mantoux, author of the widely recognized classic, *The Industrial Revolution in the Eighteenth Century*, how imports can stimulate the creation of new industries,[35] including those established to copy those very imports and ultimately replace them. Similarly, forms of supposedly irrational economic action, such as the English Navigation Acts, could and did serve to increase the volume of goods that English merchants, sailors, and manufacturers carried, processed (sometimes by copying), or reexported. And one can point to perhaps the most momentous example of an irrational policy leading to a rational outcome: the English government's repeated prohibition of the sale of Indian cottons in the early eighteenth century, which unintentionally resulted in the domestication and mechanization of the cotton industry later in the century.[36]

These examples, which call into question the neat division of economic activity into rational or irrational, merchant's or industrial categories, were perhaps reason enough for Weber not to have explored them at length. However, these examples or exceptions challenge more than Weber's economic dichotomies; they also challenge his cultural explanation of England's path to modern capitalism and the rest of the world's failure to forge that path. For if the economic categories into which Weber placed different forms of economic action are not as absolute as he had proposed, then neither are the cultural norms that he supposed mandated those activities. In human terms, Puritans, Weber's "chosen" people, were just as likely to engage in irrational, government-sponsored mercantile activity as members of other faiths within as well as outside the European world; we need only recall their commercial activity in colonial New England. Apparently, social contexts are greater determinants of behavior than religious texts or tenets, as much as the latter influence how groups respond to the former. If these considerations hold any truths, then the reasons for England's special path to industrialization have to be sought elsewhere. And here, again, the Dutch Republic may offer some insight.

Unlike the English government that responded to the influx of Indian calicos with a series of prohibitions in the early eighteenth century against their sale in the domestic market, the Dutch government took no such actions. Unlike in England, absent in the republic were hostile woolens workers and manufacturers who petitioned the government to move against calico sales and physically attacked calico wearers.[37] Due either to confidence in their products or to insufficient economic nationalism as some have claimed,[38] the Dutch were free traders (at home, at least) long before Adam Smith, as Friedrich List was sure to remind his readers,[39] became the leading advocate of that policy more than a century and a half later. Would the Dutch have mechanized the cotton industry if the artisans and manufacturers in rival textile industries had pressured the government to protect the home market from the influx of Indian calicos as the English did?[40] No one can provide a definitive answer to such a hypothetical question. However, what cannot be denied is that the procurement, popularity, and finally prohibition of Indian cottons catalyzed the mechanization of the English cotton industry, the last of which was missing in the Dutch experience.

None of what I have recapitulated here was news to Weber; save for a few details, this was fairly common historical knowledge at least from the time of List on, that is, beginning in the 1840s. The trouble was that it so compromised the validity of his political-economic categories and cultural contentions that he resorted to half-truths to salvage them. This may go some way to explain his conflicted reflections on the Dutch.

Bad Religions

The Dutch were not the only nationality about which Weber offered conflicting assessments. Asians generally, and Chinese and Indians in particular, elicited varying judgments from Weber. Whereas in some instances he underscored approvingly the sociohistorical parallels between Asian and European societies, in others he faulted Asians for having failed to develop the ideas, practices, and institutions that Europeans presumably introduced to the world. However, unlike his treatment of the Dutch, which was fairly evenly divided between praise and criticism, in the case of Indians and Chinese, their alleged failings far outweighed what Weber found laudable in them.

On the whole, Weber reserved his praise for Indians and singled out the Chinese for criticism. For example, at the outset of *The Religion of India* he remarks:

> For centuries urban development in India paralleled that of the Occident at many points. The contemporary rational number system, the technical basis of all 'calculability,' is of Indian origin. . . . Arithmetic and algebra are considered to have been independently developed in India. . . . In contrast to the Chinese, the Indians cultivated rational science (including mathematics and grammar). They developed numerous philosophic schools and religious sects of almost all possible sociological types. . . . For long periods tolerance toward religious and philosophic doctrines was almost absolute; at least it was infinitely greater than anywhere in the Occident until most recent times. . . . Indian justice developed numerous forms which could

have served capitalistic purposes as easily and well as corresponding institutions in our own medieval law. The autonomy of the merchant stratum in law-making was at least equivalent to that of our own medieval merchants.[41]

Weber's praise of Indian thought and institutions is detailed, extensive, and apparently sincere. This contrasts sharply with his assessment of the Chinese in similar domains. Late in *The Religion of China* Weber notes:

> But in spite of the rather intensive internal and, for a time at least, considerable foreign trade, there existed no bourgeois capitalism of the modern or even late Medieval type. There were no rational forms of late Medieval and scientific European capitalist enterprise in industry, and no formation of capital in the European manner. Chinese capital . . . was predominantly the capital of mandarins; hence, it was capital accumulated through extortionist practices in office. There was no rational method of organized enterprise in the European fashion, no truly rational organization of commercial news services, no rational money system—the development of the money economy did not even equal that of Ptolemean Egypt. There were only beginnings of legal institutions[,] . . . [but] [t]hese . . . were characterized essentially by their technical imperfection. . . . Finally, there was no genuine, technically valuable system of commercial correspondence, accounting, or bookkeeping.[42]

Moreover, despite their frequently impressive size, Chinese cities were devoid of citizens. For Weber, this absence was more than just a political matter, but an economic one of great significance: denied political independence by the emperor and mandarinate, Chinese city dwellers could not engage in large-scale economic activities without their permission or participation. This was literally political economics or politicized economics of the kind that Weber considered irrational.

If India, at least, held the promise of attaining the pinnacle of modern rationality in capitalism, what explains its failure to do so? The answer, so the titles of Weber's studies tell us, lay in Indian and Chinese religions.

According to Weber, much like Catholicism, which left its practitioners the choice of either the monastery or the sacraments as the path to salvation, neither Hinduism nor Confucianism, the major religions of India and China, offers its adherents a doctrine that advances the idea that good and hard work in an otherwise imperfect world is a means to create a little heaven on earth. This is, of course, what Weber argued that certain denominations of Protestantism had singularly achieved. Confucianism and Hinduism are incapable of developing such a religious philosophy because they both advocate one's resignation to the world, as it exists, albeit for different reasons. In the case of Hinduism, the reasons lay in the belief that, first, one's current life is the result of how one conducted oneself in previous incarnations; and, second, that salvation requires the mental transcendence of this world that is largely illusory anyway. Hence the time and energy Hindu spiritual leaders have devoted to meditation and the relative resignation of the Indian masses to their social fate in the precolonial era. In stark contrast, Confucianism posits that the world is generally good as it is and that a better life is attainable here on earth through three means: the study of the classic texts, the securing of wealth, and, most important, obedience to "traditional authorities, parents, ancestors, and superiors in the hierarchy of office."[43] In both religious traditions, however, most of these practices have been the preserve of the relatively few who have had the time and opportunity to avail themselves of them. By contrast, all that was left for the masses in the way of hope for the minimum improvement of their fated fortunes was recourse to magic. As Weber writes:

> There were spells not only as therapeutic means, but especially as a means aimed at producing births and particularly male births. . . . [S]pells against enemies, erotic or economic competition, spells designed to win legal cases, spiritual spells of the believer for forced fulfillment against the debtor, spells for the securing of wealth, for the success of undertakings. All this was either in the gross form of compulsive magic or in the refined form of persuading a functional god or demon through gifts. With such means the great mass of the aliterary and even the literary Asiatics sought to master everyday life.[44]

And, as we can imagine, for Weber there was no greater cultural failing than reliance on magic.

Whatever our initial reaction to Weber's characterization of Confucianism and Hinduism, we can discern the logic that led him to it. Unlike Protestantism's preoccupation with humankind's failure to fulfill God's commandments on earth, Asian religions do not create in their adherents a tension derived from the discrepancy between how the world should ideally be and how it actually is. Thus Asian religions lack a doctrine or system particularly for the middle classes that mandates righteous action in a flawed world. On its own terms, then, Weber's critique of two of Asia's most important religions is internally consistent.

Less consistent and certainly less justifiable, however, is Weber's claim that the resolution-requiring tension between the tarnished "creatural," or terrestrial, world and the divinely intended world that is primary to Protestantism is the main source not only of an adherent's rationality but also of his personality. Only through this personal tug-of-war between salvation-seeking and salvation-rejecting thoughts and actions, the choice of which ultimately determines the state and fate of one's soul, is one's personality formed. Absent this, the individual leads an unexamined life of prescribed motions without reflection.

Against such a stultifying personal and collective ethos, even commercial enterprise was powerless; it could neither encourage its participants to become more reasonable, nor thereby to develop personalities. From Weber's perspective, then, overbearing state bureaucracies, the supposed foundation of "Oriental Despotism," was the political regime that Asian peoples deserved because it suited the Asian mind. Moreover, in light of the "unrestricted lust for gain of the Asiatics in large and in small [which] is notoriously unequalled in the rest of the world,"[45] the Oriental despot truly served as the Leviathan who kept his people from devouring themselves.

Fatalistic, ritualistic, superstitious, superficial, and avaricious are some of the adjectives that come to mind from Weber's descriptions of Asians. However, these are but a few. In the following lengthy passage, Weber provides a more complete inventory of the shortcomings that kept the Chinese, in particular, from developing in the areas and in the ways in which Europeans did.

Always emphasized [in European accounts of the Chinese] are such observations as these: the striking lack of 'nerves' in the specifically modern meaning of the word; the unlimited patience and controlled politeness; the strong attachment to the habitual; the absolute insensitivity to monotony; the capacity for uninterrupted work and the slowness in reacting to unusual stimuli, especially in the intellectual sphere. . . . There is an extraordinary and unusual horror of all unknown and not immediately apparent things which finds expression in ineradicable distrust. There is the rejection or lack of intellectual curiosity about things not close at hand and immediately useful. These traits stand in contrast to an unlimited and good-natured credulity in any magical swindle, no matter how fantastic it may be. In the same way the strong lack of genuine sympathy and warmth, often even among people who are personally close, stands in apparent contrast to the great and close-knit cohesion of social organizations. . . . The typical distrust of the Chinese for one another is confirmed by all observers. It stands in sharp contrast to the trust and honesty of the faithful brethren in the Puritan sects, a trust shared by outsiders as well. Finally, the unity and unshakability of the general psycho-physical bearing contrasts sharply with the often reported instability of all those features of the Chinese way of life which are not regulated from without by fixed norms. Most traits, however, are so fixed. More sharply formulated, the bondage of the Chinese, which is produced by their innumerable conventions, contrasts basically with the absence of an inward core, of a unified way of life flowing from some central and autonomous value position.[46]

A more thorough and damning list of failings we can scarcely imagine. Weber informs us that his characterization of the Chinese is drawn from the accounts of Western missionaries and that they are fundamentally trustworthy.[47] His assurances notwithstanding, we must be sure to note what he did not mention: these sources are almost exclusively from the nineteenth century. This is not a minor point, for it raises some questions about Weber's methodological choices, not least of which is why he felt satisfied with only nineteenth-century Western sources from which to construct his figure of the archetypal Chinese individual without en-

tertaining the possibility of bias in them. For it is unimaginable that
Weber had not pondered the trustworthiness of missionary writings
about the societies in which missionaries themselves sought to spread
Christianity. It would be as absurd to claim that Weber was unaware of
these motivations as it would be to argue that he unintentionally omitted
European imperial expansion in Asia in the eighteenth and nineteenth
centuries in his accounts of Chinese and Indian societies. Rather, a generous line of reasoning might assert that in the attempt to isolate two of
Asia's major religions from other facets of social life in order to ascertain
how those doctrines shape economic activity, and then to test those
interactions against those which occur in other geographic units, Weber
necessarily downplayed the prior contacts between or mutual influences
on, in these cases, China and Europe and India and Europe in order to
make them unequivocally distinct cultural pools. Apart from its historical inaccuracy, this tendency is especially problematic when the objects of study are certain portions of humanity whose sociohistorical
activities have habitually transgressed the geographic or political divisions on which comparisons are normally based. Nations, peoples, empires, and states are all conceptually useful constructs as much to social
scientists as to politicians, but they encourage the mind to imagine them
in isolation rather than in relation to other ones. Differences between
people there certainly are, but rarely have these developed without the
contact and influences of others.

Much of the latest scholarship in world history departs from this
premise and consequently underscores the interrelations between rather
than separation of Asian and European societies, among others.[48] Some
of the themes that these scholars stress are the long history of trade,
travel, and technical transfers between the two geographic arenas, the
last of which moved primarily from east to west until the nineteenth
century. Here, then, is another plausible reason for Weber's almost exclusive reliance on nineteenth-century European missionary reports:
they avoided references to past European impressions of Asians that
were praiseful and suggested the adoption and imitation of Asian practices.[49] In other words, Weber *needed* sources that fixed Asia and Europe
as discrete entities whose differences could be traced to long-standing
and long-in-the-making internal or domestic processes, such as the

evolution of religious thought and practice, without the complications of commercial contacts, material borrowings, and imperialism. Of course, the European suppliers of such characterizations were engaged in a contemporary fiction: from the remnants of the English East Indian Company to the Opium Wars to the Open Door policy, Europeans were actively involved in Asian affairs in the nineteenth century. In short, Weber's Eurocentrism pervaded consciously or unconsciously his choice of sources no less than his conclusions.

In sum, conscious and unconscious biases are major difficulties of the comparative method in general, and of Weber's in particular. Bias can seep into the noblest social scientific inquiries not merely in the tools one uses to determine how the variables under study interact, but in how one gathers data. The measure of objectivity is not, then, as Weber had it, the neutral presentation of an investigation shorn of any attachment to how the findings can be used for particular political ends, for political ends are not the only causes of scholarly bias; theoretical, psychological, and racial agendas are no less motivating reasons. However, in faulting Weber for not having included these concerns in his discussions of bias and objectivity, we must also be mindful of the fact that the manifestation of such a consciousness on the part of a scholar of European descent was far more likely in the late twentieth and early twenty-first century than it would have been in the early twentieth century. For it was arguably only in the decades after the decolonization of European-ruled Africa and Asia and the Civil Rights movements in North America that some Western scholars have felt compelled to reflect on the biases of their particular fields as well as on their personal ones. Time will tell just how long this intellectual reflexivity will last. In the meantime, we can say that Weber's quest for and advocacy of social scientific objectivity was as commendable as it was elusive.

DU BOIS AND MARX

Returning now to what in Marx's writings appealed to or repelled our protagonists, in the case of Du Bois's engagement with Marx, the differences in economic logic between Du Bois and Weber become markedly clear. This is perhaps to put it too mildly. However, the fact that they could find apparently contradictory corroborating points in roughly the same body of work reflects as much their own predilections as it does the ambiguities in Marx's own positions.

Nevertheless, about certain matters Marx never equivocated, and one of these was his adherence to the labor theory of value. True to its name this postulate held that the "real" value of a good is determined by the amount of (average) labor that goes into its making. Marx had ironically taken this theory from some of the same political economists (later "classical" economists) against whom he railed for precisely not investigating why neither real wages nor prices conform to the labor-time embodied in commodities. For Marx, this intellectual evasion was proof not only of the bankruptcy of classical economics but also of capital's ignoble birth from and insatiable appetite for surplus labor, or that portion of a work period that exceeds the (average) amount of time necessary to produce a certain unit of good for which the laborer was contracted. The appeal to Du Bois of both the labor theory of value and of surplus labor is readily apparent: as universal claims about exploited labor they apply as much to unfree as they do to wage-earning labor, regardless of the physical traits of the worker. And as if to make certain that the point was not lost on anyone, Marx refers repeatedly to different forms of labor in the same context. The following is one such instance:

> Capital has not invented surplus-labor. Wherever a part of society possesses the monopoly of the means of production, the laborer, free or not free, must add to the working-time necessary for his own maintenance an extra working-time in order to produce the means of subsistence for the owners of the means of production, whether this proprietor be the Athenian [*kalos kagathos*], Etruscan theocrat, civis Romanus, Norman baron, American slave-owner, Wallachian Boyard, modern landlord or capitalist.[50]

On occasion Marx was willing to go beyond this mere grouping of different forms of surplus-labor-producing work to suggest not only that more than one of them can operate in the same mode of production, but that their ensemble can be fundamental to that mode of production.

Such was what he said, in more than one place, about enslaved and wage-earning labor in the capitalist mode of production. In *Capital*, Marx penned the oft-quoted line, "In fact, the veiled slavery of the wage-workers in Europe needed, for its pedestal, slavery pure and simple in the new world."[51]

Du Bois was no doubt heartened by passages such as these, which indicated that Marx had a great appreciation of slavery's contribution to modern capitalism. Still, these remarks are a marked departure from what Marx wrote elsewhere. In at least two places in *Capital*, Marx insists that capitalism requires "free" workers "in the double sense" that they "can dispose of [their] labor-power as [their] own commodity," "free from, unencumbered by, any means of production of their own."[52] Moreover, as the passage cited above makes clear, Marx situated enslaved labor in the "primitive" or "pre-historic stage of capital," despite his recognition that enslaved and wage labor coexisted for at least three quarters of a century (ca. 1780–1865), if not longer.[53] How did Du Bois handle this tension in Marx's work over the conceptual and temporal relationship between enslaved and wage-earning labor? He simply ignored it and, as we will see shortly, reconceived enslaved and other unfree laborers as "workers."

However, what Du Bois could not ignore was how little Marx said about ethnic stratification within and between working classes, and the degree to which this complicated, if not obstructed, the kind of working-class solidarity that he anticipated. In his fullest treatment of race and Marxist thought and race and the global capitalist economy, "Marxism and the Negro," Du Bois argued that racial divisions within working classes, particularly those in the United States, made appeals to working-class unity futile. The reason for this is quite simple: ethnic chauvinism benefits ethnically privileged working classes as well as racialized capital. Through either their outright exclusion from certain workplaces or complicity in the superexploitation of their labor in other instances, racially privileged working classes actively and consciously gain from the subordination of ethnically undervalued workers. This process has been especially prevalent in the Americas where, in addition to the legacy of racial slavery, the legacy of discrimination against the latest immigrant workers has also been operative. Du Bois writes:

Thus in America we have seen a wild and ruthless scramble of labor groups over each other in order to climb to wealth on the backs of black labor and foreign immigrants. The Irish climbed on the Negroes. The Germans scrambled over the Negroes and emulated the Irish. The Scandinavians fought forward next to the Germans and Italians and "Bohunks" are crowding up, leaving Negroes still at the bottom, chained to helplessness, first by slavery, then by disfranchisement and always by the Color Bar.[54]

Extrapolating from this working-class contest between older and newer "American" workers, with black workers positioned at the bottom of the social hierarchy, Du Bois further maintained that white labor, as much as white capital, bears responsibility for the socioeconomic conditions of working-class blacks.

And while Negro labor in America suffers because of the fundamental inequities of the whole capitalistic system, the lowest and most fatal degree of its suffering comes not from the capitalists but from fellow white laborers. It is white labor that deprives the Negro of his right to vote, denies him education, denies him affiliation with trade unions, expels him from decent houses and neighborhoods, and heaps upon him the public insults of open color discrimination.[55]

Needless to say, this formulation was a marked departure from Marx's diagnosis and prognosis of capitalism's impact on national working classes. For what it proposed was that in multiethnic societies like the United States, class conflict is not only that between labor and capital but also that between racially subordinated labor and ethnically privileged labor. More than even this, however, Du Bois was also suggesting that the material rewards of racism, which extend far beyond the workplace, channeled the political energies of racially privileged working classes more toward the monopolization of the physical trappings of ethnic exclusivity than to challenging capital. Rather than working-class unity resulting from production, there is working-class division resulting from consumption. Taken together, Du Bois concluded that the prospects for the realization of Marx's vision in the United States did not exist.

Under these circumstances, what shall we say of the Marxian philosophy and of its relation to the American Negro? We can only say, as it seems to me, that the Marxian philosophy is a true diagnosis of the situation in Europe in the middle of the 19th Century despite some of its logical difficulties. But it must be modified in the United States of America and especially so far as the Negro group is concerned. The Negro is exploited to a degree that means poverty, crime, delinquency, and indigence. And that exploitation comes not from a black capitalistic class but from the white capitalists and equally from the white proletariat. His only defense is such internal organization as will protect him from both parties, and such practical economic insight as will prevent inside the race group any large development of capitalistic exploitation.[56]

Little wonder that Du Bois saw no prospects for socialism in the United States. However, it was not for socialist models that Du Bois looked to Marx but for his analysis of capitalism.

Unfree Labor and Capitalism

From his published Harvard dissertation, *The Suppression of the African Slave Trade to the United States of America, 1638–1870*, to his many general histories of Africans and black Americans, including *The Negro* (1915), *The Gift of Black Folk* (1924), *Black Folk: Then and Now* (1939), and *The World and Africa* (1946), as well as his magnum opus, *Black Reconstruction in America, 1860–1880* (1935), Du Bois always saw fit to give ample space to the enslavement of Africans in the Americas. Of course, this focus stood to reason given that the story of how African captives were reduced to and defined by that condition and institution is also the pivotal story of the African presence in the Americas. Moreover, unlike the slave systems that spanned the Roman and medieval Mediterranean worlds that drew on a variety of physically distinct populations, enslavement in the Americas was unique in that it was race-specific. Among the many consequences of this peculiarity of American slavery, as Du Bois often stressed, is that nonblacks were compelled and encouraged by law and leadership to view all people of African descent as human chattel when the institution was deemed legal and unworthy of freedom when it was outlawed. Equally important, although typically downplayed by most scholars in Du Bois's lifetime, was the role that enslaved labor played in Europe's and Euro-America's economic development and expansion. To Du Bois and others who shared his perspective, the reasons for this consistent underestimation of the economic importance of modern slavery had as much to do with racial distance between the majority of Western scholars and the slaves themselves as it did to matters of economic theory.

Du Bois's first reference to the economic importance of slavery appears in his PhD dissertation. In this instance, he draws attention to multiple industries in the New England and mid-Atlantic colonies that slave traders created or stimulated rather than the profits made by southern planters from the tobacco, rice, and cotton that they forced their human property to cultivate. He notes at some length:

> The significance of New England in the African slave-trade . . . lie[s] in the fact that her citizens, being the traders of the New World, early took part in the carrying slave-trade and furnished slaves to other colonies. . . . Vessels from Massachusetts, Rhode Island, Connecticut, and, to a less extent, from New Hampshire, were early and largely engaged in the carrying slave-trade. . . . Newport was the mart for slaves offered for sale in the North, and a point of reshipment for all slaves. It was principally this trade that raised Newport to her commercial importance in the eighteenth century. Connecticut, too, was an important slave-trader, sending large numbers of horses and other commodities to the West Indies in exchange for slaves, and selling the slaves in other colonies. . . . This trade formed a perfect circle. Owners of slavers carried slaves to South Carolina, and brought home naval stores for their shipbuilding; or to the West Indies, and brought home molasses; or to the other colonies, and brought home hogsheads. The molasses was made into the highly prized New England rum, and shipped in these hogsheads to Africa for more slaves. Thus, the rum-distilling industry indicates to some extent the activity of New England in the slave trade. . . . In Newport alone twenty-two stills were at one time running continuously; and Massachusetts annually distilled 15,000 hogsheads of molasses into this "chief manufacture."[57]

Those who are familiar with Eric Williams's 1944 classic, *Capitalism and Slavery*, will recognize in Du Bois's geography of trade and industry between New England and points south on both sides of the Atlantic the precursor to Williams's triangular trade whereby a "slave ship sailed from the home country [e.g., England] with a cargo of manufactured goods," which "were exchanged at a profit on the coast of Africa for Negroes, who were traded on the plantations, at another profit, in exchange for a cargo of colonial produce to be taken back to the home country."[58] Citing Williams's work in his 1946 publication, *The World and Africa*, Du Bois echoed the findings of the Trinidadian historian and later prime minister:

> By 1750, there was hardly a manufacturing town in England which was not connected with the colonial trade. The profits provided one of the main streams of that capital which financed the Industrial Revolution. The West Indian islands became the center of the British Empire and of immense importance to the grandeur of England. It was the Negro slaves who made these sugar colonies the most precious colonies ever recorded in the annals of imperialism.[59]

By this time Du Bois had repeated such conclusions in numerous publications and addresses. The trouble is that Du Bois was typically short on demonstrating the economic benefits of empire to England and to other western European countries. Apart from references to the number of slave ships that sailed from Liverpool to Africa and the Americas in the course of the eighteenth century and the statement that the "purchase of slaves furnished a large market for British manufacture, especially textiles,"[60] Du Bois provided few details of the mechanisms by which the slave trade and the products of slave labor transformed either the English economy or the economies of other western European countries. For this Du Bois would have needed to provide the sort of diachronic and synchronic sketches of those societies that he did for African ones in *The Negro, Black Folk: Then and Now*, and *The World and Africa*. Short of these, Du Bois's assertions about the role of slavery in Western industrial development generally read like unsubstantiated claims to skeptics, race-motivated propaganda to critics. It would be left to future scholars, who drew inspiration from Du Bois, to pursue his suggestions.

In his defense, we must recognize that Du Bois never set himself the tasking of proving what he thought self-evident. As I stated earlier, one of Du Bois's scholarly objectives was to establish that people of African descent had histories worthy of being recounted, studied, and situated in world history, of which they are integral parts. Had his goal been to prove what Western political-economic development owes to the unfree and wage-earning labor of people of African descent, we can be sure that Du Bois would have tackled the subject with the same thoroughness that he brought to bear in *The Philadelphia Negro* and *Black Reconstruction in America*. Nevertheless, even if some his assertions on this subject remained largely rhetorical, others were quite convincing.

The first of these is the converse of the economic advantages that western European societies drew from their involvement in more than four centuries of enslaving Africans in the Americas: the devastation that this people-removing and people-consuming enterprise wrought on the African continent. Not only did it "cost Negro Africa from a fourth to a third of its population" in captive-seeking wars, long imprisonment, disease, and forced marches, but it "revolutionized" for the worse those societies it affected.

> Whole regions were depopulated, whole tribes disappeared; the character of people developed excesses of cruelty instead of the flourishing arts of peace. The dark, irresistible grasp of fetish took firmer hold on men's minds. Advances toward higher civilization became more difficult. It was a rape of a continent to an extent seldom if ever paralleled in ancient or modern times.[61]

Just prior to this passage, Du Bois had added, "And yet people ask today the cause of the stagnation of culture in that land [Africa] since 1600." Thus, years before the political economist Andre Gunder Frank asserted that "economic development and underdevelopment are the opposite faces of the same coin,"[62] Du Bois had essentially come to the same conclusion about the historical relationship between Europe and Africa.

A contention such as this one necessarily had implications for Africa's premodern past. For if the Atlantic and to a lesser extent the Saharan-Mediterranean slave trades bear the greatest responsibility for Africa's relatively arrested economic and political development since the seventeenth century,[63] then we can assume that prior to that time the continent's overall economic development was proceeding at the same pace as that of other continents. Du Bois said as much: "In the fifteenth century there was no great disparity between the civilization of Negroland and that of Europe."[64] However, much like his treatment of the economic benefits that western Europe and Euro-America realized from the enslavement of Africans in the Americas, Du Bois's claims about the parity of African and European civilizations are incomplete and inadequate; he did not base them on a detailed comparative study of the two geographic entities in the fifteenth century and after. Thus, on the matter of the parity of premodern Africa and Europe, Du Bois was far more suggestive than conclusive.

Still, we must appreciate the boldness, if not radicalness, of Du Bois's contention despite its shortcomings. In order to do this, we must recall the mind-set of most white Americans (and even a few black ones) in 1915, the year in which *The Negro* was first published. At this time, few were those who could fathom the genetic equality of physically different people conveniently categorized as "races," let alone their equal share of intellectual and material achievements.[65] So wholly did most assume the superiority of people of European descent over all non-Europeans in virtually all domains that they could easily use it to rationalize segregation, restrictive immigration, imperialism, and forced labor. "Most persons have accepted," Du Bois stated in *The Negro*, "that tacit but clear modern philosophy which assigns to the white race alone the hegemony of the world and assumes that other races, and particularly the Negro race, will either be content to serve the interests of the whites or die out before their all-conquering march."[66] Of course, this was hardly a new belief but one that was, at minimum, two centuries old and shared by some of the supposedly most "enlightened" minds of the Western world.

So as to silence or at least give pause to the adherents of this sort of racist thinking, Du Bois was sure to stress the one, unequivocal contribution of black people to the Western world: their labor. That Du Bois recognized its strategic power in addition to its basis in fact explains why he never missed an opportunity to remind his reading and listening audiences of black labor's multifaceted history and employment. However, Du Bois's project required more than the mere compilation and recounting of black labor's exploits to convince skeptics or to arm partisans of its importance for one stickling reason: for nearly four of the past five centuries, black labor was performed in a state of unfreedom. For this reason (in addition to the racial designation of these workers), neither mainstream (of both the conservative and liberal varieties) nor Marxist scholarship has typically rewarded unfree labor for its contribution to the modern capitalist economy. The first task, then, for Du Bois was to establish that unfree labor is nothing other than labor, despite its obviousness.

He began modestly enough. In his 1924 publication, *The Gift of Black Folk*, Du Bois asked his readers to "think of the slave as a laborer, as one who furnished the original great labor force of the new world and differed from modern labor only in the wages received, the political and civil rights enjoyed, and the cultural surroundings from which he was taken."[67] It is worth noting that Du Bois voiced this view on enslaved labor a full decade prior to his public embrace of Marxist analytical tools in what is arguably his magnum opus, *Black Reconstruction in America*. Unfortunately, in neither work did Du Bois explore the theoretical implications of this reconception of the enslaved worker as part of larger, national working classes in the Americas. Still, his act was one of the first challenges, of which I am aware, to two related points: the insistence by both Marx and Weber that capitalist social relations operate only where workers are wage earners; and their related contention that slavery was to the ancient world what wage labor is to the modern, capitalist one. For at least as far as the capitalist era is concerned, Du Bois could not deny the empirical fact that both unfree and wage labor have coexisted for the better part of its history.[68] Although he was not a scholar of slavery per se, Du Bois was well aware of the difficulty of fitting enslaved labor into prescribed socioeconomic categories, as both Marx and Weber were wont to do.

Having already discussed Du Bois's treatment of two other forms of unfree labor—debt peonage and the convict lease system in chapter 2—I want to draw our attention to another form of unfree labor that Du Bois highlighted in his writings on colonialism in Africa: African wage labor. Du Bois included African wage earners in the ranks of the unfree because for him, unfreedom is as much a political condition as it is an economic one. This is not to suggest that Du Bois downplayed the importance of forced labor in colonial Africa, which was certainly a form of state slavery that all European colonial powers employed; he certainly mentions its use in porterage, forest and brush clearing, and track laying. However, as Du Bois recognized, it would not be accurate to conceive of the colonial African wage earner as one entirely separated from the land, because the "mass of workers are still connected with tribal lands and villages, and use money wages for taxes and for luxuries rather than necessities."[69] Still, in choosing to concentrate on nominally "free" labor in contrast to non-wage-earning, forced labor in the colonial setting, Du Bois consciously draws our attention to the fact that indigenous African workers were in no way free in imperial systems that denied them political voice. After all, if the colonial regimes had encouraged African workers to become political actors, they would have lost them as cheap laborers. Contrary to their rhetoric, then, colonial regimes had to be authoritarian, when not plainly fascist. And as Du Bois was sure to note, colonial authoritarianism was established at precisely the time when skilled European and European American male workers were gaining rights, recognition, and higher wages at the workplace to go along with the franchise.[70] This is to say that as greater western European society grew more democratic in the late nineteenth century, the political systems that it introduced into its colonial possessions were fundamentally tyrannical, with governors or governors-general accorded powers of which there were no longer any equivalents in the European world's centers.

Despite or perhaps because of this discrepancy in the political rights of imperial Europe's working classes, Du Bois had an additional reason to focus on African wage earners: to situate them in the general capitalist process of proletarianization. Similar to how working classes were created in various parts of Europe, proletarianization in Africa required the denial or reduction, at least, of viable alternatives to wage work to people who formerly enjoyed tenure rights and had the means of craft production at their disposal. The differences in color and phenotype between Europe's and European Africa's wage earners served merely to obscure and justify what was fundamentally a capitalist necessity. Colonial governments and militaries thereby oversaw the legal alienation of indigenous lands to metropolitan firms, individuals, and colonial states themselves, whose total Du Bois estimated at "half the size of the United

States."[71] This was especially necessary in settler colonies whose fertile land and minerals attracted sizable European populations that needed to make workers and subordinates of the African peoples whose lands they had appropriated. In these instances, the European workers who comprised some portion of the settler populations could not see in their recently proletarianized African counterparts reflections of their forebears who underwent a similar process but the human means by which to secure a "larger share of the product of industry," for "in a sense the higher wage of the white worker is taken from the wage of the black worker and not from the profits of capital."[72] Consequently, cross-racial working-class solidarity in the colonies was the stuff of theoretical dreams.

However, the vast majority of colonial African laborers were cash crop farmers who rarely encountered colonial officials but who were certainly affected by their actions. The primary arena of administrative activity was in colonial marketing boards whose main purpose was to dictate the prices for agricultural goods that colonial wholesalers would offer growers, typically well below world market levels. In these contexts, the colonial administration either used precolonial hierarchical structures or invented new ones both to collect taxes and to provide an indigenous cover to European corporate interests. In the case of West African cocoa production in general, and the Gold Coast's (Ghana's) in particular, Du Bois argued that this collusive reduction of the value of agricultural produce on the part of colonial marketing boards aimed to render dependent otherwise independent farmers. "Since the cocoa in West Africa," Du Bois explained, "is not raised on plantations as it is in the West Indies and South America, the problem of the traders and manufacturers is to make profit by beating down the sale price and by manipulation of the world market."[73] Thus he could conclude that the "whole economy of the colony is rigged by . . . London investors."[74]

The political unfreedom of African small farmers and wage earners worked not only to the advantage of the few European wage earners in colonial Africa but also and especially to petty bourgeois recruits who could aspire to even higher social heights. Mere paper fillers and filers at home, in the colonies clerks became administrators whose actions determined the socioeconomic fates of countless colonial subjects. When their tallies (particularly of taxes) did not cause social upset, they were quick to take credit for the smooth functioning of the colonial bureaucracy; when their measures provoked indigenous resistance, colonial administrators hid behind bureaucratic anonymity and rarely saw their policies as the cause. Yet as powerful as were the psychological perquisites of colonial administration, they were insufficient inducements to venture so far from metropolitan society. To facilitate that decision, metropolitan and colonial governments were sure to include material rewards in the colonial package, at the economic and social expense of working-class Africans. And as Du Bois suggests in the following passage, they were considerable.

> There are certain unofficial advantages given to the whites, especially in the matter of living quarters which really involve a vital lessening of their health hazards. By unwritten law in Bathurst, Accra and Lagos the whites occupy the most sanitary parts of the town along the sea front with modern bungalows built out of public funds; in Freetown they live in the highlands on the hills. These beautiful living quarters are in high and segregated localities with well-planned houses, golf and tennis facilities and schools. The white officials who occupy them are given large salaries even by English standards, with liberal leaves of absence, and have an abundance of cheap menial service. In this way a high and efficient type of Englishman can be attracted to colonial service; the contrast between such persons and the poor uneducated native tends to emphasize color caste.[75]

The decision on the part of European supervisors and workers to identify with their capitalist and bureaucratic compatriots as collaborators in the "civilizing mission" in Africa affected not only their deeds on the continent but also their words, namely, their written words. For armed with pens and typewriters, colonial administrators and corporate supervisors determined whose activities in the colonial order were of value and whose inconsequential. For fairly obvious reasons, among which we can count the very economic foundations of their privileges, the distorted mirror of their self-perception, and the related general inability to interrogate themselves, colonial administrators and supervisors were unable to assess African labor at its full value.

Yet it was their reports and recollections that constituted a significant portion of the primary material of African societies from which metropolitan academics reconstructed Africa's (anthropological) present and past. And like their compatriots on the ground, for reasons of class, color, and country, they had little incentive to make African labor central to the story of what brought Europeans to the continent. The acknowledgment of African labor (and the resources they handled) would give the lie to the colonial claim that colonialism always gives and never takes. Yet, as evidenced in the following warning to Africans at the height of colonialism by Sir Harry H. Johnston, former colonial official turned academic, whom Du Bois counted among his esteemed colleagues, even colonized labor could be minimized on the grounds that it would have gone unused without European imperialism.

> The races that will not work persistently and doggedly are trampled on, and in time displaced, by those who do. Let the Negro take this to heart; let him devote his fine muscular development in the first place to the setting of his own rank, untidy continent in order. If he will not work of his own free will, now that freedom of action is temporarily restored to him; if he will not till and manure and drain and irrigate the soil of his country in a steady, laborious way as do the Oriental and the European; if he will not apply himself zealously under Europeanization to the development of the vast resources of Tropical Africa, where hitherto he has in many of his tribes led a wasteful unproductive life; then force of circumstances, the pressure of eager, hungry, impatient, outside humanity, the converging energies of Europe and Asia will once more relegate the Negro to a servitude which will be the alternative—in the continued struggle for existence—to extinction.[76]

What can we expect of a man who believed that the "Negro in a primitive state is a born slave"?[77] However, we have no reason to doubt the sincerity of what Johnston expressed here without the slightest hint of irony or awareness of any contradictions: rather than a literal imposition on African societies that compelled them to fund a colonial apparatus that disadvantaged them and to provide profits for colonial firms, colonialism was, above all, a generous lesson in good labor. Johnston's perspective was quintessentially that of a manager, which credited super-visors far more than workers with production levels. And when Johnston and other colonial officials and academics invoked racial differences to justify African subordination, we see the manner in which white su-premacy required the minimization of black labor, if not its denial alto-gether. The challenge that these myths posed to Du Bois and other black intellectuals was how to rescue black labor and humanity from a schol-arly enslavement no less damning than the condition itself, at a time when the number of black intellectuals was quite small and confined to black institutions and in the absence of a destructive political-racial crisis such as a world war. For his part, Du Bois employed at least three strate-gies to combat the racial logic that banished black labor and humanity to the nether reaches of capitalism and modernity. These were what we may call racial role reversing, racial or identity confessing, and racial cost accounting. Each of these warrants a brief discussion.

Strategies of Recognition

Although Du Bois employed these rhetorical-political strategies in a number of writings and addresses throughout his career, he highlighted them in one instance in particular: his famous historiographical chapter of Reconstruction scholarship, "The Propaganda of History," in *Black Reconstruction in America,* which he described as follows: "This chap-ter . . . which in logic should be a survey of books and sources, becomes of sheer necessity an arraignment of American historians and an indict-ment of their ideals."[78] Yet not every point that Du Bois makes in the chapter is so combative, although many are. What I am calling racial role reversing is far more an invitation to his white colleagues to imagine al-ternative perspectives or outcomes other than those drawn from racial logic than it is tough talk. We read:

> Suppose the slaves of 1860 had been white folk. Stevens would have been a great statesman, Sumner a great democrat, and Schurz a keen prophet, in a mighty revolution of rising humanity. Ignorance and poverty would easily have been explained by history, and the de-mand for land and the franchise would have been justified as the birthright of natural freemen. (726)

Put in different terms, if enslavement in the Americas had been multiracial, most white scholars and their reading publics would take vastly different views of Atlantic slavery and postemancipation American societies, because they would identify with their ancestors who had lived through those experiences. This is to say that there is a relationship between scholarship and identity or scholarship and emotional attachment to the people who are the objects of study, greater than what has been generally recognized in the academy. Precisely because whites could not know the experience of slavery legally (although indentured servitude at times approximated it), their descendants, both lay and credentialed, have had little or no cause to identify either with the slaves or with their condition. Consequently, they have tended to advance, consciously or unconsciously, arguments and perspectives relating to blacks that they would not embrace if the people in question had been their racial kin. However, Du Bois was fair-minded enough to know that if he drew attention to the whiteness in white scholarship, he would have to acknowledge the blackness in his own. Hence, his racial confession:

> Naturally, as a Negro, I cannot do this writing without believing in the essential humanity of Negroes, in their ability to be educated, to do the work of the modern world, to take their place as equal citizens with others. I cannot for a moment subscribe to that bizarre doctrine of race that makes most men inferior to the few. But, too, as a student of science, I want to be fair, objective, and judicial; to let no searing of the memory by intolerable insult and cruelty make me fail to sympathize with human frailties and contradiction, in the eternal paradox of good and evil. (725)

Although it may seem strange to call a racial confession what is simply Du Bois's statement of facts, it is both racial and confessional but not for the obvious reasons. For one, only a scholar of color at the time would have had reason to draw attention to his race and its relationship to his scholarly perspective, due in equal measure to his minority status in the academy and the questioning of his intellectual and emotional abilities on the part of the collective white professorate. Consequently, a black academic's declaration of his fundamental belief in human equality would have been taken both as a racial and radical one for the simple reason that so few whites would have professed the same conviction. Still, there is a certain irony and contradiction in the fact that a black intellectual should have been the one to do so when he had the least need to. However, could it have been otherwise? Could most whites, credentialed or not, have even acknowledged racial assumptions as such given that they were largely second nature and considered articles of faith? Or would most of them even have wanted to declare such beliefs for fear of being vulnerable to the charge of engaging in self-serving or predetermined scholarship? Regardless of the answers to these questions, the very raising of them suggests that the conviction of racial superiority hinders one from exploring those lines of thought that do not support that conclusion. There is, in other words, a built-in ignorance in arrogance of any sort. Consequently, black writing, of the type that Du Bois supplied, is a partial antidote to racially arrogant and deficient scholarship.

Finally, Du Bois drew attention to the opportunity costs of race conscious scholarship. An economics term, "opportunity cost" is the loss in alternatives that one incurs in making a particular choice. In "The Propaganda of History," Du Bois highlights three opportunity costs of historical writing on the Civil War and Reconstruction. One was the willingness to recognize the central role that slavery and its expansion played in instigating the Civil War. Another was the acknowledgment of the fact that "in proportion to population more Negroes than whites fought in the Civil War" (716). And the third was the possibility that black elected officials in Reconstruction governments did their constituents some good in the decade or so that they were allowed to represent them. In each case, the opportunity cost of race-conscious scholarship was the crediting of black people with any activity that whites deemed beyond their capacities or worth.

However, to Du Bois, the use of history as propaganda or for "our pleasure and amusement, for inflating our national ego, and giving us a false but pleasurable sense of accomplishment" applies as much to the slavery era as it does to the postemancipation period; as much to the time of the early settlement of the Americas as to the decades of political independence in the late eighteenth and early nineteenth century (714). For in three of these four eras, there were two constants according to

Du Bois: the "black worker was the ultimate exploited; . . . he formed the mass of labor which had neither wish nor power to escape from the labor status, in order to directly exploit other laborers, or indirectly, by alliance with capital, to share in their exploitation"; and "black labor became the foundation stone not only of the Southern social structure, but of Northern manufacture and commerce, of the English factory system, of European commerce, of buying and selling on a world-wide scale; new cities were built on the results of black labor, and a new labor problem, involving all white labor, arose both in Europe and America" (15, 5).

Based on such an understanding of slavery and other forms of unfree labor, Du Bois could not help but see in the minimization or outright dismissal of the economic contribution of merchant's capital to western European and North American industrialization something more than a theoretical position; it smacked of a racial one as well. For how else could he interpret the refusal to recognize the fact that by the terms of slavery and colonialism those who supplied western Europe and North America with many of its most coveted commodities were denied the right not only to profit from their labor but also to transform them into retail goods, for these activities were almost wholly monopolized by Europeans and Euro-Americans. As I pointed out earlier in this chapter, this was precisely the position that Weber took on the economics of slavery and colonialism.

Even if we give Weber the benefit of the doubt and attribute his position on the economics of these systems more to the limitations of theory than to racially motivated conclusions, we cannot fail to recognize the scholarly challenge that Du Bois posed to him: namely, that some scholars, for any number of reasons, cannot be counted on to provide certain facts and interpretations. In practical terms, this means that neither the social sciences nor the humanities can pretend to seriously engage in social "facts" until the composition of the academy is diverse, which Du Bois would have measured by race, class, and political convictions. In suggesting this, Du Bois was neither self-serving nor unaware of the risks involved. After all, he was the one who criticized some black scholars for their "natural partisanship" for fellow black people (724). Yet their biases were no greater than those of their white counterparts who monopolized the production of knowledge. In short, Du Bois agreed with Weber that scholarly objectivity requires passion for the subject but dispassion in one's findings. However, he argued that diversity of perspective is the only means of achieving the latter.

BOTH WEBER AND DU BOIS agreed with Marx on some points and rejected others. Weber concurred with Marx on the inability of merchant's capital to catalyze any sort of social transformation, but he disagreed with him on the primacy of economic interests in the motivations of elites, even under capitalism. Conversely, Du Bois shared with Marx the belief that the labor embodied in a commodity is or should be the ultimate determinant of its value, but, unlike Marx, he did not privilege wage labor in the application of the labor theory of value. Du Bois in addition called into question Marx's expectation of cross-ethnic and cross-national working-class solidarity.

These divergent responses to certain elements of Marxist thought took Du Bois and Weber in diametrically opposite political-economic directions. Whereas Weber took his agreement with Marx on the alleged socioeconomic conservatism of merchant's capital both to consistently downplay its role in capitalism's history and maintenance and to remove the social impact of its European variety on India and China in the eighteenth and nineteenth centuries, Du Bois made his disagreement with Marx on the place of unfree labor and racism in capitalism's origins and reproduction the centerpieces of his admittedly fragmentary theory of capitalism. Nonetheless, Du Bois did elaborate on a theme that he felt accounted for Marx's and Weber's, no less than many others', undertheorization of merchant's capital: the inability to see in the human commodities of merchant's capital populations agents capable of transforming the capitalist mode of production. Much of this myopia was due to the combination of at least two factors that Du Bois either suggested or stated directly: the fact that the number of European and Euro-American wage earners engaged in commodity production was growing relative to the number of unfree workers so employed, even if the number of the latter was still greater than the ranks of the former for most of the nineteenth century; and that the racial distance between European and Euro-American theorists of capitalism and the majority of unfree workers in the capitalist world economy worked to keep those theorists from fully appreciating and exploring the economic and sociopolitical import of unfree labor historically and in the nineteenth and twentieth centuries in particular.

To Du Bois, this sort of thinking was unacceptable for a variety of reasons, not least of which is the disservice that it has done to the political-economic experiences of people of African descent for the past five centuries. According to its rendering of those experiences, the input of slaves, "natives," and other unfree people contributed nothing to the political-economic development of western European and North American societies. Du Bois rejected this conclusion virtually to the same degree that Weber endorsed it. Here was the gulf that separated Weber's and Du Bois's economic reasoning. Next, we turn to the gulf that separated their political thought.

CHAPTER FOUR

Leaders and the Led

In light of their contrasting emphases on the elements of the modern capitalist economy, one could understandably assume that Du Bois's and Weber's political stances were equally oppositional. Differences there certainly were but not as great as they would become in the World War I years. For, until then, there were at least three political orientations that they shared. First, they were both nationalists, although Du Bois's racial nationalism was both defensive and pan-African, spanning the nation-states and empires wherever black people found themselves. Second, they were both opponents of conservative forces in their respective countries. For Weber, these were the Junkers, who aimed to maintain their political dominance even as their economic importance waned, whereas for Du Bois, this was Booker T. Washington and other public figures, black or white, who counseled black Americans to submit to the American socioracial order without protest. And third, as gifted middle-class intellectuals who were also astute students of domestic and world politics, they felt that people like themselves should be the ones to formulate and set national and international policy agendas. However, this shared belief did not require them to hold political office, despite their late in life decisions to attempt to do just that. Accordingly, neither one believed that politics and hence political influence are confined to the electoral process or to political appointments, which is why both remained vigorous public commentators on current events and exponents of their respective political visions until their deaths. By contrast, on the subject of revolutionary Russia, Weber and Du Bois disagreed sharply, as a comparison of their writings about the country demonstrate. Among other insights, this comparison reveals the principles that guided their political analyses and which political system they each considered the best that could be hoped for.

WEBER'S NATION

Of the two politically engaged academics, Weber was certainly the more uncompromising nationalist. If we take what he expressed in his famous Freiberg address as the measure of his nationalist convictions, Weber handily wins the contest. In it he declared:

> Our successors will hold us answerable to history not primarily for the kind of economic organization we hand down to them, but for the amount of elbow-room in the world which we conquer and bequeath to them. In the final analysis, processes of economic development are *power* struggles too, and the ultimate and decisive interests which economic policy must serve are the interests of national *power*, whenever these interests are in question. The science of political economy is a *political* science. It is a servant of politics, not the day-to-day politics of the persons and classes who happen to be ruling at any given time, but the enduring power-political interests of the nation.[1]

By "elbow-room in the world," Weber's audience immediately understood what their speaker was calling for: overseas expansion. For Weber, German imperialism would fulfill two essential "power policy" aims, one economic, the other political. The economic goal was fairly straightforward: colonial possessions as markets for German manufactures and sources of raw materials. "The acquisition of overseas colonies," Weber remarked on this score, "facilitates the compulsory monopolization of trade with these colonies and possibly with other areas."[2]

Moreover, "imperialist capitalism," Weber declared, without any comment on its extramarket mechanisms, "has offered by far the greatest opportunities for profit[,] . . . far greater than those normally open to industrial enterprises . . . which oriented themselves to peaceful trade."[3] However, as Mommsen explained, Weber rated commercial protection above profit in his advocacy of German imperial expansion, because he "feared that international trade would gradually . . . be restricted to trading within specific economic zones of interest. These economic interest zones would keep out all third-party trade by high tariff walls, thereby permitting free access only to the commercial interests of the nation controlling a zone. Consequently, free international competition would be gradually replaced by a struggle of the great powers for economic outlets overseas."[4]

Yet the economic potential of imperialism was of secondary importance to Weber; first and foremost was what he prophesied would be its political impact. In its pursuit, he foresaw two benefits for two beneficiaries. In one case, imperialism was supposed to be the means by which the German bourgeoisie fully entered the realm of high politics, which until the close of World War I was dominated by the Junkers, the large landowners of Prussia. The Junkers had earned the right to lead the country above all because of their military strength and bureaucratic efficiency. However, as noted earlier, their economic policies in particular—the recruitment of Polish workers to tend their fields and tariff protection for their grain—threatened the national interests, as Weber understood them, of Germany's other constituencies. One of these was the class that was responsible for the country's first economic miracle, and of which Weber was a proud member and representative: the German middle class. As the economic leader of Germany, the German middle class, in Weber's view, should lead the country politically. In words that echoed Marx's, Weber added in his Freiburg address, "It is dangerous, and in the long-term incompatible with the interests of the nation, for an economically declining class to exercise political rule. But it is more dangerous still when classes which are moving *towards* economic power, and therefore expect to take over political rule, do not yet have the political maturity to assume the direction of the state."[5]

To the degree that one person could be held responsible for the sad political state of the German bourgeoisie, that person was none other than the architect of German unification, Otto von Bismarck. "Rule by a great man," Weber remarked, "is not always a means of educating the people politically."[6] At most, Bismarck and the Prussian landed elite that he both embodied and represented were willing to use bourgeois parties and representative institutions to rubber stamp their political decisions, but they would not tolerate independent political action by plebian elements regardless of their wealth and social aspirations. (However, despite their general contempt for bourgeois upstarts, the Prussian elite had no compunctions about using nouveau riche money in marriages of convenience to shore up the fortunes of the ruined among it.) Hence, if the German bourgeoisie was going to gain the political skills that the Bismarckian system deprived it of, it would have to hone them at the margins of the Prussian bureaucracy, that is, in the colonial offices in Berlin and abroad. Weber remarked in *Economy and Society*, "'Imperialist' capitalism . . . has always been the normal form in which capitalist interests have influenced politics."[7] Weber would have agreed, then, with Hannah Arendt's pronouncement made some twenty-five years after his own that imperialism "must be considered the first stage in the political rule of the bourgeoisie rather than the last stage of capitalism."[8]

It was not in the political interests of the German bourgeoisie alone that Weber advocated an aggressive imperialist policy but in that of the German working class as well. Or, rather, in what should have been its political interests. For Weber, imperialism would remedy a deficiency in the German working class: expansionist sentiment. Too busy demonizing its employers rather than its European and American working-class rivals, the German working class was indifferent when not hostile to Bismarck's belated imperial project.[9] Aside from insufficient nationalism, Weber attributed the slowness of the German working class to appreciate the benefits of imperialism to that project's indirect and veiled fruits. This was unlike ancient imperialism, in which

every full citizen could directly grasp the interest in imperialist policy and power. Nowadays, the yields flowing from abroad to the members of a polity, including those of imperialist origin and those actually representing 'tribute,' do not result in a constellation of interests so comprehensible to the masses. For under the present economic order, the tribute to 'creditor nations' assumes the forms of interest payments on debts or of capital profits transferred from abroad to the propertied strata of the 'creditor nation.' Were one to imagine these tributes abolished, it would mean for countries like England, France, and Germany a very palpable decline of purchasing power for home products. This would influence the labor market in an unfavorable manner.[10]

In his Freiberg address, Weber suggested that the English working class in particular, in contrast to its German counterpart, understood what it gained from the British Empire because it had fought longer for the spoils of capitalist profits both at home and abroad. Here was a case of the class struggle resulting in working-class identification with the imperial system. Whether this transformation of working-class consciousness was the result of England's early industrialization and subsequent early working-class mobilization, Weber did not say. What he did imply, contra the young Marx but in accordance with Du Bois, is that the class struggle tends to placate, rather than radicalize, an industrial working class over time. That is, with working-class gains in wages, rights, protections, and privileges, there also grows the tendency for that class to align itself with the classes above it in the social hierarchy, an alignment facilitated by the entry of some working-class children into those echelons through scholastic achievement. And to the extent that a national bourgeoisie is, or should be, more prone to pursue imperialist ends, a bourgeois-identifying working class will also support the acquisition of overseas territory, according to Weber. At that point, a national working class will have substituted the domestic class struggle with the nationalist imperial struggle in the global arena. With this vision in mind, we can also interpret Weber's advocacy of German overseas expansion as a preemptive social imperialism that aimed to forestall the class crises that would require the distraction of German colonial efforts in the first place.

Before turning to the domestic component of Weber's politics, we would do well to consider the theoretical implications of his call for an aggressive German imperialism. One of these is quite clear: imperialism is not always irrational. Or, to put this in different terms, irrational means can result in rational ends. This is a far cry from his disparaging remarks about "adventurer's" and "pariah" capitalism, which he associated with Jews and other peoples in *The Protestant Ethic and the Spirit of Capitalism*, and quite a departure from his opinion of mercantilism in *General Economic History*. Apparently, for the purposes of cultivating nationalism, imperialism, and its primary economic mechanism, merchant's capitalism, can be beneficial to any nation, even to Protestant ones. This point suggests that Weber was willing to reconsider, under certain circumstances, two other claims that he made in those works: that imperialist expansion is contrary either to the spirit of capitalism or to the Protestant ethic; and that the profits of unfree labor are negligible in comparison to those derived from the employment of wage labor. On this score Weber asserted elsewhere, "In general and at all times, imperialist capitalism, especially colonial booty capitalism based on direct force and compulsory labor, has offered by far the greatest opportunities for profit. They have been greater by far than those normally open to industrial enterprises which worked for exports and which oriented themselves to peaceful trade with members of other polities."[11]

This was even more than Marx was willing to admit about the profits of imperialism. Still, passages such as this one leave us wondering why Weber's remarks on the subject in *Economy and Society* are far more "positive" about imperialism than those he made in *The Protestant Ethic and the Spirit of Capitalism* and in *General Economic History*. One distinct possibility is that Weber was simply seeking to justify his own political position in the former work by disguising it as a universal one. Again, Weber would not have been alone on this score, despite his insistence that personal and scholarly positions should not mix.

Another related explanation of Weber's different assessments of imperialism in *Economy and Society* from those that he advanced elsewhere might have been that there was no harm in admitting its theoretical and practical advantages there. The year in which Weber penned the above remarks on imperialism, 1911,[12] was virtually the midway point between the initial publication of *The Protestant Ethic and the Spirit of Capitalism* and the delivery of the lectures that became *General Economic History*. By then, Weber had more or less successfully removed imperialism from the origins and maintenance of industrial capitalism but had not yet come to regret the role that German imperialism had played in the origins of World War I. In other words, at the time that Weber was recording his scant reflections on imperialism in *Economy and Society*, imperialism was not yet considered troublesome among Europe's middle classes and aristocracies.

The year 1911 was also at a few years' remove from the troubling reports of the means by which the German colonial army put down indigenous contestations of its rule in South West Africa (now Namibia) and Tanganyika (now Tanzania).[13] About these events, Weber uttered not a word, despite the staggering death tolls involved. How should we interpret Weber's silence on the human costs of the project of which he was a leading voice? As consent? As embarrassment? As an attempt to avoid a conflict of interest between his academic analysis and his own political wishes? Colonial violence was only one of the themes that Weber left unexplored in his reflections on imperialism; there were a host of others, many of which were fundamentally legal questions: Which or whose laws would govern social organization in the colonies? Would colonial law recognize indigenous claims to property or land custodianship? Would colonial law recognize indigenous colonials as citizens in their own land? Would they be entitled to participate in colonial governance? In limiting himself to the consideration of imperialism's political-economic objectives, Weber was able to skirt the equally important matters of imperialism's social mechanisms and how they affected his sociological observations and political positions.

However, the opening focus of Weber's Freiberg address was not imperial policy and its international implications but a particular domestic matter addressed earlier: Weber's opinion of the Polish seasonal workers whom East Prussian landowners recruited and employed on their estates. Here, I only want to add that we also read his anti-Polish remarks as a strategic calculation to pair the Polish scare with a Junker one. This would be an instance of attacking the messenger so as to attack the dispatcher. For, as Weber recognized, one could only blame Poles for so much, and certainly not for being Polish. The real culprits of the alleged endangerment of eastern Prussia's cultural level were not the Poles themselves but the employers of Polish agricultural workers, the Junkers. The political unifiers of Germany had now become its cultural dismantlers, with some exaggeration of course. In a couple of places in his Freiberg address, Weber alluded to but did not mention them by name or the threat that their economic policies posed to the integrity of the nation. He told his audience, "From the standpoint of the nation, large-scale enterprises which can only be preserved at the expense of the German race deserve to go down to destruction."[14] And: "The expanded economic community is just another form of the struggle of nations with each other, one which has not eased the struggle to defend one's culture but made it more *difficult* because this enlarged economic community summons material interests within the body of the nation to ally themselves with it in the fight *against* the future of the nation."[15]

This was a very serious charge: in employing Polish agricultural labor, the Junkers were acting as willing collaborators with their subordinates in aiding Germany's enemies. They were fifth columnists of sorts in the constant struggles over seemingly everything that characterizes Weber's modern world. To his thinking, then, there were definite limits to capitalist rationality: profits, privilege, and prestige should never trump patriotism.

Yet, despite their hire of cheap Polish labor and their insistence on the legislative protection of their agribusiness interests, Weber knew that to charge the Junkers with treason would have weakened the impact of his compelling points; exaggeration runs that risk. And the Junkers were still Germans, after all, and German in ways that their hired hands could never be. Thus, in his presentation of the cultural situation of eastern Prussian agriculture, Weber had to make Polish inequities greater than the power of those who hired them. Here was yet another reason to racialize the Poles.

NATIONHOOD AND MANHOOD

Turning now to Du Bois's nationalism, it was of an entirely different sort from Weber's and, in certain respects, its converse. For where Weber was preoccupied with the homogeneity of the German nation, Du Bois was concerned with black America's and the black world's attainment of manhood. Of course, elements of each man's nationalism could be found in the other's: Weber's advocacy of German imperialism could certainly be interpreted as an expression of German virility as measured by the military campaigns that territorial expansion required no less than by the respect of rival Great Powers that military action would garner; and Du Bois's desire to restore the manhood of African humanity was certainly race-specific, even if he considered that process of male maturity a universal phenomenon. Moreover, as diasporic or pan-nationalisms, Weber's pan-Germanism, like Du Bois's pan-Africanism, sought to advance the political-cultural and masculinist aims of people of German and African descent wherever they lived. However, it was precisely at these points of convergence that the differences in Du Bois's and Weber's nationalisms became apparent. For, unlike Weber's nationalism, which defined the German nation as much, if not more, by who was not included in it than who was, Du Bois's nationalism did not aim to denigrate those who did not or were not identified as black. Consequently, Du Bois, like other black nationalists of the nineteenth and early twentieth century, could speak positively about the cultural and institutional achievements of a variety of populations, including those that had been or were at present perpetrators of gross injustices against black people.

There was an irony, of course, in the black nationalist position but also a maturity: the recognition that an entire people could not be held responsible for what a few of their members had perpetrated. However, in light of the fact that the nationalisms of the populations whom black nationalists admired were not similarly generous and, hence, tended to rely on stereotypes of black people, among other groups, rather than on analysis, black nationalists had to actively combat antiblack propaganda. Little wonder, then, that the fourth clause of the constitution of the American Negro Academy (ANA), the black nationalist think tank that Du Bois cofounded with Alexander Crummell, called for "aid[ing], by publications, the dissemination of the truth and the vindication of the Negro race from vicious assaults."[16]

However, this noble aim of the ANA served to undermine its very credibility in a racist society. As noted in the previous chapter, the reasons for this were clear: in an era in which the majority of white scholars and laypeople did not question the inferiority of black people, arguments that challenged that conviction were presumed to be biased, particularly when made by black commentators. In this climate, the ultimate proof of black intellectual "objectivity" was the black scholar's willingness to agree with her white counterparts that blacks are, in fact, culturally inferior to whites. Short of this, the black intellectual ran the risk of being charged with offering excuses for poor black performance in a variety of arenas and according to an equal number of measures. For to argue that even some portion of black performance is a function of white action was to call into question the then supposedly "objective" perspective on black performance and the objectivity of those who shared that perspective.

However, even if the wall of white supremacy remained publicly unmoved by the force of the arguments made by members of such black organizations as the ANA, black people who were aware of both were moved. At a time when any shortcoming of an individual black person tarnished the image of all other black people, the achievement of any one black person was simultaneously perceived as a collective advance. This logical conflation of the individual and the collective had at least two significant sociopolitical implications for black communities in the United States as well as throughout the black diaspora. One was the attitude taken by many educated blacks that because of their intellectual achievement they had license to represent and to lead the "race." And another, derived from the first, was that educated blacks alone had the credentials to challenge white supremacist thoughts and assumptions. Again, the logic of both tendencies was entirely understandable: in an age when whites could dismiss out of hand the approaches and perspectives of any black person, those of credentialed blacks held the greatest potential to counter white opinion. With these considerations in mind, Du Bois felt confident to write the following in "The Talented Tenth":

> Can the masses of the Negro people be any possible way more quickly raised than by the effort and example of this aristocracy of talent and character? Was there ever a nation on God's fair earth civilized from the bottom upward? Never; it is, ever was and ever will be from the top downward that culture filters. The Talented Tenth rises and pulls all that are worth the saving up to their vantage ground. This is the history of human progress.[17]

Those unfamiliar with the early Du Bois might be understandably disturbed at this display of unabashed elitism and self-promotion. And no less shocking was his selective reading of history to argue that this "aristocracy of talent and character," now trained, like himself, in the university system, has been the primary shaper of history: conveniently sidelined are revolutionary upheavals, such as the Haitian and French Revolutions, in which the "masses" were central players, no less than in civil wars, such as the American Civil War, which Du Bois himself would later chronicle. In part, but only in part, does the context of "The Talented Tenth" explain the strategy that Du Bois employed in it: it was an elaboration of his "Of Mr. Booker T. Washington and Others" and "Of the Training of Black Men" chapters from *The Souls of Black Folk* that aimed to undermine Washington's position as the "one recognized spokesman of his ten million fellows."[18] However, "The Talented Tenth" differed from those chapters in Du Bois's claim there that a liberal arts education is the foundation of "manhood" generally and of black manhood in particular.

Kevin Gaines reminds us that "manhood" in the way that Du Bois and others used the word in the early twentieth century was a "signifier for citizenship, militancy, humanity (as opposed to the stereotype of animalism) and the protection of black women."[19] Save for the second and last components, which suggested physical demonstrations of manhood, the remaining two conformed to middle-class notions of the term, despite the fact that working-class black men could also lay claim to it: middle class, because, unlike the labor of working-class men, which was physical, citizenship and "humanity" were largely the result and reward for having undergone a particular type of training that did not require physical labor. In a word, this was university training at one of the many black colleges and universities that were established in the aftermath of the Civil War, such as Du Bois's alma mater, Fisk University, or Booker T. Washington's Tuskegee Institute. And one aspect of that training in particular was typically taken as the mark of having earned a degree as much as the degree itself: namely, the decipherment and use of sophisticated technical language. For lack of a better term, we might call this aspect of university training "high literacy" to distinguish it from the more practical literacy that characterizes working-class life. To Du Bois and others who subscribed to similar ideas, only literacy that provides "knowledge of the world that was and is" and forces one to reflect on the "relation of men to it" is the kind that makes men of its participants.[20] And the ultimate proof of one's manhood as measured by the criteria of high literacy and formal educational level is the quality, quantity, and variety of one's written work. By such standards, Du Bois was more of a man than Booker T. Washington, but Washington maintained control of Du Bois's research money.

Was there more, however, to Du Bois's grounding of black manhood in a liberal arts education than his aim to dethrone Washington? Or, in other terms, was Du Bois's conception of manhood more than just a self-serving exercise of using his brains and credentials to hit Washington below the belt, where it hurt?[21] In Du Bois's defense we can say yes, there was more substance to his linking of manhood and a liberal arts education than the mere desire to score political points. And for proof of this, we can point to two sources: Alexander Crummell and the University of Berlin.

CHARACTER AND *KULTUR*

Measured by their respective influences on Du Bois, Crummell's was weightier than the University of Berlin's, for of none of his German professors did he ever write, "Instinctively I bowed before this man, as one bows before the prophets of the world."[22] Who was this man of whom Du Bois thought so highly that he was awed by his presence? By vocation Alexander Crummell was a Cambridge-trained minister who presided over churches in both the United States and Liberia. Away from the pulpit, Crummell was a writer and lecturer, whose words were mainly devoted to the history, conditions, needs, and prospects of black people throughout the diaspora. In a word, Crummell was an unapologetic black nationalist. However, the mid- to late nineteenth-century black nationalism to which Crummell subscribed was markedly different from that which reemerged in the twentieth century in the interwar years and after. Whereas twentieth-century black nationalism was mainly working class and lumpen proletariat in composition, as likely to be Marxist or Muslim as Christian, publicly reverential of African practices and philosophies, and highly critical of Western middle-class values, nineteenth-century black nationalism was just the opposite, point for point: elitist, Christian (Protestant), critical of most African practices, and firmly committed to adopting and spreading Western middle-class values.[23] Still, despite the marked differences between these two expressions of black nationalism, they were united by two common convictions: that racism in the forms of colonization, enslavement, and segregation united people of African descent historically, socially, economically, and politically; and that it was the duty of all blacks to help their fellows improve their lives for the collective betterment of the "race."

By the criteria of these dictates of black nationalism, Du Bois, like Crummell, remained a black nationalist throughout his life, although the elements on which he drew alternated between the nineteenth- and twentieth-century varieties. In the early twentieth century, however, Du Bois continued to subscribe to the nineteenth century's version of black nationalism on which Crummell's imprint was unmistakable. For proof, we need only compare Crummell's thoughts on leadership with those that Du Bois expressed in his "Talented Tenth" essay: "Observe, then, just here that 'every good and every perfect gift comes from above.' And what I wish to say in its interpretation is this, viz., that all the greatness of men comes from altitudes. All the improvement, the progress, the culture, the civilization of men come from somewhere above. They never come from below!"[24]

We see here Crummell's use of scripture (James 1:17) to argue that some of God's creation might attain earthly heights akin to his lordly place in the heavens. And just as the Lord bestows grace on his worshippers, so the chosen few civilize the masses. Crummell continued:

> Just as the rains and dews come down from the skies and fall upon the hills and plains and spread through the fields of the earth with fertilizing power, so, too, with the culture of human society. Some exalted man, some great people, some marvelous migration, some extraordinary and quickening cultivation, or some divine revelation, 'from above' must come to any people ere the processes of true and permanent elevation can begin among them. And this whole process I call civilization.[25]

Of course, there is a terrific irony in a black man (whatever his academic credentials) subscribing to such a view at a time when the number of "extraordinary" blacks (as measured by scholastic degrees) was so minuscule that many whites could use Crummell's very words to justify their numerical preponderance in that category, despite their active or passive efforts to hinder black achievement. Otherwise, we have proof here of Crummell's adherence to the social theory that great men with great ideas (or that great ideas find certain men, which make them great) are the prime movers of history and who from the nineteenth century on have increasingly been university trained.

We also gather from this passage that Crummell held that central to civilization is the process of superior minds enlightening duller lights. However, this was only part of the civilizing process; no less important was the substance of what was imparted. Typical of a man with his training, Crummell included in his inventory of civilization "letters, literature, science, philosophy, poetry, sculpture, architecture, yea, all the arts."[26] In a word, the bedrock of civilization is the liberal arts, with just enough knowledge of the physical sciences to erect impressive structures. Beyond this, Crummell asserted that the study (and presumably production of) the liberal arts results in the attainment of manhood. In his critique of his fellow clergyman, the Reverend Dr. Wayland, who argued that industrial education was the appropriate educational model for black people, Crummell put forward the argument that most people associate with Du Bois and his debate with Booker T. Washington on the same subject:

> How pitiable it is to see a great good man be fuddled by a half truth. For to allege 'Industrialism' to be the grand agency in the elevation of a race of already degraded labourers, is as much a mere platitude as to say, "they must eat and drink and sleep;" for man cannot live without these habits. But they never civilize man; and *civilization* is the objective point in the movement for Negro elevation. Labor, just like eating and drinking, is one of the inevitabilities of life; one of its positive necessities. And the Negro has had it for centuries; but it has never given him manhood. It does not *now*, in wide areas of population, lift him up to moral and social elevation. Hence the need of a new factor in his life. The Negro needs light: light thrown in upon all the circumstances of his life. The light of civilization.[27]

Crummell's logic is clear enough not to warrant further comment; and we can certainly understand how it led him to the conclusion that a "race of thoughtless toilers are destined to be forever a race of senseless *boys*; for only beings who think are men."[28] Still, we should be sure to note that his claim about the link between a liberal arts education and manhood was not merely an idealistic assertion but one that alleged certain practical outcomes, particularly for working-class blacks. According to Crummell, the study of the liberal arts would cultivate in working-class blacks an "intelligent impatience at the exploitation of [their] labor" and the "courage to demand a larger share of the wealth which [their] labor creates for others."[29] Thus, for Crummell, a liberal arts education fashions men as much from its intellectual effects as from its political-economic ones.

A second source of the connection that Du Bois drew between a liberal arts education and the attainment of manhood was the German educational system whose philosophy and curriculum he eagerly absorbed while a doctoral student at the University of Berlin. This source was more implicit than explicit, however, given that the founders of the modern German university system did not explicitly claim that one of their objectives was to make boys into men, despite the degree to which this goal was already implied by the gender composition of the student body and the age of most of them.[30] Nevertheless, the founders did assert that the goal of education generally and the university in particular was to transform the being of the student. This they termed *Bildung*, which was more than simply a student's training in a particular field of study but his engagement with especially classical texts for the purposes of undergoing a wholistic transformation. Fritz Ringer has described it like this:

> It is epitomized in the neohumanist's relationship to his classical sources. He does not only come to know them. Rather, the moral and aesthetic examples contained in the classical sources affect him deeply and totally. The whole personality is involved in the act of cognition. If the materials to be learned are properly selected, their contemplation can lead to wisdom and virtue. They can attract, elevate, and transform the learner. He can thus acquire an indelible quality, also called, *Bildung*, which is a potential rival to the characteristics of the aristocrat.[31]

We have in Ringer's description of *Bildung* the meaning of such Du Bois expressions as the "higher aims of life," the "quest of Goodness and

Beauty and Truth," and "the end of which [*Bildung*] is culture." But the question remains whether there was a direct German inspiration for Du Bois's claim that the end result of *Bildung* is manhood. In his classic study of the German university system and its professorate from the height of the imperial era to the rise of the Nazis, Fritz Ringer named only Reinhold Seeberg, an "academic theologian," as one who indirectly linked *Bildung* and manhood. However, in Seeberg's case, it was not *Bildung* that he connected to manhood but its relative, *Weltanschauung*. As Ringer explained, how Seeberg and his contemporaries employed the term was to convey more than simply "worldview," its literal translation in English, but to express an outgrowth of *Bildung*:

> When the academic theologian Reinhold Seeberg spoke of the need for weltanschauung through scholarship, he was not just referring to a complete and systematic understanding of reality or to a meta-physical as distinct from a 'merely' epistemological emphasis in philosophy. He was also recommending an emotionally active stance toward the world, a personal 'synthesis' of observations and value judgments, in which the individual's purposes were related to his understanding of the universe.[32]

Put in these terms, *Weltanschauung*'s relationship to *Bildung* is readily clear. From there, Seeberg went on to assert the connection between the cultivation of *Weltanschauung* and the attainment of manhood.

> Weltanschauung is the spiritual man's right of citizenship in the world of geist and therefore the justification of his dominion over the sensible world. It enables man, even without specialized infor-mation, to understand the meaning and value of the several areas of human endeavor. It alone makes man a man in the full sense of the word, for it is proof of his spirituality (*Geistigkeit*) or of his god-likeness.[33]

Whether Du Bois had ever read Seeberg we cannot say with any certainty. We can be sure, however, that Du Bois heard and read thoughts such as these while a student in Berlin, for they were generally shared by the German academic community. Yet, in the final analysis, Du Bois had little need to try to establish a link between a liberal arts education and manhood when he could and did avail himself of another argument: the fact that Washington's confidants and closest collaborators had themselves taken degrees in the liberal arts. In his "Talented Tenth" essay, Du Bois remarked, "Indeed some thirty of his chief teachers are college graduates, and instead of studying French grammars in the midst of weeds, or buying pianos for dirty cabins, they are at Mr. Washington's right hand helping him in noble work. And yet one of the effects of Mr. Washington's propaganda has been to throw doubt upon the expediency of such training for Negroes, as these persons have had."[34]

There was little if anything that Washington could have offered in his own defense to Du Bois's points, for these were mere matters of fact. Any response on his part would have required addressing why his own practice did not accord with his public pronouncements. However, if Du Bois was the victor in his debate with Washington over the curriculum for black young people, he did not have the time to celebrate the win; another well-publicized lynching of a black man took place in his now home city of Atlanta, which made curricular disagreements and talk of manhood seem inconsequential if not surreal if black people could not defend their physical beings. Much as the 1899 lynching of Sam Hose affected him, the 1906 Atlanta lynching made Du Bois painfully aware of the powerlessness of social science to combat racial violence and a society that condoned it.[35] His despair would have been even greater had he not a year earlier assembled a group of black intellectuals at Niagara Falls to formulate a programmatic response to American racism. The birth of the Niagara movement was not only the precursor of the National Association for the Advancement of Colored People of which Du Bois was also a founding member, but also of Du Bois's decision to leave the academy so as to be able to engage more directly in shaping public opinion and policy.

FROM BLACK TO BLACK AND RED

Recently, Bill Mullen has persuasively advanced a significant reinterpretation and reperiodization of Du Bois's leftward turn from his comfortable elitism. According to Mullen, the Russian Revolution and the

Soviet Union to which it gave birth were the pivotal processes that moved Du Bois toward socialism in the last forty years of his life, almost a decade earlier than his first visit to the Soviet Union. In Mullen's words, "The Russian Revolution of 1917—and its failures—was for Du Bois the specter that haunted everything, including his interpretation of the past, his lived experience of the present, and his typology of the future world. It is the ineluctable moment that tragically defines both the horizons of the century of world revolution and Du Bois's place in it."[36] The transformation began, Mullen argues, with Du Bois's engagement with a number of socialist positions in the immediate aftermath of the Russian Revolution as he encountered them in leftist publications, political meetings, letters, and personal conversations with the likes of William Walling, Lala Lajpat Rai, and Claude McKay. Probably the most significant of these positions was Lenin's call for simultaneously combating majoritarian ethnic chauvinism within nation-states and promoting the political independence of nationalities within multiethnic and overseas empires and supporting working-class internationalism in all of these sites.[37] It was a tall order, and one that proved too tall for Europe's working classes prior to and since World War I, just as it did and has to the Euro-American working class since emancipation, the partial roots of which Du Bois chronicled in *Black Reconstruction*. Still, Mullen maintains, by 1926, the year of his first trip to the USSR, Du Bois had adopted the Leninist position of the twin revolutionary struggle of the world's nationally privileged and ethnically disadvantaged working classes.

While I largely agree with Mullen's reinterpretation of the context and content of Du Bois's third and more serious adoption of socialist analysis and political vision, I continue to believe that what we might call Du Bois's Africa turn was instrumental in facilitating his leftward one. I am referring to the decade spanning roughly 1906 and 1917: 1906 being the year in which Du Bois heard Franz Boas's commencement address at Atlanta University, where Du Bois was teaching, in which he told his audience, as Du Bois paraphrased it, "You need not be ashamed of your African past";[38] and 1917, the year in which he published the second installment of "The Souls of White Folk." Closer to the end of that period, Du Bois also published "The African Roots of War" and *The Negro*, his short attempt to synthesize his reading on African history and the early institutionalization of Europe's colonial regimes on the

continent. Despite his earlier identification as a pan-Africanist, I believe
that it was only in this period that Du Bois became a historically informed one, beyond his knowledge of then-recent colonial events.

However, in his article and essays on colonialism in this period, Du
Bois focused his attention as much on the economics of that system as
he did its racial arrogance. For example, his reason for believing that the
primary cause of World War I was found in Africa pivoted on the ways
in which racism justified the superexploitation of human labor.

> The day of the very rich is drawing to a close, so far as individual
> white nations are concerned. But there is a loophole. There is a
> chance for exploitation on an immense scale for inordinate profit,
> not simply to the very rich, but to the middle class and to the labor-
> ers. This chance lies in the exploitation of darker peoples. It is here
> that the golden hand beckons. Here are no labor unions or votes
> or questioning onlookers or inconvenient consciences. These men
> may be used down to the very bone, and shot and maimed in 'pu-
> nitive' expeditions when they revolt. In these dark lands, 'industrial
> development' may repeat in exaggerated form every horror of the
> industrial history of Europe, from slavery and rape to disease and
> maiming, with only one test of success,—dividends.[39]

The realization of superprofits outside of Europe, particularly in
Africa, became a pressing one, according to Du Bois, due to two late
nineteenth-century developments: the politicization of western Europe's
working classes, which were demanding larger shares of capital's profits;
and a recently politically united and economically expansive Germany,
which sought a redistribution of Europe's overseas colonies befitting its
new political-economic status. However, in a certain respect, the precise
reasons for the scramble for Africa were secondary to what Du Bois dis-
covered about the economics of colonialism or the economics of capitalism: if allowed, capital will not pay the worker enough to reproduce
herself physically, if it pays her at all. And for its part, racism facilitates
and justifies the lowering of this payment threshold (on the grounds that
such workers are undeserving of high rewards), which not only increases
capital's profits, but has the additional result, as remarked in chapter 3, of
blunting the class struggle by enticing workers of a dominant racial

group, with material and psychological perquisites, to identify more with their racial kin but class superiors than with their class kin in different skins. Du Bois coined the term "democratic despotism"[40] to capture this phenomenon of a racially privileged working class's greater allegiance to capital than to underrewarded labor of people of color.

I want to highlight two other points here as well. The Du Bois who was condemning moneymaking in the above passage from "The Souls of White Folk" was not the same Du Bois who criticized it some years earlier in *The Souls of Black Folk*. In the latter, the basis of his criticism drew on his conviction that the goal of making money is a debasement of the purpose of human existence. He asks in that work, "In all our Nation's striving is not the Gospel of Work befouled by the Gospel of Pay? So common is this that one-half think it normal; so unquestioned, that we almost fear to question if the end of racing is not gold, if the aim of man is not rightly to be rich."[41] Du Bois was particularly concerned with what effect this obsession with moneymaking was having and would continue to have on black folk who were not far removed from an institution that did not reward their labor. By contrast, in "The African Roots of War" and "The Souls of White Folk," Du Bois's concern was no longer with the moral repercussions of the amassing of wealth on the part of the accumulator but with its toll on the workers whose labor makes wealth possible. Du Bois had clearly undergone a fundamental shift in his understanding and estimation of capitalist production in the roughly fifteen years separating *The Souls of Black Folk* and "The Souls of White Folk," which supports Mullen's contention that the Left generally, and the black Left in particular, had influenced Du Bois to adopt more critical approaches to capitalism, both domestic and international.

However, we should be sure to recognize that Du Bois's new focus on the human creators of wealth was also the result of his foray into African history and the then-current mechanisms of European colonialism on the continent. Apart from contesting racist assumptions about precolonial Africa and the supposed benefits of Europe's "civilizing mission" there, Du Bois's dual project also provided him with a basis of comparison of noncapitalist African societies with those brought into the European capitalist orbit, through both the Atlantic slave trade and "slavery . . . taken to Africa," as Du Bois characterized European colonialism. Thus, it was Du Bois's historically informed pan-Africanism combined with a Left-inspired anticapitalism that enabled him to re-conceive of the enslavement of Africans in the Americas and Europe's land and labor grab in late nineteenth-century Africa as among the mainsprings of global capitalism. In yet other terms, it was Du Bois's application of Marxist principles to the African Atlantic that prepared him for an alternative to capitalism even before the Russian Revolution offered him a model.

THE CALL OF RUSSIA'S REVOLUTIONS

As I stated at the outset of this study, the 1905 Revolution in Russia played some part in ending the correspondence between Du Bois and Weber. In order to follow and make sense of the course of events as they were reported in Russian newspapers and secondary documents, Weber taught himself enough of the language in the short span of three months. Clearly, Weber, like many others, thought these developments were worthy of considerable intellectual attention and commitment. Why was this? The answers are many, but certainly one of the most com-pelling was the fact that the Russian Empire was the last and largest bas-tion of unreformed (save for the abolition of serfdom in 1861) reaction in Europe. Having literally weathered Napoleon's incursions early in the nineteenth century and a palace coup attempt two decades later, the tsarist regime by the mid-nineteenth century "represented the greatest embodiment of obscurantism, barbarism and oppression in Europe, the inexhaustible reservoir whence the reactionaries of other nations were able to draw strength and consequently became the bugbear of Western liberals of all shades of opinion."[42]

Heeding Isaiah Berlin's description of what nineteenth-century Russia represented to liberal Europe, we have an additional reason for Weber's deep interest in Russian events: their impact on political devel-opments in Germany and in other central and western European coun-tries. We should also bear in mind that with the dismemberment and political demolition of Poland by Prussia, Russia, and Austria at the end of the eighteenth century, Russia now bordered Germany. Consequently, events in Russia literally touched Germany and influenced another movement that, we will recall, was of utmost concern to Weber: the flow of Poles in and out of Germany. Thus, for both political and demographic or national reasons, Weber felt compelled to track events in Russia.

Yet Weber was not so forthcoming about his interest in Russia. Among the reasons that he provided was a variation of what North Americans would recognize as a frontier thesis, similar to the one that he put forward in his address in St. Louis a couple of years earlier. In his version, the United States and Russia are "perhaps the 'last' opportunities for the construction of 'free' cultures 'from scratch,'"[43] despite having reached the Pacific limits of North America and Asia respectively and having wrested these territories from the political control of their indigenous inhabitants. By "free cultures," Weber meant societies in which the ability to own or occupy land and to escape customary mechanisms of social immobility are great enough to forestall the formation of aristocracies; but only to forestall that development because, with the growing disparities of wealth and power that all societies engender, save, perhaps, the most communal, the establishment of aristocracies is just a matter of time, according to Weber. Referring specifically to the Russian case in this instance, Weber added, "And this is why despite all the differences of national character and—let us be honest about it—probably those of national interests, too, we cannot do other than look with profound inner emotion and concern at the struggle for freedom in Russia and those who engage in it—of whatever 'orientation' and 'class.'"[44] Per Weber's suggestion, let us explore the "struggle for freedom," the "orientations" or ideologies of different segments of Russian society, and the class membership of those who subscribed to these different orientations as Weber discussed them in his Russia essays.

THE PROMISE OF LIBERALISM

Unlike his use of the adjective *free* as in "free cultures," which implied the escape from concentrated landownership and the monopolization of political power that are the hallmarks of aristocracies, by "struggle for freedom" in the Russian context Weber meant something considerably different. Here he was referring to challenges to the entire tsarist edifice, which, as its name reflects, was more than some anachronistic monarchy, although it was certainly that. *Tsar* or *czar*, like *kaiser*, was taken from Caesar, the name of a number of Roman emperors, and in adopting the title, Russia's tsars intended to be autocrats. This was no mere pretense but had been codified in the seventeenth century: 'To the Emperor of all the Russias belongs unlimited autocratic power. Submission to his supreme will, not only out of fear but also for conscience sake, is ordained by God himself.'[45] By these terms of tsarism, only the tsar was free; all others were subject to his freedom. These tenets of tsarism resulted in two tendencies in imperial Russian politics: the perception of supporters of the system that any questioning of the pillars of tsarism—the tsar himself, the army, the church, and the imperial bureaucracy—was blasphemous and treasonous and therefore warranted crushing or banishment; and the typically external origins of the impetus for reform, rebellion, or revolution. The 1905 Revolution fit this pattern, for it is hard to imagine that the uprisings in the countryside and in the cities would have reached the pitch and intensity that they did without Russia's loss to Japan just months earlier, or that Nicholas II would have nominally legalized freedom of speech and assembly in his October Manifesto or that he would have "upgraded" the hastily convened Duma, or National Assembly, "from a consultative to a legislative body."[46] These measures, in effect, reduced him to the ranks of a constitutional monarch.

A "truly constitutional Russia" was precisely what Weber wanted to see emerge from the upheavals of 1905, even if it resulted in a "stronger and . . . more restless neighbor."[47] The question was which force or combination of forces would bring a constitutional regime to fruition once the intensity of foreign and domestic pressures had abated. Being the proud bourgeois that he was, Weber looked to his class counterparts in a land where some 90 percent of the population lived wholly or in part from agriculture: the liberal lesser gentry. What, in Weber's mind, made this class uniquely qualified to carry through a constitutional revolution in Russia? Weber supplied a number of reasons. First, it had administrative experience in local representative assemblies (*zemstvos*) that had been officially established in 1864 soon after the abolition of serfdom. Second, unlike the other mobilized sectors of Russian society that lacked property, the lesser gentry was landed and saw in the expansion of individual property rights the path to economic and social development. Third, its members were largely idealists who sought Russia's transformation into a representative democracy not for what they could gain from it either economically or politically but because liberalism's "vocation [i]s fighting against both bureaucratic and Jacobin *centralism* and working at the permeation of the masses with the old individualistic basic idea of the 'inalienable rights of man.'"[48] Fourth and finally, its participation was indispensable to the success of any protest or social movement. On this last point Weber was emphatic: "Every general strike and putsch failed from the moment when the bourgeoisie and specifically that part of the bourgeoisie which is most important in Russia, namely the landowning zemstvo circles, had refused any further participation."[49] Their uneven participation in the 1905 Revolution, due in no small part to the fact that their property was threatened, destined that revolutionary upheaval to fall short of its goals by Weber's logic.

Other contenders for leadership in transforming or merely reforming Russian society were lacking one or more of these attributes in Weber's opinion. The peasantry, for example, the vast majority of the empire's population and on whom the "future not only of the Constitutional Democratic movement but, more importantly, of its fundamental program, and beyond that the chances of a liberal 'development' in the West European sense," was hindered by two tendencies: its hesitation to adopt individual property rights and its disinterest in formulating a national political-economic program. Weber attributed the first disability to the Russian peasant's lifelong membership in his "native" or adoptive rural commune (*mir* or *obschina*) whereby "he has the right to his share of land, and it, in principle, has the right to his labor."[50] In exchange for the security of being able to return to the mir whenever he chose, the mir could "oblige him to do so at any time by not renewing his passport."[51] Although the mir system was not without its inequities, the fact that the village assembly determined the distribution of unused and newly acquired lands meant that "individual" property rights were subordinated to communal considerations. To most peasants who worked modest plots from which they could subsist, meet communal and imperial obligations in labor, money, or crops, and market a small surplus when there was one, the mir provided social insurance that they wanted to retain at all costs. Conversely, to peasants with more substantial holdings or lucrative side ventures, the mir was a real obstacle to the accumulation of more wealth in land or movable capital. For his part, Weber sided with those peasants (and their supporters) who sought to establish individual property rights, prognosticating that the "Russian peasant will have to continue to carry his cross in torment and anger until a combination of modern agrarian capitalism and the modern small farm on inherited soil trying to gain a foothold in the market has finally emerged victorious in Russia too, and thus the last refuge of communism in Europe and of the peasant revolutionary natural law which arises from it is finally buried."[52] Exactly how the adoption of agrarian capitalism would enable small farmers to avoid torment and anger, Weber did not elaborate.

Weber saved his harshest words for tsarists and Marxists, two ostensibly opposed political camps who were nonetheless wedded by having committed the "original sin of every kind of radical politics[,] . . . the ability 'to miss opportunities.'"[53] In light of some of the overarching themes in Weber's Russia essays, it seems that the rest of the sentence could have read, "opportunities to compromise or form alliances with the bourgeoisie." Tsarists proved uncompromising in at least two ways: in their refusal to question autocratic rule and in their resistance to reform measures, save for those that were introduced by the tsar. Given that notions of citizenship, civil rights, shared governance, and a social contract between the tsar and his subjects were foreign to tsarists, these attitudes were to be expected. However, the inflexibility of the tsarist system did not make it politically stable, particularly when it was forced to make concessions to reformers and then renege on them. This is what happened in 1905. Repeatedly in his Russia essays, Weber noted how politically disastrous this "game of tag" was to the regime itself as much as to the empire. For example:

The machinery grinds on as if nothing has happened. And yet things have been done which cannot be undone. The insincerity by which liberties are officially granted, and at the moment when one is about to avail oneself of them, are taken away with the other hand, *must* become the source of constantly repeated conflicts and fierce hatred, and be far more provocative than the old blatantly crushing system of repression. You cannot play a game of tag with a nation's political liberties, by holding them out to it as one holds out a ball to a child and, when it reaches for them, making them disappear behind your back. It is the same with the *'constitution'* which the Manifesto of 17 October promised, however many provisos accompanied the promise.[54]

With the outbreak of World War I in roughly a decade, Weber's assessment of the instability of the tsarist system would prove correct.

Tsarists, however, were not the only ones guilty of making false promises to supporters and opponents alike; Marxists were no less dishonest, according to Weber. And like tsarists, Marxists vacillated between smugness and hysteria, albeit for different reasons. The first was born from the assuredness of their analysis and of ultimate victory.

> Like the thoroughgoing Jesuit, the devout Marxist is imbued by his dogma with a blithe superiority and the self-assurance of the somnambulist. Disdaining to strive for lasting political success, and confident of being above reproach, he accepts with equanimity and a mocking laugh the collapse of all hopes—his own included—of overcoming the mortal foe he shares with other groups; is always exclusively concerned with the preservation of the pure faith and—if possible—the increase of his own sect by a few souls; and seeks the 'unmasking' of 'those who are also catholics' here, of 'traitors to the people' there, in neighboring groups.[55]

This is to say that Marxists were so convinced of the correctness of their position and vision that they could be fairly indifferent to the immediate concerns of allies, followers, and even success. Theirs were the politics of conviction taken to an absurd extreme.

However, when Marxists were in need of foot soldiers, they proved more than willing to descend from their lofty heights and resort to craven strategies to garner support. Weber made this damning indictment in a passage worth quoting at length:

> 'Correct' Social Democracy drills the masses in the intellectual parade-ground step and, instead of directing them to an otherworldly paradise, which, in Puritanism, could *also* claim some notable achievements in the service of this-worldly 'liberty', refers

them to a paradise in this world, making of it a kind of inoculation against change for those with an interest in preserving the status quo. It accustoms its charges to the unquestioning acceptance of dogmas, submissiveness towards party authorities, to ostentatious mass strikes which achieve nothing, and to the passive consumption of the tiresome invective of their journalists, which is as harmless as it is ultimately ridiculous in the eyes of its opponents, but provides its authors with a comfortable living; it accustoms them, in other words, to a 'hysterical indulgence in emotion', which takes the place of economic and political thought and action. On this barren ground, once the 'eschatological' age of the movement has passed and generation after generation has clenched its fists in its pockets in vain or bared its teeth heavenwards, only intellectual torpor can grow.[56]

Contempt can frequently inspire such compelling prose. Although a number of Weber's claims warrant dissection, the one that is particularly hard-hitting is the assertion that leftist writers profit from playing on and with the emotions of their mainly working-class followers. Unlike the owners of the means of production, who realize returns on the employment and production of wage laborers, these petty bourgeois manipulators of the means of communication turn profits from the working class's purchase of their publications and from dues, donations, and drives for Marxist parties. Thus, despite their claims to uphold their interests, Marxists, like capitalists, according to Weber, take advantage of the working class. This was a sobering claim.

THE PROMISE OF SOCIALISM

After his first visit to the Soviet Union in 1926, that is, some twenty years after Weber wrote his Russia essays, Du Bois would have found Weber's criticisms of Marxists, Russian, German, or otherwise, remarkably petty and typical of anti-Marxist detractors. Whereas the latter saw only self-serving motives in the actions of Marxists, Marxists themselves and their sympathizers saw testaments to their convictions and principles. After all, given the state repression that Marxists of all stripes faced in the nineteenth and twentieth centuries in those countries that were not governed by communists, there was little to be gained but a lot to be lost from subscribing to the thought of Karl Marx. Of course, in not having lived to see the Bolsheviks emerge victorious from the civil war but having witnessed the failure of German Marxists to imitate the Russian example, Weber died assured of the accurateness of his assessment of Marxism in theory as well as in practice, and if he had lived another five years or more, the rise and rule of Joseph Stalin would only have confirmed his beliefs.

By contrast, Du Bois argued that the Marxists who led the Russian Revolution were men driven by a vision far more noble than that which has moved any capitalist: to found a society on the needs and aspirations of working people rather than on the profit from their labor. Russia, asserted Du Bois circa 1950, "is seeking to make a nation believe that . . . the people who . . . work are the ones who should determine how the national income from their combined efforts should be distributed; in fine, that the workingman is the State; that he makes civilization possible and should determine what civilization is to be."[57] Soon thereafter he added, "Russia is trying to make the workingman the main object of industry. His well-being and his income are deliberately set as the chief ends of organized industry, directed by the State" (42). Elsewhere, Du Bois broadened the objectives of Soviet socialism as putting "public" or "human" welfare before profit. This, of course, was a claim that capital could not make.

Moreover, in light of Du Bois's contention that fundamental to capitalism's rise and maintenance have been "Negro slavery in America, the cotton kingdom, and the Industrial Revolution, and then . . . the factory system, world commerce, and colonial imperialism," he would have found Weber's insinuation that Marxists profit from worker dissatisfaction in ways comparable to how capitalists cheat workers out of the full value of their labor as both pathetic and insulting. Unfortunately, Du Bois would use the sins of capitalism to blunt any justifiable criticisms of the Soviet Union. For in Du Bois's estimation, the achievements that Marxism inspired in the Soviet Union far outweighed its failings, particularly as the former were attained in the face of the capitalist world's relentless assaults on the country. First and foremost among these achievements were the provision of basic needs in the way of housing, health care, education, and employment either free of charge or for nominal fees. As an educator and a black one at that, Du Bois was markedly impressed by the Soviet commitment to universal education, which, in short order, reduced illiteracy to a negligible percentage and increased university enrollment by a substantial one. Moreover, the majority of these new students were the sons and daughters of peasants and industrial workers, not just the sons of landowners, merchants, professionals, and civil servants, as they had been in the nineteenth century and earlier. For Du Bois, the Soviet commitment to education reflected a fundamental difference in attitude toward the "common people" between capitalist and socialist societies: the fear of an educated populace in the former and the cultivation of one in the latter. On this point, Du Bois made a compelling observation.

> If anyone doubts this planning for democracy in this nation, the system of Soviet education would seem a sufficient answer. If a mass of people are to be misled and used by others for selfish and anti-social interests, they must not be educated save in limited ways. This explains why black slaves in the United States were denied by law the right to learn to read and write; it explains the determined limitation of native education in all colonies. But in Soviet Russia from the beginning, the Revolution stressed education. (112–13)

As for the content and diversity (particularly in the social sciences and humanities) of the Soviet curriculum, Du Bois did not elaborate.

Equally, if not more important, and in striking contrast to how these services were offered by capitalist governments, was the Soviet state's provision of these services to its citizens irrespective of race, gender, ethnicity, or religious background, or so Du Bois believed. For obvious reasons, this was an extraordinary accomplishment to Du Bois as it was to other visitors to the Soviet Union. And based on his travels there, this was not merely the letter of the law, but actual practice.

> Men and women irrespective of physical traits or color of skin, even including occasional African Negroes[,] could associate freely; travel in the same public vehicles and go to the same restaurants and hotels; sit next to each other in the same colleges and places of amuse-

ment; marry wherever there is mutual liking; engage in any craft or profession for which they are qualified; join the same societies; pay the same taxes and be elected to any office without exception. No other nation on earth can boast of such a situation. (122)

Certainly not the United States in the mid-twentieth century.

Du Bois believed the same to be true for gender equality in the Soviet Union, declaring, "No modern nation has equaled the Soviets in the emancipation of women." "Women," he continued, "married or single, could vote and hold office; could work at any task at the same wage as men with the same chance of promotion; they shared all rights of property, and the same rights as men in divorce and care of children" (125). Soviet women, so it seemed to Du Bois, had made great strides in escaping the "damnation of women," as he called it: having to choose between motherhood and a career.

If he had been asked to account for how the Soviet Union was able to attain the level of social equality that he observed there, Du Bois would have named the Revolution's eradication of the sources of inequality: property, profitability, and payment. By Du Bois's lights and those of other leftists, remove these from the social equation, and the content of class, gender, race, and other measures of social valuation are correspondingly emptied. Hence, the Soviet state's nationalization of property and enterprises and its provision of basic services to its citizens.

Du Bois was sure to underscore, nevertheless, that not all state ownership or intervention is the same and that most forms differed significantly from the Soviet Union's model of socialism. On this he wanted no confusion.

Socialism is state control of industry through a planned economy. Usually social theorists have assumed that the chief if not sole beneficiary of socialism, would be the mass of the working class of the socialized nation. But German state socialism under Bismarck and its successors had shown that a state economy might be partially socialized for the benefit of landlords and a hereditary nobility and only in part for the benefit of labor. And now came Mussolini and Hitler with a socialized state in which again, labor was only a partial beneficiary, while the bulk of the benefits went to a ruling oligarchy with a dictator. (86)

Although he did not explicitly state it, in light of his recognition of the many forms that state management and planning could take, Du Bois argued that in order for a society to earn the label "socialist" working people themselves had to be makers of policy, not just passive followers of directives supposedly made in their best interest. The medium by which working input was channeled and conveyed in the Soviet Union was the soviet, or council, the first of which emerged in St. Petersburg during the 1905 Revolution and spread to other cities. In theory, urban and rural soviets discussed pressing matters and "elect[ed] delegates to local governing bodies, who in turn elect[ed] [representatives] to district bodies, and they to provincial bodies; and thus up to the All-Union Congress of Soviets" (111). Although the base of the soviet pyramid was naturally the locus of greater mass involvement in the political process than the ascending tiers, Du Bois believed that its upper reaches, despite having preemptive powers over the former, were responsive to the base's concerns and positions thanks to the channels of communication that the soviet structure afforded.

> The 70,000 village and shop Soviets were allowed the utmost freedom of discussion. There was practically nothing they were not allowed and even encouraged to discuss and deal with, so far as it touched their interests; but neither village nor district nor province had any rights which the higher body could not curtail or veto; in other words, the Russian primary unit or intermediate governmental body was not given legal rights which belonged exclusively to them and with which 'States' Rights', the higher authority could not interfere. Thus the Russian Federated Government avoided the tyranny of local rule but laid itself open to imposed authority. Here, however, authority could never act in ignorance, because the criticism on local and national matters was literally boundless and continuous. (110)

Despite the theoretical appeal of the soviet political arrangement, Du Bois could not bring himself to call it democratic. At most he could argue that "such a state would eventually become a democracy," but this was an admission that it was not yet one (110). However, this concession made his rationalization of one-party rule ring particularly hollow: "but the absence of parties today is not necessarily a denial of democracy any more than the presence of parties ensures democracy" (112). It is true that political parties in themselves are not guarantors of democracy, but their absence is no guarantee of democracy either.

Whereas Du Bois felt it necessary to respond to the criticism of one-party rule, he felt no such compulsion to address autocratic rule, or, more specifically, Joseph Stalin's rule of the Soviet Union. At the time of Du Bois's composition of "America and Russia: An Interpretation," Stalin had presided over the Soviet Union for over twenty years, a long time for a man who fought to end monarchical rule in Russia. One would have expected Du Bois to square this apparent contradiction with the vision of socialist democracy, but he kept his silence. Apart from the all too human desire not to despair of the source of one's hope, Du Bois's silence on this incongruity of socialist practice suggests that he was either not the democrat that he presented himself to be or that he was willing to relax democratic standards under certain conditions. In the case of this second possibility, certain conditions included those of a socialist regime. Otherwise, Du Bois's silence on Stalin's rule was consistent with his support of the "purge" or orthodoxy trials of the 1930s and his obsessive denunciations of Leon Trotsky, whom he branded "one of the great traitors of history" (81).

Du Bois's decision not to scrutinize Stalin's direction of the Soviet state was also consistent with his support of Stalin's plan for the peasantry: collectivization. On the face of it, collectivization made sense in its aim to consolidate small and dispersed landholdings, to introduce mechanized equipment such as tractors and threshers for sowing and harvesting, and to apply the latest agronomic findings to agricultural production generally. In exchange, peasants were required to share equipment and other inputs among themselves, to cultivate specified crops, and to sell them at state-determined prices. Of these requirements, the one that caused the greatest resentment, even more than the relinquishment of customary plots, was the obligation to accept what the government offered them for their crops, especially when many peasants knew or surmised that these prices were well below urban and world market prices. As a result, many peasants, as Du Bois admitted, withheld their yields and livestock to drive up prices. Stalin struck back: "Those who refused to cooperate were removed to distant places and put to work abroad building, cutting timber or mining" (77). This was as close as Du Bois would come to Soviet prison camps.

Du Bois expressed little concern about the plight of the Soviet Union's peasantry, an indifference or even hostility that contrasts sharply with his sympathies for former slaves. In large part, the difference was due to his especially low opinion of the country's former serfs before, during, and after the Revolution. Before the Revolution the *mujik*, or Russian peasant, "was picturesque, but he was the worst farmer in Europe. He was ignorant, the victim of age long slavery, misled by a religion which taught superstition instead of morals, and ordinarily he did not produce enough to support himself" (75). During the Revolution, Russia's peasants "supported" the Bolsheviks, who promised them land, and "fought the Whites [tsarists and Cossacks] to prevent land from being taken away." Nevertheless, "they yielded to their age-old vices of laziness, drunkenness, and greed" (75). Finally, in the aftermath of the Revolution, Soviet peasants proved counterrevolutionary in Du Bois's estimation: "Once the state distributed the land they regarded it as their personal property to be used as they pleased. They resented taxation or advice or direction as to the sale of their crops or the prices asked" (75).

What is interesting about Du Bois's characterization of the Russian peasantry is how it compares to Weber's. Whereas they both agreed that it was self-interested and hence short-sighted, they differed over the reasons for this: Du Bois attributed it to individualistic and profit-seeking inclinations; Weber, to overweening collectivism. Thus, we have Weber, the bourgeois liberal, asserting that the Russian peasantry was too communistic and Du Bois, the socialist, claiming that it was too capitalistic. Of course, Du Bois's view of the peasantry was also that of many of the Russian revolutionaries themselves, including Stalin. Consequently, we have to wonder if agreement with the Soviet leadership overrode Du Bois's willingness to entertain alternative interpretations of peasant resistance to collectivization.[58]

However, despite Du Bois's unwillingness to criticize any of the terms of collectivization, he was surprisingly critical of two aspects of the Soviet regime that were also Weber's major objections to socialism: increased bureaucratization and the curtailment of individual freedom. The admission appears in an unexpected place in "Russia and America," when Du Bois is speculating on what an Asian socialism would look like in contrast implicitly to the Soviet model.

> It would take a new way of thinking on Asiatic lines to work this out; but there would be a chance that out of India, out of Buddhism and Shintoism, out of the age-old virtues of Japan and China itself, to provide for this different kind of Communism, a thing which so far all attempts at a socialistic state in Europe have failed to produce; that is a communism with its Asiatic stress on character, on goodness, on spirit, through family loyalty and affection might ward off Thermidor; might stop the tendency of the Western socialistic state to freeze in bureaucracy. It might through the philosophy of Gandhi and Tagore, of Japan and China, really create a vast democracy into which the ruling dictatorship of the proletariat would fuse and deliquesce; and thus instead of socialism ever becoming a stark negation of the freedom of thought and a tyranny of action and propaganda of science and art, it would expand to a great democracy of the spirit. (150–51)

In light of Du Bois's normally steadfast defense of the Soviet Union, this was a bombshell, and one that, if taken literally, threatened to undermine much of his praise of that socialist system. However, rather than venture any further, Du Bois stopped at the water's edge.

THE FALSE PROMISE OF SOCIALISM

Du Bois's enthusiasm for socialism generally and its Russian form in particular contrasted sharply with Weber's pessimistic view of both. Earlier we saw how and why Weber questioned the sincerity of Russian socialists in his Russia essays: he viewed them as self-serving profiteers of unrealizable dreams. In his 1918 essay "Socialism,"[59] Weber criticized the petit bourgeois and middle-class participants in the radical socialist wing of the western European labor movement for slightly different but related reasons: they were the socially maladjusted and escapists of their class. We read:

Indeed it is remarkable that—in flat contradiction of the dictum that salvation can only come from the real workers uniting in the trade union federation and not from politicians or any outsiders— there are vast numbers of intellectuals with a university education. What are they looking for in syndicalism? It is the *romanticism* of the general strike and the *romanticism* of the hope of revolution as such which enchants (*bezaubert*) these intellectuals. If one looks at them, one can see that they are romantics, emotionally unfit for everyday life or averse to it and its demands, and who therefore hunger and thirst after the great revolutionary miracle—and the opportunity of feeling that even they will be in power one day.[60]

Reserving comment on the irony of Weber's reference to the emotional state of socialist intellectuals, a number of the points that he raised in the above passage cannot be dismissed out of hand as so much bourgeois claptrap. We might begin with his deliberate use of the verb *bezaubern* to describe how the promise of the "general strike" and the "hope of revolution" captures the imagination of socialist intellectuals. Like its usual rendering in English, "to enchant," *bezaubern* denotes that the object in question has a magical effect on a person or group. And as discussed in the previous chapter, Weber asserted that magic is at play when reason is absent or suspended. Thus, for something or someone to enchant someone else requires the suppression or suspension of reason. By extension and in slightly different terms, this formulation suggests that unreason is synonymous not only with magic, but illusion. Therefore, people who become enchanted by whatever force are people who believe in illusions. Such is how Weber categorized socialists.

By contrast, people like himself are disenchanted (*entzaubert*) or realistic. These terms are vastly different in meaning and feeling, which is why "disenchanted" is really an insufficient English rendering of *entzaubert*. Moreover, whereas disenchantment suggests the loss or relinquishment of an expectation, however acquired, realism, despite its implicit referencing of the abandonment of most illusions, suggests the gain of a mature view of the world, such as it is. Thus, for Weber, unlike its connotation in English, disenchantment is the unavoidable consequence of sober thinking, of rational assessments, as opposed to romantic ones that are the stuff of magical thinking. Socialists are also, then, believers in magic.

What evidence did Weber marshal to support his contention? Not the medical or psychiatric records of socialist intellectuals but rather the sociological constraints of socialist theory and practice. One of these Weber alluded to in the passage cited above, and the matter discussed with regard to Du Bois's politics, is the significance of the large, frequently inordinate representation of middle-class intellectuals in socialist ranks. That this fact had to have an impact on socialist institutions was as plain to Weber as it was avoided by socialists themselves. For implicit in Weber's observation were a host of related questions: Do middle-class intellectuals and industrial and agrarian workers share similar motives in becoming socialists? Can middle-class socialists authentically commit class suicide, both materially and culturally, so as to reduce the social distance that separates them from their working-class comrades? And can middle-class socialists be trusted not to use their literary training to dominate the upper echelons of socialist institutions, be they party, movement, or state? No, was Weber's implicit or explicit answer to all of these questions, not merely because he thought socialism impracticable, which he did, but primarily because he saw that portion of human society that had taken part in the Industrial Revolution as now undergoing a no less transformative managerial or bureaucratic one, regardless of a state's professed ideology. As he put it in *Economy and Society*, "It does not matter for the character of bureaucracy whether its authority is called 'private' or 'public.'"[61] Thus, he could write about socialism:

> What this means is that share companies with salaried managers are taking the place of individual entrepreneurs, and that businesses belonging to the state, municipalities and single-purpose associations are being set up which are no longer based, as before, on risk and profit of a single (or indeed any) private entrepreneur. . . . Above all . . . this kind of socialization means . . . an increase of *officialdom*, of specialist, commercially or technically trained clerks. . . . It is in the publicly owned concerns and those of single-purpose associations, however, that the *official*, not the worker, rules completely and

exclusively; here it is more difficult for the worker to achieve anything by strike action than it is against private entrepreneurs. It is
the dictatorship of the official, not that of the worker, which, for the
present at any rate, is in the advance.[62]

And to further drive home the warning to committed socialists and no-
vitiates, Weber added elsewhere:

In large states everywhere modern democracy is becoming a bu-
reaucratized democracy. This is how things have to be, for democracy is replacing the noble, aristocratic or other honorary officials
with a body of paid officials. It is the same everywhere, within the
parties too. This is inescapable, and is the fact which socialism, too,
has to reckon with: the necessity for long years of specialist training,
for constantly increasing specialization and for management by specialist officials trained in this way. The modern economy cannot be
managed in any other way.[63]

And all complex societies had to be managed in some way in order to
earn that label, according to Weber.

Still, I do not believe that Weber was speaking as a capitalist ideo-
logue here (although I seriously doubt the sincerity of his claim that if
the Russian Revolution "were to succeed and we were to see that culture
is possible on this basis, then we would be converted") but as a student
of the world, past and present, and its trends.[64] Nor did he assume that
socialist bureaucracies were necessarily more oppressive than capitalist
ones, given his suggestion elsewhere that the latter served as one of the
models of the former: "Normally, the very large modern capitalist enterprises are themselves unequalled models of strict bureaucratic organization."[65] Yet what he thought that socialists in particular had not taken
seriously into consideration, in light of their twin goals of achieving a
state-guided yet equality-grounded society, was the fact that the organizational requirements of its realization would undermine the original
political-economic vision. Why? Because the *demos* [citizenry] itself, in
the sense of a shapeless mass, never 'governs' larger associations, but
rather is governed. What changes is only the . . . measure of influence

which the *demos*, or better, which social circles from its midst are able to exert upon the content and the direction of administrative activities by means of 'public opinion.'"[66] This tendency results in what Weber alternately termed "passive democratization," or the "*leveling of the governed* in face of the governing and bureaucratically articulated group, which in its turn may occupy a quite autocratic position, both in fact and in form."[67]

This "leveling of the governed" was based on more than the organizational structure of bureaucracy but equally on the credentials and psychology of the "governing and bureaucratically articulated group." Generally, holders of examination certificates (although some owed their positions to political appointments and nepotism), bureaucrats could claim greater or even expert knowledge in a given domain over those whom they managed. Weber implied that, save for in wartime, the social tensions between supervisors and rank-and-file employees were more antagonistic than what any ideology of social solidarity, such as nationalism or socialism, could forge between the two classes. The following, for example, is his description of the sort of workplace conflicts that are typical of bureaucratic management.

> On the other side, professional specialization and the need for specialist education are growing at all levels in production *above* that of the workers, down to the charge hand and the overseer, while the relative number of persons belonging to this stratum is growing at the same time. Admittedly, they too are 'wage slaves', but they are mostly not on piece-wages or weekly wages, but on a fixed salary. Above all, the worker naturally hates the foreman, who is perpetually breathing down his neck, far more than the factory owner, and the factory owner in turn more than the shareholder, although the shareholder is the one who really draws his income *without* working, while the industrialist has to do very arduous mental work, and the foreman stands much closer still to the worker.[68]

Again, Weber maintained that this scenario was no less imaginable in a socialist system, where the state acts as industrialist and where "shareholders" are the workers themselves.

Regardless of the ideological inspiration for Weber's reflections on the modern bureaucratic revolution and its impact on the socialist alternative to capitalism, we must credit him for his insights into the likely constraints on democracy at both the workplace and formal political spaces under socialism. In a word, Weber posited that the means of administration were more powerful than the means and politics of production. This was a staggering contention, and one that should have given pause to anyone envisioning a radical transformation of modern society. It left Weber skeptical of the possibility of revolutionary change "in the sense of the forceful creation of entirely new formations of authority," which he thought most people confused with coups d'etat.[69] This was how he characterized the Bolshevik Revolution and the abortive German revolution that it inspired. It was mainly, therefore, with an eye on the managerial and bureaucratic requirements of the modern era that Weber saw in socialists believers in illusions and unreality, particularly those drawn from the middle class who refused to come to terms with the fact that by training and status they risked doing more harm than good to the socialist project.

PERSONALITY AND POLITICS

Returning now to Du Bois and imagining his reactions to Weber's observations on the future of managerial bureaucracy, the reasonable assumption is that it would have been mixed. We have no indication that he would have disagreed with the organizational patterns of all manner of modern institutions. However, he would have remarked that those with formal training *should* be the ones to occupy the supervisory and coordinating positions over those beneath them. Perhaps Du Bois would not have put it so indiscreetly, especially in his later years, but in light of the structure of the advocacy organizations that Du Bois either cofounded or was a central member of, from the ANA to the NAACP, he apparently thought this institutional stratification was appropriate to the charge: not one of them had a mission statement that imagined mechanisms by which nonofficials could influence or participate in policy making.[70] No allowance was made, either in conception or in bylaws, to enable low-level members or outside supporters to shape organizational agendas, long-term visions, or decision-making structures. The absence of such mechanisms suggests any number of biases among which we would have to include the likely possibility that Du Bois and his immediate collaborators could not imagine the common black woman or man playing a central role in organizations supposedly founded for their liberation. This is why I believe that it is fair to label Du Bois a vanguardist,[71] and this also explains why these organizations were all unapologetically top-down.

Although it is possible that Du Bois would have rejected the implications of the term "vanguardist," he could not have distanced himself from its practice: in word and deed this was the organizational pattern that Du Bois endorsed. For, in addition to believing that this structure was the most effective way of combating social injustice in primarily its racial and class expressions, he apparently believed that the very struggle itself, as well as its concrete and anticipated results, far outweighed any criticism of structural inequities within the organizations; after all, the goal was the eradication of racism in all its manifestations. The pyramidal structures of these organizations also fit Du Bois's personality, if it is appropriate to introduce that aspect of his person in this context. When describing himself in his last autobiography, *In Battle for Peace*, in the context of his 1950 run for the Senate as the American Labor Party candidate, Du Bois remarked that he was "no orator or spell-binder, but only one who could reason with those who would listen and had brains enough to understand."[72] He went on to add that he had been "reared in the New England tradition of regarding politics as no fit career for a man of serious aims, and particularly unsuitable for a college-bred man. Respectable participation in political life as voter, thinker, writer, and, on rare occasions as speaker, was my ideal."[73] From these remarks, one gathers that Du Bois's low opinion of mass politics was as much its requirement of the politician to engage in demagoguery as it was that he smile regularly, back slap, be quick with a witty aside, and kiss babies. Du Bois could never have been so disingenuous.

Nevertheless, Du Bois made a distinction between demagoguery and using the pen and podium to advance particular political positions. In light of the connotation that the word *propaganda* came to have in the Cold War era, the deliberate dissemination of patently false or distorted information so as to sway others to act accordingly, Du Bois's identification of himself as a propagandist was unfortunate.[74] The label gave his immediate and future political opponents grounds to dismiss or seriously call into question both his academic and popular writings on the grounds that they were first and foremost politically motivated. Deliberately lost in this view of Du Bois was his commitment to chronicling *the* truth as he saw it, no less than what he meant by propaganda: the highlighting of certain facts to persuade an audience of the wisdom of specific political positions. To jettison these considerations when evaluating Du Bois's work is to be guilty of the very infraction with which one charged him.

Without recourse to propaganda, Du Bois had no other means of affecting social change in a society that was desperately in need of transformation, according, at least, to those to whom it denied full citizenship. For in having disavowed violence after World War I as a means of catalyzing social transformation, Du Bois had also questioned the model of revolutionary change as established by the American, French, Haitian, and Russian Revolutions. However, without such dramatic social upheavals that forced the defenders of the status quo to surrender, it is hard to imagine how imperialism, monarchy, slavery, and capitalism would have been otherwise defeated, however temporarily in the last case. Herein were the philosophical and practical dilemmas of advocating nonviolent social change: the very principles of social justice for which one was fighting were originally won through violence. In the absence, then, of violent confrontations between categorically opposed sides, reform, not revolution, was ostensibly Du Bois's prescription for social change, nationally no less than internationally.

But what was the nonviolent intellectual-activist supposed to do when significant sectors of his own society, including key elected and appointed officials in the government charged with representing him, brand nonviolent social action subversive and therefore open to prosecution? This was precisely the question that Du Bois and other American peace activists had to ask themselves as their government harassed, stymied, and indicted them primarily in the decade between the end of World War II and the beginning of the Civil Rights movement. To this, the normally prescriptive Du Bois could really not offer any answer. Rather, he resorted to the similar appeals to reason with which he began his academic and activist work more than half a century earlier: he cajoled, pleaded, petitioned, embarrassed, and warned his opponents of the folly of their ways. His age may provide part of the answer (he was, after all, in his eighties in the 1950s) but only part of the reason for his return to his original political tactics. The more compelling reason was that the political atmosphere of the early Cold War era was just as politically un-forgiving as that of the first decade of the twentieth century; in each, dissent was silenced by intimidation, detention, or death. However, there was one surprising difference between the two, at least for black spokespeople: at the turn of the twentieth century they were not labeled un-American by their political opponents for decrying racism. They were called subhuman, biologically inferior, and fit to be lynched but not un-American, if only because they were not considered eligible for full citizenship. But in the 1950s, even this resident alien status, as we would now term it, was denied those who questioned the American political-economic system in any way, regardless of race. They were all, rather, agents of an alien society.

By the force of such logic, Du Bois's audience could turn a deaf ear to his critique of American culture and politics despite its agreement with him on certain points. Thus, even if the American reading public was willing to concede that early post–World War II America was "be-coming a police state, with secret espionage, tapping of private telephone conversations, and filling of dossiers of accusations against thousands of persons unaccused by police or courts, but denounced by gossip, rumors, hearsay and the testimony of professional informers"; that "because of the billions of dollars . . . spent on war," little public money was left for education, housing, health, infrastructure, and social insurance; that the federal government increasingly allows businessmen to "control . . . the most important functions of life . . . at public expense"; that "newspapers, magazines, radio and television bombard the public with inducements to spend money, to such an extent that the public wants things they do not need and often wants them for the wrong reasons"; that "we pay our farmers to raise less or destroy part of what they have raised"; and that blacks and other racial minorities "have been the defenders of democracy in the United States, of which they themselves were so widely deprived," it could not accept that the state appropriation of major industries of natural resources and communications would result in the "emerge[nce] of a new freedom in Art and Literature and a flowering of Science not dreamed of since the seventeenth century."[75] An American audience would not only consider this last assertion patently false, but also an insult to national pride and proof, furthermore, of Senator Joseph Mc-Carthy's claim that Ivy League Brahmins, in and outside of government, were increasingly mesmerized by the spell of the Soviet model of bureaucratic social engineering with which they sought to substitute capitalist individualism and entrepreneurial freedom.[76]

But Du Bois would have anticipated such resistance to his critique of American cultural life and his suggestion that its failings could be rectified by the adoption of a socialist program; after all, he had spent the greater part of his life chronicling, analyzing, and criticizing the very reasons racial, class, and national inequalities were so central to the modern world and to the place of the United States in it. Consequently, it is doubtful that Du Bois could have framed his arguments in a way that would have appealed in greater measure to the working-class Americans whom he was trying to convince of the validity of his observations and conclusions rather than offend them. Even if he "nationalized" his critique of early postwar America by underscoring the degree to which the persecution of political opposition undermined the protection of freedom of conscience on which the country was supposedly founded, it seems unlikely that he could have averted being categorically dismissed as a communist by his target audience rather than seen as an American social reformer or even revolutionary.

THE FUTURE OF LIBERAL POLITICS

In contrast to Du Bois's writings on Russia that were largely a paean to what he believed to be a successful and workable socialist model, Weber's Russia essays were as critical of the socialist prospect as they were of a dying tsarism. However, apart from providing him a "live" case to argue the advantages of a constitutional monarchy, Weber's Russia essays moved him to write as much about the practice and principles of modern politics as about what the optimal political arrangement might be for Germany in particular and great powers in general. Yet, unlike Du Bois, Weber refused to idealize what he considered the better political formula, for he found the unwillingness to grapple with ugly political realities irresponsible and, as we shall see, to think or act irresponsibly was to Weber a grave political sin. "What matters," he wrote in his justly famous essay "The Profession and Vocation of Politics," "is not age but the trained ability to look at the realities of life with an unsparing gaze, to bear these realities and be a match for them inwardly."[77] The context and deeper meaning of these sentiments will become clearer in the pages that follow. Suffice it to say here that Weber sought to be both a realist and dialectician in his major writings on politics, commitments that did not permit illusions. For Weber, then, there are no political utopias, only those political formulas with the fewest ostensible flaws.

As I have already noted, this was his basic criticism of socialists: their willful refusal to recognize human imperfections, their own included. So enamored were they with the romanticism of revolution that they refused to come to terms with its institutionalization or routinization, the second stage of any social project, which was based as much on coercion and violence as the capitalist system they justifiably condemned. To Weber, this was simply the reality of politics, which no slogan or program could reverse. For if the state, as he famously asserted, "is that human community which (successfully) lays claim to the *monopoly of legitimate physical violence* within a certain territory," then those who govern a state, regardless of professed intentions, do so thanks to that monopoly.[78] It was for this reason in particular that he had no patience for Bolshevik or Sparticist "call[s] for one *last* act of force to create the situation in which *all* violence will have been destroyed for ever": they were patently false.[79]

And they were no less false if uttered by administrators and managers of capitalist democracies who, like socialist ones, could point to "their noble intentions" in the performance of their assignments. If anything, Weber found their claims even more intolerable than those of their ideological leaders and sympathizers, because they could lead these bureaucrats to inflate their own political importance. Certainly, as Weber took pains to reiterate, an administrative infrastructure is indispensable to the establishment and maintenance of any political regime, but bureaucrats are not statesmen, and they are not supposed to be.

> The official's honor consists in being able to carry out . . . instruction[s], on the *responsibility* of the man issuing [them], conscientiously and precisely in the same way as if it corresponded to his own

convictions. Without this supremely ethical discipline and self-denial the whole apparatus would disintegrate. By contrast, the honor of the political leader, that is, of the leading statesman, consists precisely in taking exclusive, *personal* responsibility which he cannot and may not refuse or unload onto others. Precisely those who are officials by nature and who, in this regard, are of high moral stature, are bad and, particularly in the political meaning of the word, irresponsible politicians, and thus of low moral stature in this sense—men of the kind we Germans, to our cost, have had in positions of leadership time after time. This is what we call "rule by officials."[80]

In slightly different Weberian terms, whereas officials live by politics, statesmen live for politics; whereas statesmen are visionaries, officials are order takers and task fulfillers. However, in light of the increasing bureaucratization of political parties themselves to which Weber alludes in this passage, and given the number of political appointments (hundreds of times greater than the number of representatives) that the winning party secures as the spoils of victory, elected representatives could not but succumb to the tendency toward officialdom. In fact, so pronounced did Weber find the official's mentality among political actors across the ideological spectrum that he went so far as to suggest that one of their primary motivations for participating in electoral or even revolutionary campaigns is to be able to assume key bureaucratic posts and offer others to their friends and allies. Yet Weber's reading of practical politics was based on neither a strictly cynical view of human nature (although his was certainly not generous) nor one that did not recognize unselfish convictions but was rather grounded in the structure of politics itself. In a word, those who have been authentically moved to political action on principled convictions have been historically few. However, in order to have some social impact, those few have had to win over the hearts and minds of followers. But unlike those selfless leaders, and irrespective of the sincerity of their belief in his abilities and vision, followers expect some rewards for their support of their leader. In recognition of this fact, leaders are forced to satisfy those expectations typically at the expense of their original convictions. Ideals are thus doubly compromised.

Does this mean that convictions have no place in politics? No, be-cause, as Weber put it, without them "what is possible would never have been achieved."[81] His counsel was that a commitment to *responsibility* had to be first among a statesman's political convictions. To Weber, a po-litically responsible actor is one who enters the political arena to pursue a cause, recognizes the "everyday shortcomings in people," and openly "an-swers for the (foreseeable) *consequences* of [his] actions" without apology or excuse.[82] Although all these elements of political responsibility were equally fundamental to Weber, the last one was especially important to him because he found that convictions-led political actors have the ten-dency to "hold the world . . . or the stupidity of others, or the will of God who made them thus" responsible for the failure to realize their social vision but never their unreal expectations.[83] Nor can they come really to terms with the "fact that the achievement of 'good' ends is in many cases tied to the necessity of employing morally suspect or at least morally dangerous means, and that one must reckon with the possibility or even likelihood of evil side-effects."[84] Only responsible political actors, Weber maintained, grapple with these concerns.

Having made the case for the necessity of responsibility in politics (to which he also added passion and judgment, or the "ability to main-tain one's inner composure and calm while being receptive to realities, in other words *distance* from things and people"),[85] Weber then had to propose who was most likely to exhibit these qualities. His first answer was the parliamentary leader, but he quickly lost his faith in this figure for reasons that remain unclear. His second and final (due to his death) candidate was the plebiscitary or popularly elected leader like the American president. However, in keeping with his desire to be a respon-sible political commentator, this was not an uncritical endorsement of the American political system whose flaws he found most troubling. Let us briefly consider how Weber viewed both figures.

Charisma and Democracy

Both parliamentary leaders and popularly elected leaders had to be demagogues, which for Weber was no source of shame but a simple ne-cessity: political leaders had to attract a following beyond the party apparatus and the halls of parliament. Yet charisma, while a necessary attribute of the political leader, was insufficient for the task; Weber insisted that a requirement for statesmanship was political experience. For the political leader drawn from parliament, political experience included negotiating budgetary agreements, crafting legislation, active participation on established committees, and the convening of special investigative panels as need arose. Among other benefits, these duties would provide the future statesman with experience in political administration but not of the bureaucratic kind. Whereas bureaucratic administration, in Weber's opinion, sought to hoard and hide information from the public, parliamentary administration aimed to bring it to light for the purposes of educating itself and the public about the information that a government has in its possession. This is what he so admired about the English parliamentary system whose *"supervision and control"* of the flow of bureaucratic information-gathering "force[d] the administration to work *publicly*" rather than secretly.[86] So important to Weber was this "right to inquiry" into behind-the-scenes government action that he seemed to rate it above even lawmaking among parliamentary duties. Yet Weber soon lost faith in the seasoned parliamentarian becoming a statesman, despite his role as an effective bulwark against bureaucratic abuse. How do we explain this sudden change of heart?

The short answer is that Weber had reassessed the relative strength of party leaders—"notables," "bosses," and "officials"—and charismatic parliamentarians and came to the conclusion that the former had a variety of means to stifle the political careers of the latter. How? Mainly by not selecting charismatic political figures as candidates and by withholding financial and print support from their campaigns. Even the independently wealthy political aspirant whose economic profile made him most eligible to hold political office could not withstand such a denial of political support. Weber learned this firsthand when he was encouraged to run for political office by fellow members of the Democratic Party after addressing them in Frankfurt in December 1918. Weber obliged, only to have party officials remove his name and replace it with one of their choice. Was this experience what cooled Weber to the idea that the parliamentary party system was capable of producing statesmen? Was this literally a case of the personal becoming political and then theoretical? David Beetham thinks not but remarks that the "incident can only have reinforced [Weber's] long standing concern about the domination of politics by those who lived of it."[87]

Yet, even if Weber ultimately concluded that parliamentarians were unlikely to become statesmen given the weight of either the guild-like or bureaucratic structure of their political parties, he still argued that they had important roles to play in plebiscitary democracies, the most important of which was to conceive of a "peaceful way of *eliminating* the Caesarist dictator when he has *lost* the trust of the masses."[88] The risk of this occurring was quite high for two compelling reasons: the pursuit of political power requires ambition, and ambition is one form of vanity; and political cause and charisma tend to part company after they have captured the popular imagination, leaving only charisma without a cause. In a particularly powerful and prescient passage, he described these tendencies in this way:

> The sin against the holy spirit of [the politician's] profession begins where this striving for power becomes detached from the task in hand and becomes a matter of purely personal self-intoxication instead of being placed entirely at the service of the 'cause'. For there are ultimately just two deadly sins in the area of politics: a lack of objectivity and . . . a lack of responsibility. Vanity, the need to thrust one's person as far as possible into the foreground, is what leads the politician most strongly into the temptation of committing one or other (or both) of these sins, particularly as the demagogue is forced to count on making an 'impact'. . . . His lack of objectivity tempts him to strive for the glittering appearance of power rather than its reality, while his irresponsibility tempts him to enjoy power for its own sake, without any substantive purpose.[89]

Nevertheless, political charisma's inclination to lapse into egoism was not the fault of politicians alone; the voting and even nonvoting public was no less to blame. That Weber had become an advocate of the popular and direct election of the highest political office in modern democracies did not mean that he was suddenly a champion of the perspicacity of the "people." On the contrary, he continued to believe that the "*un*organized mass, the democracy of the street, is wholly irrational" and that it is primarily responsible for the "possibility that *emotional* elements will become predominant in politics."[90] Why the middle class or landed, industrial, or commercial elites were any less susceptible to emotional appeals Weber saw no reason to elaborate; this was simply one of those self-evident characterizations of the working class that came naturally to those of Weber's class and training. Only "modern monarchs practicing 'personal government' . . . exhibit the same [emotional] features" as the masses, Weber went on to add.[91] In light, then, of the collective personality flaw of the masses, it is presumably desirable that the "ordinary voter . . . has no active role [in politics] at all, and notice is only taken of his person during elections or in public advertisements formulated for his benefit at other times."[92]

To Weber, these were the natural or realistic limits of democracy plain and simple: given the time, energy, and willingness to compromise that referenda on all important political questions require, democracy by questionnaire was impractical, which is why policy "is always made by a small number of people in any case."[93] Outside of periodically casting their vote, citizens were supposed to comply with the policy decisions of their political leader, whose job it was to persuade them of the wisdom of his choices. If his powers of persuasion or the results of his policies proved wanting, the electorate had to swallow their discontent until the next round of elections. This was indeed their "spiritual proletarianization," as Weber put it, which matched their economic one. At most, and this was no small demand at the time, Weber could call for the end of Prussia's tiered electoral system, which afforded those with the highest income the voting power many times greater than that of the far larger numbers of their less fortunate fellow citizens. But this was Weber's only concession to the people. Here is how Mommsen described Weber's conception of plebiscitary democracy:

> Hence, democracy is conceived as a functionalist system that gives the people no more and no less than the guarantee that the direction of governmental affairs is always in the hands of leaders who, at least formally, are optimally qualified for this task. There will no longer be any question of active participation by the people, in any form, in the material formulation of the political objectives to be pursued by the

community. This will be the sole responsibility of the political leaders, who create the necessary following for the realization of their goals through their demagogic qualities. The democratic constitutional state was perceived essentially as a technical organization for the purpose of training political leaders and enabling them to rise to power and to rule.[94]

The only alternative to this arrangement was a "democracy without a leader," a condition that was as unimaginable to Weber as it was to Du Bois. However, Du Bois would have gone on to warn Weber, with the same words that he ended his observations on German politics in 1893: "It is thus plain that the political leadership of Germany for the next fifty years will require talent of an equal if not higher order than that of the last fifty. Indeed, to this great task the genius of no one man, Bismarck or other, will suffice; it calls for the genius of the nation."[95] On this score, Du Bois proved particularly farsighted.

DESPITE THEIR STARK ideological differences, Du Bois and Weber agreed on the role of the people in the political process: to support trained or charismatic leaders, not to select or supply them. In the kindest terms, the people were a collective supporting cast, not the stars of the political production. Whereas Weber maintained that the limited role of the people in a democratic political system was a function of the facts that only small numbers of actors really wield political power in any political regime and that an even smaller number of them possess charisma, Du Bois held that a similarly minuscule number have received the requisite intellectual training to lead and to envision a better world. Those who either profit from social hierarchy or who are too debilitated by its demands would not be among them. For Du Bois, this future world would be a more egalitarian one in which physical and cultural differences would no longer serve as the bases and justification for differences in wealth and power. In a word, only in a socialist society would difference be gutted of value. Believing that the former Soviet Union had achieved this among other accomplishments, Du Bois could not allow himself to be more critical of his model society.

For Weber, this expectation of socialist society was rank utopianism because no political regime, beyond a certain size, could willfully banish social differences or distinctions. And even if this were hypothetically achieved in one society, it would encounter a formidable obstacle in attempting to extend the principle of equality across political and national borders; national sentiment is not so easily surmounted. In light of this reality, Weber attempted to formulate a political program that would best advance a state's national interests while minimizing its internal tensions. His proposal was the democratically elected charismatic man of independent means whose wealth would allow him both to live for (rather than by) politics and put the nation's best interests before his own or those of his class. This seemed to be a regression to a Bismarck figure of the kind that he criticized (along with his steadfast supporters) in quite strong terms for the greater part of his adult life but with the addition of demagogic talents. Perhaps Weber's hope was that this next Bismarckian incarnation would be less threatened by charismatic rivals, including his eventual successor. Whomever he had in mind, a Bismarck or a Gladstone, Weber wanted him to be a truly extraordinary figure, despite his normally cynical view of unrealistic wishes. Sadly, Weber proved to be correct about the rise of a plebiscitary leader but not about the content of his message or program.

CHAPTER FIVE

Unequal Treatment

By any measure, the work that appeared on Max Weber and W. E. B.
Du Bois from the late 1950s to the mid-1960s set new standards and
choices for how scholars would treat the two thereafter. In fact, we can
be more specific and call 1959 the watershed year in Du Bois and Weber
studies, for it was in that year that two pathbreaking works on these
scholar-activists were published: Wolfgang Mommsen's *Max Weber und
die Deutsche Politik, 1890–1920*,[1] an exhaustive and critical exploration of
Weber's political thought from young adulthood to the year of his death;
and Francis L. Broderick's *W. E. B. Du Bois: Negro Leader in a Time of
Crisis*, the first critical introduction to Du Bois's life and work that Du
Bois himself lived to see in print. The uncanny parallels continued into
the following year with the publication of Reinhard Bendix's *Max Weber:
An Intellectual Portrait* and Elliot Rudwick's *W. E. B. Du Bois: Propagandist of the Negro Protest*. These were followed by Du Bois's own contribution to his life story in the form of his fourth and final autobiography,
*W. E. B. Du Bois: A Soliloquy on Viewing My Life from the Last Decade of Its
First Century*, the "basic draft" of which he wrote in 1958–59 but which
was initially published "in somewhat shortened versions in 1964 and
1965, in China, the U.S.S.R. and the German Democratic Republic,"[2]
before it appeared in its original and unabridged form in 1968. Finally,

also in 1964, the centennial conference of Max Weber's birth was convened in Heidelberg and counted among its presenters and respondents Talcott Parsons, Raymond Aron, Herbert Marcuse, Max Horkheimer, Jürgen Habermas, Wolfgang Mommsen, and Reinhard Bendix, among others.[3] These were indeed rich years for Weber and Du Bois studies.

The works produced on Du Bois and Weber in these years also set the tone for how future scholars of the two men would handle one issue in particular: the intersection or separation of their political positions and academic work. Generally speaking, the tendency among Weber scholars has been to treat the two domains separately, as Weber himself prescribed and a rule to which he, too, presumably adhered. Conversely, the tendency among Du Bois scholars has been to underscore the intersection of his politics and scholarship, not least because Du Bois himself recognized that even the sincerest attempt on a scholar's part to separate the two will, on some level, fall short of her or his intentions. In his opinion, scholarship is an uneven mix of bias and objectivity, the recognition of which should deepen the scholar's resolve to commit to the latter, not cause her to abandon the effort altogether. Sadly, however, it appears that Du Bois's honesty on this matter cost him his academic credentials in the eyes of some, long before he turned to Marxism in the 1910s for a new understanding of the interplay of race and political economy. For it remains the unspoken rule in the academy that a scholar is not supposed to admit any bias (outside of that which is unconscious and, consequently, unintentional), and if he should do so, the admission is fair grounds for his or her work not to be taken seriously or, at worst, dismissed altogether. As I see it, this is one of the reasons for the marked differences in treatment of Weber's and Du Bois's scholarly work.

In this survey of the scholarly approaches to the work of Weber and Du Bois that I present here, I do not claim to be exhaustive for that literature is vast. Still, what I can highlight here are some of the trends and patterns in the scholarship over the past few decades that I have detected.

HEIDELBERG, 1964

To begin with the work on Weber, it is generally of three kinds in my view: the uncritical introductions to his work that avoid mention of his political convictions; studies that either recognize or focus on his politics but suggest by silence that it had no bearing on his scholarship; and finally, those that underscore the intersection of his politics and scholarship and suggest that the latter is, at times, propaganda.[4] These happen to be the approaches taken by the three invited speakers at the centenary conference of Weber's birth in Heidelberg: Talcott Parsons, Raymond Aron, and Herbert Marcuse.

Despite having been "assigned" the topic of his address, "Evaluation and Objectivity in Social Science: An Interpretation of Max Weber's Contributions," Parsons stated that he found it "entirely congenial" for two reasons: "First, it provided an occasion to reconsider the meanings of Weber's two famous conceptions of 'value freedom' (*Wertfreiheit*) and 'value relevance' (*Wertbeziehung*)"; and second, it "provided an occasion for reviewing the general structure of Weber's treatment of social systems."[5] Parsons went on to add that the assigned topic allowed him to explore the "central significance of the sociology of law for the design of Weber's work as a whole."[6] There is nothing extraordinary in this straightforward and accurate description of his Heidelberg address. So, too, it would seem, is his next remark: "This accorded with Weber's personal intellectual history, since he began his career in jurisprudence."[7] However, to those familiar with Parsons's work there is a remarkable aspect to the inclusion of this matter of fact: it is a reference to an aspect of Weber's life that had some bearing on his scholarship. Parsons only rarely and sparingly divulged any personal information about the lives of the scholars whose theories he analyzed and employed. In, for example, his justly celebrated *The Structure of Social Action*, we learn nothing of the lives of the four scholars whose work and thought he interprets apart from their nationalities. In another instance where he does tell us something about Weber's background, he limits his revelations to the fact that Weber "came from the most highly cultured portion of the German upper middle class" and that "from an early age he took a passionate interest in political affairs."[8] What bearing these personal details had on Weber's scholarly predilections and interests Parsons leaves us to guess. In this sense Parsons was quite the believer in scholarly purity: scholarly ideas, like their formulators, stand above human prejudice and ulterior designs.

Parsons could take this avoidance of relevant, personal details to extremes. In an essay where he applied Weberian concepts and insights to the rise of Nazism in Germany—"Max Weber and the Contemporary Political Crisis"—Parsons makes no mention of Weber's own political views, which is why his musing on what "Weber's personal attitude toward National Socialism would have been, had he lived to see it,"[9] comes as a surprise; Parsons gives us no indication elsewhere in the essay that Weber held political positions in any way related to the topic. In any event, in light of Parsons's insistence on a clear separation of scholarship and politics, we can understand his "disappointment" with the discussion that followed his paper because "only in one connection was the relationship between Weber's methodological work and his substantive sociology mentioned by any one of the discussants."[10] Their concern was far more with Weber's politics, the buzz theme occasioned by the then relatively recent publication of Wolfgang Mommsen's work, than with Parsons's more theoretical topic.

If the organizers of the Heidelberg conference[11] had based their decision on whom to invite to give the second address on the possession of the greatest knowledge of the subject matter—Weber's politics—they should have chosen Mommsen. However, they made the decision to invite scholars living outside of Germany as the principal presenters, and one suspects that many of the guests would have questioned the choice of such a young scholar anyway.[12] Of course, Raymond Aron, the French political scientist and sociologist who was invited to give the second address—"Max Weber and Power-Politics"—was no novice to the subject. Some three years before the publication of Parsons's *The Structure of Social Action*, Aron had devoted a chapter of his *German Sociology* to a discussion of Weber. Despite being a fraction of the length of Parsons's treatment of Weber, he readily acknowledged Weber's politics in it. Plus, he found them entirely understandable, if not commendable.

Weber's realistic political theory was intended to serve the greatness of Germany. He was certainly a nationalist. He belonged to the generation which had entered politics after the unification of Germany, and which regarded the extension of Bismarck's work as its supreme task. The unity of Germany was to be the starting-point for its role in world affairs. I do not wish to minimize Weber's nationalism, although this term usually denotes attitudes very different from his. Nothing in his writing would offend or wound a foreigner. He conceived the greatness of Germany, which was his supreme aim, less as the triumph of force than as the expansion of a civilization. In his view, the civilizations of the West had developed within the framework of great States. The Germans would be responsible before history if they allowed Russian autocracy or Anglo-Saxon pragmatism to dominate the world.[13]

In his Heidelberg address, delivered some thirty years after he penned these words, Aron had significantly modified his views on Weber's politics and offered a far more critical assessment of them. There he asked rhetorically and certainly with the extremes to which it had been taken by the Nazi regime in mind, "Can the power of the nation be an ultimate goal, the god to whom one sacrifices everything?"[14] Aron even called Weber's worldview into question, which saw humanity as engaged in a life or death struggle of competing forces—good versus evil, morality versus immorality, peace versus war—and which only served to heighten Weber's sensitivity to perceived threats to Germany's national interests. "I cannot help thinking," Aron mused in Heidelberg, "that Weber, obsessed by the vision of struggle everywhere and at all times, came thereby to transform an incontestable but temporary rivalry of power into a war of gods."[15] Finally, and perhaps most damning, Aron argued that Weber's political positions did not rise to the level of his scholarly achievements: "It remains to say that Weber, who as a sociologist is as up to date today as yesterday, was not always, as a politician, in advance of his times."[16] This remark, however muted, undoubtedly stung the other Weber admirers who heard it, for if there was one criticism of their hero that they could not tolerate, it was the suggestion that he was ordinary on some matters.

The remarks of the conference's third and final presenter, Herbert Marcuse, stung only slightly less, primarily because they were largely expected from a man of the Left. Marcuse's argument was fairly simple, if not always his language: one can detect a middle-class bias in Weber's scholarly work no less than in his politics. Proof of this, Marcuse argued, is found immediately in Weber's sociological point of departure: industrial capitalism as the culmination of Western reason. It alone developed a conception of rationality that puts a premium on the calculability or "mathematization" (*Mathematisierung*) of not only the costs and benefits of given actions and goals but also the means and ends of realizing them. Industrial capitalist rationality also drew from and strengthened one of its forebears, political bureaucracy, which it subjected to capitalist logic. However, this enhancement of bureaucratic political power threatened to devour its economic offspring. The most effective measure, according to Weber, to contain bureaucratic overreach was the activity of a dynamic capitalist economy. Without that, modern industrial society would succumb to the antithesis of Western rationality, namely, socialism.

To Marcuse, such understandings of rationality, capitalism, bureaucracy, and socialism were bourgeois through and through. For one, they failed to take into account the irrationality of capitalism as measured by its human and environmental costs, its reduction of human life to calculations of profit and loss, and its reification of the market as the site of free exchange rather than of coercive contract. When capitalism is assessed according to these considerations, it appears far less rational than how Weber described it. If Weber was unwilling or unable to perceive capitalist unreason, it was because, Marcuse argued, he was too "profoundly . . . attached to . . . the equation of technical and bourgeois-capitalist reason." He continued:

> This prevented [Weber] from seeing that it was not 'pure' formal technical reason, but the reason of domination that was building the 'houses of bondage,' and that the *perfection* of technical reason can very well become the instrument of man's liberation. To put it another way: Weber's analysis of capitalism was not value-free enough, in that it imported values and norms specific to capitalism into the 'pure' definitions of formal rationality.[17]

One example was particularly revealing to Marcuse: Weber's belief that political and economic or political-economic elites in both capitalist and socialist societies, who monopolized the means of production and administration in their respective societies, regarded those whom they employed and managed in a similar light. To Marcuse, this was patently false. Unlike capitalist elites, who view the economically dependent as means to profitable ends, socialist ones recognize that a "truly 'rational' administration would be the utilization of social wealth in the interests of the free development and satisfaction of human needs—[which] technical progress makes . . . into an ever-more-real possibility."[18] For Marcuse (as for Du Bois), it was the aim or intent of those who managed a social system, more than their formal position in the social hierarchy, that determined whether they were acting to promote their individual interests or collective ones. However, on some level, Weber must have recognized this distinction in light of the hopes that he had for the plebiscitary leader; he simply did not want to make the same allowance for socialist leadership.

Understandably, Weber supporters did not take kindly to Marcuse's remarks. Much like the storm that Mommsen's work set off when it appeared,[19] Marcuse's criticisms of Weber had a similar effect. In the discussion following Marcuse's presentation, Benjamin Nelson employed the strongest language against Marcuse's "insistent forthrightness in blaming so many of the ills of recent times on the 'rationalism' which Weber, in his view, espoused in so undialectical a fashion."[20] Another discussant suggested that Marcuse's was "cheap criticism of one of the greatest thinkers of this century."[21] Even Raymond Aron, whose topic at the conference, "Max Weber and Power Politics," supposedly took Weber's political positions head-on, described Marcuse's paper, a couple of years after the meeting, as "seem[ingly] motivated by a kind of fury against Max Weber, as if he were still alive and indomitable."[22]

However, what Aron failed to remind his readers was that he, too, was criticized in Heidelberg for harboring comparable ill will for Weber. Eduard Baumgarten, who seemed incapable of comprehending that Weber's own attacks on German patriotic figures and institutions did not make him any less of a nationalist (but perhaps even more of one), charged Aron and Mommsen of deliberately citing incomplete and therefore misleading excerpts of Weber's work to make him appear to be more of a nationalist than he truly was. And in a brilliant stroke of intellectual deflection, Baumgarten added that such criticism of Weber was an admission that "we are children of our fears which result from our experiences, and our reproaches to him would be better directed against ourselves."[23]

Irrespective of the tenor of Baumgarten's comments, they were emblematic of those voiced by Weber defenders at the conference—that

Weber's critics have exaggerated the force of some of his arguments and declarations by selecting certain passages and excluding others that temper his remarks. However, as noted earlier, on some matters, Weber did not express any later reservations or qualifications to his earlier claims, as he did in the cases of, say, rationality and bureaucracy. A short list of these would include the overall superiority of Western institutions and thought, the corresponding deficiencies in Asian cultural systems, the necessity of imperialism for Western great powers, and the primacy of German nationalist interests in policy decisions. Weber did not advance any of these claims provisionally, as Bendix suggests was Weber's wont;[24] and nowhere did he retract them. And in light of the fact that such thinking was shared by Nazis, whom we rightly condemn, we cannot label them mere "mis-steps" or occasional "crude and gauche" lapses, as Nelson suggested that we do. For when are racism and subjugation only missteps? When the victims in question are, say, Slavic and African, not Jewish and western European? The absurdity of Nelson's claims is in no way mitigated by taking into account the complete sentence in which he made them, but it does reveal what he considered to be the stakes of the matter:

> During the past few days we have been deluged with proofs that Weber was no flawless paragon. Weber could and did become crude and gauche in some of his forays into *Machtpolitik*. Surely we have not been gathered here in his beloved Heidelberg to hear this one side of the story. Nor is this in any profound sense how his life and work demand to be understood.[25]

And:

> The mis-steps that he made in all good faith in responding to the awesome challenges of his day do not weigh heavily in the balance against the immense services that he rendered to mankind. . . . To hold him responsible for the advent of 1933 or the nightmare of Auschwitz, as a number of his aroused countrymen are now doing, is to commit error and wrong at one and the same time. One may be allowed to hope that posterity will make amends for this misguided gesture. His countrymen should not wish to do less for one who

struggled so valiantly, albeit so vainly, to guard them against the disasters which lay ahead.[26]

Two points strike us immediately in Nelson's remarks: his concern that inordinate attention paid to Weber's aggressive and subjective positions would be used to taint or even overshadow his presumably far more substantial scholarly contributions; and his concern that some had already used Weber's retrospectively embarrassing positions to argue that he played a significant role in preparing the German public to embrace Hitler and his program. To take Nelson's second preoccupation first, I believe that he was mainly referring to Mommsen's study, *Max Weber and German Politics*, and specifically to Mommsen's statement, "The charismatic plebiscitary leadership 'with machine' materialized in 1933 in a completely different form from that which Weber had in mind. Nonetheless, we have to concede that Weber's theory of charismatic leadership combined with the radical formalization of the meaning of democratic institutions helped, if only marginally, to make the German people inwardly willing to acclaim Adolf Hitler's leadership position."[27] Little did it matter that Mommsen made it clear that he firmly believed that Weber would have denounced Hitler and the Nazi program.[28] The mere fact that he had drawn a link between Weber and the notorious charismatic leader of the Third Reich was sufficient cause for Nelson to dismiss the message and the messenger altogether. For similar reasons, we imagine, Nelson was not moved to address Marcuse's charge of bourgeois bias in Weber's sociological and political work.

Yet in partial defense of Nelson and the faction for which he spoke, Marcuse was no more willing to grapple with some of Weber's important insights, particularly those into the impact of institutionalization and bureaucratization on the original aims and goals of reformist and revolutionary movements, than Nelson was open to contending with Marcuse's. Presumably, Marcuse, like Nelson, reasoned that if he had conceded any point to Weber, his promoters would have used it as grounds to call into question any and all of his criticism of Weber. In order to preempt that likelihood, Marcuse refused to entertain the validity of any of Weber's emphases. And here is where the debate was left in 1964 and after. And here it has arguably been since Weber's death, with his friends, colleagues, and their students drawing a bold line between his scholarship and politics and his primarily Marxist critics charging that both are thoroughly bourgeois.[29] Our concern here, however, is not with that debate but with how the scholarly treatment of Weber contrasts with that of Du Bois, and with how Du Bois himself would have addressed the question of the relationship between Weber's politics and scholarship. Let us begin with this last question.

DU BOIS, 1959–1960

As we will recall from chapter 2, Du Bois shared with Weber the position that the production of bias-free scholarship should be the aspiration of all scholars. However, he also recognized that unconscious biases seep unavoidably into their work precisely because they are unconscious. "Convictions," or what Weber termed presuppositions, Du Bois wrote in the opening pages of *The Philadelphia Negro*, "on all great matters of human interest one must have to a greater or less degree, and they will enter to some extent into the most cold-blooded scientific research as a disturbing factor."[30] Still, Du Bois insisted throughout his life that the pursuit of the "truth" must guide the historian, not indulgence in myth making or myth maintenance. As he declared in the final chapter of *Black Reconstruction in America*:

> In the first place, somebody in each era must make clear the facts with utter disregard to his own wish and desire and belief. What we have got to know, so far as possible, are the things that actually happened in the world. Then with that much clear and open to every reader, the philosopher and prophet has a chance to interpret these facts; but the historian has no right, posing as scientist, to conceal or distort facts; and until we distinguish between these two functions of the chronicler of human action, we are going to render it easy for a muddled world out of sheer ignorance to make the same mistake ten times over.[31]

And Du Bois demanded that the same principle apply to biographical portraits, where the temptation to engage in hero worship is perhaps even greater than in studies of populations.

One is astonished in the study of history at the recurrence of the idea that evil must be forgotten, distorted, skimmed over. We must not remember that Daniel Webster got drunk but only remember that he was a splendid constitutional lawyer. We must forget that George Washington was a slave owner, or that Thomas Jefferson had mulatto children, or that Alexander Hamilton had Negro blood, and simply remember the things we regard as creditable and inspiring. The difficulty, of course, with this philosophy is that history loses its value as an incentive and example; it paints perfect men and noble nations, but it does not tell the truth.[32]

If the words and the tone that he used in *Black Reconstruction in America* are any guide, we can imagine Du Bois similarly chiding Weber scholars for engaging in hero worship rather than tackling troubling claims. Unfortunately for Du Bois, his first two biographers, Francis Broderick and Elliot Rudwick,[33] heeded his counsel arguably too well, and painted decidedly unflattering portraits of the man while he was still alive no less. These studies, it should be noted, differed from Mommsen's study of Weber (and those of other Weber scholars) in at least one critical sense: whereas Mommsen did not use his revelations on Weber's politics to impugn his scholarship, Broderick and Rudwick did just that, sparing only *The Philadelphia Negro*. In a word, they had come to bury Du Bois, certainly not to save him. Accordingly, what Du Bois and his champions took to be his intellectual and institutional successes Broderick and Rudwick considered evidence of his failures. These, they argued, were due mainly to Du Bois's irreconcilable (according to them) desire to be both an activist and an academic, a researcher and a reformer. Unable to master either one of them, Du Bois excelled, as Rudwick put it, in an intermediate or combinatory endeavor as a master essayist who "stirred up controversies, commented on current events related to the race problem, provided arguments for racial egalitarianism, and formulated theoretical blueprints which other men were to bring into actuality."[34]

There was more, however, to Broderick's and Rudwick's criticisms of Du Bois than the fact that he refused to establish a clear boundary between his political and institutional work and his academic and popular writings, which left all of them wanting. What troubled them even more were his political positions themselves, one of which was his advocacy of the preservation and cultivation of distinct black American cultures and communities while fighting against antiblack discrimination in an interracial organization, the NAACP. Why Rudwick interpreted Du Bois's stance as a "paradox" and Broderick characterized it as "racist" rather than as expressions of ethnic pluralism and pan-identities reveal more about their own politics than Du Bois's. Clearly, they found black nationalist/pan-African sentiments far more troubling and menacing than they found, say, Irish American, Irish Republican, and Irish diasporan appeals or American, Israeli, and diasporan Jewish identity. The reason, which we can infer from their criticisms of Du Bois's "racial nationalism," is that, unlike other people's nationalisms of both the domestic and diasporic varieties that are inspired primarily by ethnic pride, black nationalism is necessarily racist because it is largely a reaction to white racism and consequently rejects integration and the efforts of well-meaning whites in presumably much the same way that white nationalists are intolerant of the integration of people of color. Unwilling to explore the limited meaning and results of American racial integration by the mid-twentieth century, any more than the subtle forms of racism practiced by white liberals, Broderick and Rudwick could only portray Du Bois as a phenomenal, yet tragic puzzle.

What was more, Du Bois's personality, they argued, though partially shaped by the racist society in which he lived, grew to become a larger obstacle to his efforts to mitigate racism than that bigotry itself. Arrogant, aloof, condescending, childish, petty, petulant, snobbish, sensitive, selfish, and self-important were some of the ways in which Broderick and Rudwick described Du Bois's character. Personal challenges such as these could hardly make of Du Bois an organization man, much less the producer of impartial scholarship. From this very damning tag-team portrait of Du Bois, Broderick could conclude that it was solely due to Du Bois's adeptness in self-promotion that scholars and laypeople would continue to pay attention to what he wrote, said, and did: "In his own lifetime, Du Bois has become an almost mythical figure, and no one has contributed to this myth more sedulously than Du Bois himself."[35] As hard-nosed scholars, Broderick and Rudwick had set themselves the task of demythologizing Du Bois.

RESCUING DU BOIS

Despite the efforts of the editors of *Freedomways*,[36] Henry Lee Moon,[37] Shirley Graham Du Bois,[38] Myron Weinberg,[39] and Julius Lester,[40] in the mid-1960s and early 1970s to balance Broderick's and Rudwick's pronouncements on Du Bois's life and work with what they felt to be both more accurate and sympathetic portraits, the shadow of the first studies remained largely intact until the appearance in 1976 of Arnold Rampersad's *The Art and Imagination of W. E. B. Du Bois*. This was mainly because, unlike the interim works that were either reminiscences or appreciations of Du Bois's person and passions, Rampersad's was a university press–published monograph. Moreover, Rampersad's was not a frontal assault on Broderick's and Rudwick's scholarship but a subtle one that was no less devastating in effect. For what Rampersad demonstrated was the degree to which many of Du Bois's thoughts and attitudes, which Broderick and Rudwick presented as peculiar to him, could be traced to the white institutions and personalities with which and with whom he had contact. His oscillation between elitist judgments of the common, working person and his democratic identification with her was the secular form of the Congregational preaching he heard in his youth; his twin desires to be both academic and advocate, scholar and policy shaper were shared by his teachers at Harvard and at the University of Berlin: William James, Albert Bushnell Hart, and Gustav Schmoller; and his nationalism, in its international, domestic, and local forms, was no less shaped by Bismarck, Treitschke, and Herder. Of course, in no way was Rampersad arguing that Du Bois was some impressionable tabula rasa onto which other people's ideas had been neatly inscribed. But what he did make clear is that many of Du Bois's bedrock ideas with which Broderick and Rudwick took issue were drawn from the larger white world in which he was raised. Thus, if any of his views warranted criticism, so, too, their sources.

Rampersad's equally important contribution to Du Bois scholarship was his insight into Du Bois's academic and fictional work: as studies in which Du Bois explored his sociopolitical visions, challenges, and dilemmas. These reflections served as the backdrop of Du Bois's biography of

John Brown in particular, which he researched and wrote in the period separating his launching of the Niagara movement and the cofounding of the NAACP. In that portrait, Rampersad argues, Du Bois the scholar was contemplating his own life-changing decision to become a full-time activist as he chronicled the life of one who sacrificed his life to end slavery.

> Brown had conceived of himself as a literal instrument of the Lord and had served his master to the death. A less religiously dogmatic soul, Du Bois nevertheless saw himself as also serving ideals compatible with religious godhead. His staring into the dark well of Brown's legacy should not be dismissed, therefore, as an exercise to remind others of a dedicated abolitionist martyr. The study was an outward, objective tracing of his inner anguish over how best to serve himself, his people, the world, and the spirituality before which he abased himself. Trapped in the gilded cage of his education and scholarship, he pondered the personal consequences of the radical life.[41]

A farther cry from Broderick's summation of *John Brown* as unoriginal, pleading, and "flimsy" is hardly imaginable.

Like Rampersad, Joseph DeMarco aimed in *The Social Thought of W. E. B. Du Bois* to correct what he concluded were Broderick's and Rudwick's problematic interpretations of Du Bois's thought and activities. In this case, the focus was on Du Bois's thinking about racial membership and racially inspired action. Through close readings of Du Bois's major monographs and essay collections (including *The Suppression of the African Slave Trade to the United States, John Brown, Darkwater, Dusk of Dawn*, and *Black Reconstruction*) and his most significant articles, DeMarco identified three primary forms of racial expression—cultural, economic, and psychological—that were central to Du Bois's work, academic and political, with the last form initially undergirding the first two but then taking on a life of its own. Moreover, despite Du Bois's realistic tendency to write about race as the interplay of these three dimensions of the concept, DeMarco argued that, at specific junctures, Du Bois emphasized one or a combination of two over the other(s): a cultural emphasis spanning the twenty years from college and graduate school to roughly the time of his mobilization of the Niagara movement; and an economic conception of race largely characterizing the remaining years of his life, which led him to the conclusion that only socialism aims to dismantle the economic foundations and psychological residues of race thinking.

Most notably, DeMarco devoted an entire chapter of his study to Du Bois's *Black Reconstruction in America* to contest presumably Broderick's criticism of Du Bois's "half-assimilated and misapplied Marxist terminology" in the work, as well as to determine the degree to which a Marxist-inspired analysis of the Civil War era could shed light on the sociopolitical developments that led to it, occurred during its course, and followed it. Although DeMarco questioned the appropriateness of Du Bois's use of terms like "dictatorship" to characterize some Reconstruction governments (South Carolina's, in particular), he nevertheless argued that Du Bois's employment of terms that Marx normally reserved for wage earners to enslaved toilers was justified on the grounds that they, too, were economically exploited and that, more important, they acted on their class interests more than southern white workers. Proof of this lay in their readiness to offer their skills and labor to the Union forces, the enemies of their class enemies, while southern white small farmers and artisans fought for their class enemies but racial kin. The import of Du Bois's analysis was lost on Broderick and other critics of *Black Reconstruction in America* who failed to recognize, as De Marco did, the sociological point that Du Bois was making: in bi- or multiracial societies collective working-class action is virtually impossible as long as the racially privileged portion of that class continues to consider itself superior to other racial constituents of it. If Du Bois had adhered to, rather than modified, a strict Marxist interpretation of the Civil War, he would not have been able to explain southern white working-class racial attitudes except as reflections of elite racial manipulation. Certainly, he attributed part of those attitudes to that, but Du Bois understood that racial manipulation alone could not explain the historical consistency of the southern white working class's choice to mobilize around race rather than class; at some point, it has to be considered the forger as much as the follower of its own destiny. Consequently, if the southern white working class chose to not combine forces with recently emancipated workers, their decision indicated to Du Bois that another variable was at work that a strict class analysis did not take into account. This is the psychology of race membership, or the "psychological wage," as Du Bois termed it, that white workers enjoyed over their black counterparts, and one that they shared with white capital. Rather than appreciate the theoretical innovations that Du Bois introduced to interpret a pivotal moment of American history with far-reaching consequences, critics of *Black Reconstruction in America*, such as Broderick, questioned his overall project of applying Marxist theory to American social realities, past or present.

DeMarco was not the only Du Bois scholar who devoted a substantial portion of his analysis to *Black Reconstruction in America*; Cedric Robinson did the same in his pathbreaking *Black Marxism*, also published in 1983. Although Robinson's study of Du Bois was not a monograph, I include it in this review of what I consider to be the most significant work of the scholar-activist because of its contribution to the reevaluation of Du Bois's thought no less than its place as the first of three works on Du Bois by black leftists in the early and mid-1980s, along with Gerald Horne's *Black and Red: W. E. B. Du Bois and the Afro-American Response to the Cold War, 1944–1963* and Manning Marable's *W. E. B. Du Bois: Black Radical Democrat*. Together these three works finally put to rest the misreadings, misinterpretations, and, in some cases, misinformation that Broderick and Rudwick provided in their studies of Du Bois. This was, it should be noted, a nearly thirty-year process.

In contrast to DeMarco, who underscored Du Bois's observation that the white American working class was more likely to mobilize around race than class when there was a black presence in the labor force, Robinson drew attention to two other of his contentions: that slave-cum-free people orchestrated the revolution of their own emancipation without the guidance of recognized, mass leaders; and that it was precisely in the act of emancipation that formerly enslaved people began to define the elements of freedom: land, education, and the right to political participation. These arguments were marked departures as much from the Leninist position of the necessity of a revolutionary vanguard as from Du Bois's own black uplift philosophy, both of which agreed to varying degrees that subordinate people were largely incapable of affecting their own liberation without the planning and vision of radical intellectuals. And this position was all the harder to overcome when the subordinate population in question was enslaved, for many who were sympathetic to its plight felt that in light of the degradation of the work that it was forced to do, the sadism of the overseers who routinely punished its ranks, and the illiteracy that the legal system imposed on it, it could not realize the overthrow of the slave system. In a word, enslaved people could rebel and even plan an uprising, but they could not achieve their own emancipation. As Robinson highlighted, in the chapter "The General Strike" in *Black Reconstruction*, Du Bois laid bare the fallacy of this contention.

It was left to Gerald Horne to lay to rest another fallacy advanced by Broderick and Rudwick, and even to a lesser degree by DeMarco as well: that in the last twenty years of his life Du Bois abandoned the political cause of black America and replaced it with participation in a number of questionable movements, the culmination of which was an increasing alignment with the Communist Parties of both the Soviet Union and the United States. Horne demonstrates the error of and political bias in such a view by referencing the fact that black Americans were generally far more sympathetic to the Left at home and abroad because it was the foremost political faction to make racial equality a centerpiece of its platform. They also understood that the Left's publicity of American racism abroad in particular was one of the most effective means of putting pressure on the U.S. government to penalize discriminatory practices and push it to extend basic liberal principles to black Americans. For these reasons, black America largely hailed Du Bois's postwar political activities even if it remained skeptical of how the adoption of communist measures could transform a proudly and powerfully racist America and saw through the conservative campaign to discredit Du Bois's politics as communist-inspired as little more than self-serving claptrap. In refusing to chronicle the postwar conservative backlash and its impact on black America, Broderick and Rudwick were able to portray the later Du Bois as a Don Quixote of sorts, a rebel without a cause, who fought the shadows of racial injustice that were largely on the wane. As Horne suggests, omissions of this magnitude demonstrate the degree to which the political biases of a scholar affect how he re-presents a particular historical moment. It was ironic that both Broderick and Rudwick should have repeatedly commented on Du Bois's difficult personality when their own treatment of Du Bois revealed so much about theirs. "In discussing Du

Bois's conflicts and appeal," Horne maintains, "his personality is not a material issue, especially when one views his peers."[42]

Horne's study facilitated the appearance of the work that was arguably the first complete treatment of Du Bois's life: Manning Marable's *W. E. B. Du Bois: Black Radical Democrat.* Though of comparable length to the studies by Broderick, Rudwick, and DeMarco, Marable's surpasses them all in terms of its balanced treatment of all phases of Du Bois's long life. More than this, Marable's study contextualizes Du Bois's thought and activities in ways that the earlier studies (excepting Rampersad's) do not. Thus, we learn that Du Bois's conservative streak was due as much to Alexander Crummell as to western Massachusetts Calvinism; that Du Bois was a cultural pluralist probably since his teen years in Great Barrington; that Du Bois's long-standing criticism of American labor unions and Left parties centered respectively on their indulgence of white working-class and middle-class racism; that Du Bois and countless others were victims of state and federal statutes that banned either the Communist Party itself or ideas that were associated with it, including racial equality and world peace; and that Du Bois received greater acclaim as a scholar-activist in Europe (particularly in the former Eastern Bloc countries), Asia, and Africa than he did in the United States during his lifetime. These and other facts and factors are conspicuously absent from Broderick's, Rudwick's, and DeMarco's studies of Du Bois.

Still, despite Marable's recognition of the many forces and ideas that Du Bois had to negotiate in his lifetime, he resisted the temptation to excuse all of Du Bois's decisions because he was aware of the context in which they occurred, to paraphrase the French adage. For, although appreciative of his "firm moral and political dedication to human equality," he ends his analysis of Du Bois on a critical note: "His decision to 'close ranks' during World War I was a disaster; his segregated cooperatives plan was unworkable; his assessments of Japanese imperialism in the 1920s–30s were faulty; and his understanding of Ghanian society under Nkrumah during the 1950s was too uncritical," not to mention his "tendency to equate any type of state-dominated economies with the process of socialist construction."[43]

To Adolph Reed Jr., however, Marable's study was not critical enough of Du Bois largely because it did not provide an adequate description of the prevailing intellectual currents of the era in which he was born and reared. In a word, like Weber (although he did not cite the German scholar), Reed sees the period beginning soon after the Civil War as one marked by the rise of the managerial class. Now professional by virtue of their special training, performance on written examinations, specific areas of expertise, and degrees, managers occupied the offices of government bureaucracies, stock-offering corporations, universities (both in administration and among the faculty), legal firms, and hospitals. Their credentials also reinforced a belief shared by virtually all who acquired them, regardless of personal political beliefs, that they were cerebrally superior to the uncredentialed. "Du Bois shared," asserts Reed, "the perspective of his progressive peers for whom popular activism was marked with the stamp of dangerous irrationality. Both mainstream corporate liberalism and much of what understood itself as socialism were predicated upon models of orderly, technicistically rational societal development—without the disruptive participation of the rank-and-file citizenry."[44]

Furthermore, the self-serving content of this belief was hardly lessened in the case of Du Bois and in the cases of other liberals and leftists by their aim to use their intellectual talents to help the less fortunate, for their noble cause still left unquestioned the conviction that intellectuals have a monopoly on good ideas and programs. To Reed, this assumption was one of Du Bois's "core unifying principle[s] of his thought, notwithstanding his various changes of political affiliation and program between 1900 and his death in 1963."[45] To avoid or to apologize for Du Bois's elitism is to engage in a vindicationist sanitization of the real Du Bois, according to Reed.

Even if Reed's work can be read as a leftist return of sorts to the type of double criticism of Du Bois's politics and scholarship that Broderick and Rudwick first supplied, one major difference between their studies and Reed's is that Reed's was a response to what he argued were a number of uncritical interpretations of Du Bois's work in both arenas rather than the inception of that critical perspective. Moreover, the fact that Reed's critique of what was then the past twenty years of scholarship on Du Bois was intended to be a corrective of overly positive assessments of him suggests that Du Bois studies had finally reached a relative balance by the mid-1990s. Certainly, David Levering Lewis's two-volume biography of Du Bois marked that achievement.[46]

Still, the manner in which Reed critiqued Du Bois's political thought and the general academic treatment of the subject illustrate quite well the differences between how the majority of Du Bois scholars present his scholarly work and political positions and how the majority of Weber scholars present his: as inseparable in Du Bois's case but separable in Weber's. As I noted earlier, Du Bois and Weber themselves played significant parts in this difference of treatment: whereas Weber was emphatic in his demand that scholars not bring their political desires into their scholarship, Du Bois was nowhere as adamant. However, the fact that Du Bois did not always refrain from inserting his political judgments into his academic studies does not necessarily mean that he discarded the findings that did not advance his political ends or that he failed to uncover certain "truths" as a result. Rather, it means that he was simply quite direct and honest about the political conclusions he drew from his research. Still, in wearing his politics on his sleeve, so to speak, Du Bois presented his critics with an opportunity to slight or dismiss his scholarship on the grounds of his political biases when what they truly objected to were both his politics and his scholarship. And those doing the attacking or silencing are under no obligation to reveal their own biases. Thus, the critique of either Du Bois's politics or scholarship has remained a simultaneous critique of the other.

Unfortunately, many Du Bois admirers have not helped to rupture this circular reasoning because they agree with his political positions and, by extension, with his scholarship. Consequently, they have seen little reason to delineate the merits of the latter. However, in not stating explicitly the value of Du Bois's scholarship and the contributions that he made to the social sciences, some of Du Bois's boosters enable those who condemn his politics to continue labeling his scholarship partisan. This is why the studies by Reiland Rabaka and Aldon Morris,[47] among others, are so important and necessary. However, Morris's, unlike Rabaka's more expansive treatment of Du Bois's sociological work both temporally and disciplinarily, runs the risk of lending support to the belief that liberalism, or some variant of it, is the sole sociopolitical orientation to which a scholar can subscribe to produce sensible scholarship, as Du Bois was primarily a liberal during the period of his life that Morris's study covers. Of course, to advance the cause of human equality, equality before the law, and equality of opportunity in a society that has historically denied those very liberal principles to black people and to other people of color, as Du Bois did, was not only courageous, but indeed radical. However, in not mentioning Du Bois's sociological work, or at least the work that Du Bois himself described as such,[48] in the period when he was openly questioning whether capitalism could fulfill even the promise of liberalism, Morris leaves us wondering whether he considers that body of work by Du Bois as reputable as that which he undertook in the early twentieth century. In any event, to place Du Bois among sociology's great figures requires rethinking the relationship between scholarship and politics, at the very least.

ALTHOUGH CRITICAL SCHOLARSHIP ON Weber and Du Bois began at roughly the same time, the difference in the scholarly treatment of the two has been marked. In a word, whereas Weber scholars have largely presented him as the consummate academic, largely free of any troublesome biases and equally neutral about the results of his findings, Du Bois has consistently been portrayed as a political figure whose academic work was a prelude to his more momentous calling as a public intellectual. In addition to underestimating Du Bois's efforts to bridge scholarship and politics, in much the way that Verein members did, this viewpoint, in the context of a comparison with Weber, leaves unshaken the often implicit suggestion that Weber had the unique ability to separate his strong political views from his scholarship in ways that few others could, Du Bois included. That such a verdict is perversely unfair and needs to be corrected is one of my aims in this work.

Conclusion

As I stated at the outset of this study, what drew me to it were Du Bois's and Weber's markedly different conceptions of the origins and features of modern capitalism. Whereas for Weber its roots were in the emergence of Europe's culture of rationality spurred on by the unintended consequences of Protestantism's rise, for Du Bois, who early subscribed to a variant of Weber's thesis, its roots were in the colonization of the Americas and the enslavement of Africans, where Weber's Protestant rationality did not operate in the ways that Weber had described. Clearly, Weber and Du Bois were referencing the opposite poles of the capitalist experience no less than different people. There was a striking irony, nevertheless, in Weber's scholarly avoidance of modern imperialism, given that he was a vocal advocate of Germany's overseas territorial expansion, a process that relied on racism and coercive labor regimes. Thanks, perhaps, to Du Bois's unawareness of Weber's pro-imperialist politics, in addition to Weber's apparently sincere interest in Du Bois's scholarship on American urban and agricultural life, no less than to his expressed agreement with Du Bois that the global color line would remain a persistent problem, these differences did not overshadow their common goal of advancing sociology as an academic discipline.

However, even this shared vision could not save an already fragile intellectual relationship from the events on the horizon for each of them. As Weber turned his attention to the Russian Revolution of 1905 and grew more critical of the political-economic extremes of tsarism and Marxism, Du Bois became more actively involved in antiracist organizing and in studying African history. It was also at this juncture that Du

Bois was increasingly exposed to Marxist critiques of capitalism, which he applied to European imperial regimes in Africa and elsewhere. For Germany's part in the carving up of the African continent and for that country's odious actions in its African colonies, Du Bois leveled some of his harshest words against German imperialism specifically and white racism generally. As far as Du Bois was concerned, in the decade prior to the outbreak of World War I, European culture had gone from being the global standard of excellence to an example of rank barbarism. Indirectly included in this assessment were many members of the European professorate.

Scholars who address either the Du Bois–Weber exchange or the impact of Germany on Du Bois's intellectual development tend to avoid the question of why their contact was so short-lived and why Du Bois reversed his position on Germany and Europe generally so soon after having praised both the country and European culture so highly. The reasons, I argue, are found in Europe's imperial expansion and racism, particularly on the African continent. These are coincidentally the very issues that the majority of Weber scholars avoid in their discussions of Weber's thought and interpretations, despite his strong pronouncements on both. It appears that the majority of Weber scholars largely believe that, true to his own admonitions, Weber managed to keep his politics out of his scholarship. According to such an assumption, Weber was the quintessential scholar who was able to successfully balance a passion for research with a dispassion for its results.

This contrasts sharply and unfairly with the scholarly treatment of Du Bois, even by his admirers. In the main, they have stressed his role as a public intellectual, who boldly denounced racism and economic exploitation. Of course, this emphasis makes sense, given that it was the role that he played for the greater part of his life. However, frequently downplayed in this framing of Du Bois is his pioneering sociological work at the turn of the twentieth century and into its first decade, which challenged both popular and academic racist beliefs about black people, Asian, and Latin American populations. It was precisely because his scholarly "presuppositions" were grounded in human equality of the world's populations that Du Bois's methods of investigation, no less than his conclusions, were far more rigorous and reasonable than those of scholars like Weber, who relied on selected, yet vast secondary material to draw global conclusions about various populations. Hence the irony that Du Bois is considered the political academic, when he is remembered as an academic at all, and Weber the pure scholar. Hence also, my hope that this study moves Weber scholars to grapple with the highly political and biased content of Weber's scholarship and Du Bois scholars to assess Du Bois's scholarly contributions in conjunction with rather than in contrast to his political activism.

NOTES

Introduction

1. W. E. B. Du Bois, *The Souls of Black Folk* (Chicago: A. C. McClurg and Co., 1903; repr. (New York: Vinatge/The Library of America, 1990).

2. Max Weber to W. E. B. Du Bois, 30 March 1905, in *The Correspondence of W. E. B. Du Bois*, vol. 1: *Selections, 1877–1934*, ed. Herbert Aptheker (Amherst: University of Massachusetts Press, 1973), 106–7; emphasis in original. Lawrence Scaff has also included this letter and four others in an appendix to his *Max Weber in America* (Princeton, NJ: Princeton University Press, 2011).

3. Both Herbert Aptheker, Du Bois's literary executor, and David Levering Lewis, Du Bois's preeminent biographer, maintain mistakenly that Du Bois's and Weber's North American encounter took place at Atlanta University when, according to Lewis, Weber "came to the campus to participate in the conference on crime during his American visit in 1904." David Levering Lewis, *W. E. B. Du Bois: Biography of a Race* (New York: Henry Holt & Co., 1993), 225. In fact, in his first correspondence with Du Bois, dated 8 November 1904, which he sent from New York City, Weber refers to where and how they met and provides the reason he was unable to visit him in Atlanta. Weber wrote, "I learned from you at St. Louis that you hoped to be back at Atlanta after the 20th of October. Unfortunately my wife could not stand the climate of the South and so I failed to see your University and to make your acquaintance,—the few minutes in St. Louis not counting in this respect. I hope to be allowed to do so another time." See Scaff, *Max Weber in America*, appendix 2, 255. Weber was sure not to mention to Du Bois that he and Marianne did manage to make it to Tuskegee Institute but were unable to meet Booker T. Washington, who was away from the university at the time of their visit. For Marianne Weber's impressions of the Webers' visit to Tuskegee, see her biography of her husband, *Max Weber: A Biography*, trans. and ed. Harry Zohn

(New York: John Wiley & Sons, [1926] 1975), 295–96. The English translation of Weber's address in St. Louis was published as "The Relations of the
Rural Community to Other Branches of Social Science," *Congress of Arts and
Science, Universal Exposition, St. Louis* (Boston: Houghton-Mifflin, 1906),
vol. 7, 725–46. A version of his paper appears as "Capitalism and Rural Society
in Germany," in *From Max Weber: Essays in Sociology*, trans., ed., and introd.
H. H. Gerth and C. Wright Mills (New York: Oxford University Press, 1946),
363–85.

4. See Nahum D. Chandler, "The Possible Form of an Interlocution:
W. E. B. Du Bois and Max Weber in Correspondence, 1904–1905," *CR: The
New Centennial Review* 7, no. 1 (2007): 213–72.

5. Weber to Du Bois, 8 November 1904, in Du Bois Papers, reel 3, Du
Bois Library, University of Massachusetts–Amherst. I would like to take this
opportunity to thank the archivists of the Du Bois Papers for having found,
photocopied, and sent what they have of the Weber–Du Bois correspondence.

6. W. E. B. Du Bois, "Die Negerfrage in den Vereinigten Staaten," in
Writings by W. E. B. Du Bois in Periodicals Edited by Others, ed. Herbert
Aptheker (Millwood, NY: Kraus-Thomson, 1982). Joseph Fracchia's English
translation of Du Bois's essay first appeared in *CR: The New Centennial Review*
6, no. 3 (2006). Nahum Dimitri Chandler has included it in a collection of Du
Bois's essays, *The Problem of the Color Line at the Turn of the Twentieth Century:
The Essential Early Essays*, ed. Nahum Dimitri Chandler (New York: Fordham
University Press, 2015).

7. Commenting on the totality of the Du Bois–Weber correspondence,
Chandler notes, "In all we have more or less direct evidence, from the extant
correspondence, that there were at least nine letters exchanged between Du
Bois and Weber from November 1904 to May 1905. Six of those letters have
survived, in whole, in part, or perhaps in draft form: we know of five from
Weber, all of which have been maintained among the papers of Du Bois; and,
so far, we have only an incomplete one from Du Bois, also among his papers."
Nahum Dimitri Chandler, "The Possible Form of an Interlocution: W. E. B.
Du Bois and Max Weber in Correspondence, 1904–1905," *CR: The New Cen-
tennial Review* 6, no. 3 (2006): 196.

8. Weber to Du Bois, 1 May 1905, in Du Bois Papers, reel 3, Du Bois
Library, University of Massachusetts–Amherst.

9. Weber to Du Bois, in Aptheker, *The Correspondence of W. E. B. Du
Bois*, vol. 1, 106.

10. Ibid.

11. Weber to Du Bois, 17 November 1904, in Du Bois Papers, reel 3, Du
Bois Library, University of Massachusetts–Amherst.

12. Max Weber and Dr. Alfred Ploetz, "Max Weber, Dr. Alfred Ploetz, and W. E. B. Du Bois" (Max Weber on Race and Society II), *Sociological Analysis* 34, no. 4 (Winter 1973): 312. I thank Jill Briggs for bringing this exchange to my attention.

13. See Max Weber, *Economy and Society: An Outline of Interpretive Sociology*, vol. 1, ed. Guenther Roth and Claus Wittich (New York: Bedminster Press, 1968), 164; and Max Weber, *General Economic History*, trans. Franklin H. Knight (Glencoe, IL: Free Press, [1927] 1950), 277. However, in fairness to Weber, we must point out that despite drawing attention to the advantages of wage labor over slavery, he did not categorically exclude either slavery or other forms of unfree labor from the ranks of capitalist enterprises, provided that their operations were "continuous" as opposed to singular or sporadic. Hence his inclusion of the Carthaginian, Roman, and North American plantation systems under the heading, "Capitalistic Development of the Manor," in *General Economic History*, 79–84. Some years earlier, Weber was even more emphatic about placing unfree labor within capitalism and took issue with those scholars who did not: "Slave agriculture, when the slaves are normal objects of exchange (it makes no difference whether particular labourers have been actually purchased or not), and the land worked is privately owned or leased, is of course capitalist from the economic point of view. . . . Today the concept of 'capitalist enterprise' is generally based on . . . the large firm run with free wage-labour, because it is this form which is responsible for the characteristic social problems of modern capitalism. From this point of view it has been argued that capitalist economy did not play a dominant role in Antiquity, and did not in fact exist. However, to accept this premise is to limit needlessly the concept of capitalist economy to a single form of valorization of capital—the exploitation of other people's labour on a contractual basis—and thus to introduce social factors. Instead we should take into account only economic factors. Where we find that property is an object of trade and is utilized by individuals for profit-making enterprise in a market economy, there we have capitalism. If this be accepted, then it becomes perfectly clear that capitalism shaped whole periods of Antiquity, and indeed precisely those periods we call 'golden ages.'" *The Agrarian Sociology of Ancient Civilizations,* trans. R. I. Frank (London: New Left Books, [1909] 1976), 50–51. Still, Weber was of the opinion that, generally speaking, wage labor is the most extensive labor regime of modern capitalism just as some form of unfree labor was the common labor regime of ancient capitalism.

14. And it confirms Gurminder K. Bhambra's observation that "colonialism is crucial to the scenes of inquiry that are the contemporary social sciences and yet, for the most part, it is largely outside their field of vision." *Rethinking*

Modernity: Post-Colonialism and the Sociological Imagination (Hampshire: Palgrave Macmillan, 2007), 16. I thank Cecilia Green for recommending Bhambra's work to me.

15. Max Weber, *The Protestant Ethic and the Spirit of Capitalism* (London: Routledge, [1904–5] 2002), 20.

16. Gabriel Kolko made this point in his "Max Weber on America: Theory and Evidence," in *Studies in the Philosophy of History: Selected Essays from History and Theory*, ed. George H. Nadel (New York: Harper & Row, 1965).

17. W. E. B. Du Bois, *The Suppression of the African Slave Trade to the United States of America, 1638–1870* (Millwood, NY: Kraus-Thomson, [1896] 1973), 31.

18. And as Patrick Manning recently remarked, this imbalance between the numbers of enslaved and wage-earning workers in the Atlantic world still held true more than a century later: "Another testament to slavery's significance on a worldwide scale can be obtained by comparing the enslaved workforce to that of the emerging system of industrial wage labor. At the end of the eighteenth century, some six million persons of African descent lived in the Americas, with more than four million of them in slavery. Add to these an African population of at least four million in slavery and those in slavery in the Old World diaspora and one sees that this huge slave workforce dwarfed the number of industrial laborers earning wages in Europe and North America, who totaled at most a few hundred thousand at this time." *The African Diaspora: A History through Culture* (New York: Columbia University Press, 2010), 118.

19. W. E. B. Du Bois, "The Conservation of Races," in *W. E. B. Du Bois Speaks: Speeches and Addresses, 1890–1919*, ed. Philip S. Foner (New York: Pathfinder Press, 2002), 88.

20. Kieran Allen, *Max Weber: A Critical Introduction* (London: Pluto Press, 2004), 57.

21. Aldon Morris, *The Scholar Denied: W. E. B. Du Bois and the Birth of Modern Sociology* (Oakland: University of California Press, 2015).

22. Max Weber, "Zur Psychophysik der indutriellen Arbeit," in *Gesammelte Aufsatze zur Soziologie und Sozialpolitik*, ed. Marianne Weber (Tubingen: Mohr & Siebeck, [1924] 1988), 125. I thank Andrew Zimmerman for including this reference in his "Decolonizing Weber," *Postcolonial Studies* 9, no. 1 (2006): 67.

23. Scaff, *Max Weber in America*, 113.

24. Du Bois was clearly aware, nonetheless, of Weber's thesis even if we cannot date it exactly. In his 1946 publication, *The World and Africa*, Du Bois refers to the "new era of [industrial] capitalism" as "springing from Calvinism:

thrift, industry, honesty as the best policy, along with interest and profit." *The World and Africa* (Millwood, NY: Kraus-Thomson, [1946] 1976), 67. We should also note that the understanding of industrial capitalism that Du Bois expresses in this passage contradicts what he states elsewhere in the same work.

25. W. E. B. Du Bois, "The African Roots of War," in Foner, *W. E. B. Du Bois Speaks*, 260–73.

ONE   The Free vs. the Bound

1. My position is admittedly based on my questioning of the sincerity of Weber's praise of *The Souls of Black Folk* and of his remark about the color line. The reasons for my doubts about the first will become clearer in the pages that follow. As for the second, my reasons are simple: Weber's academic work and political positions exacerbated rather than contested the problem of the color line. This will become clearer in the chapters to follow.

2. W. E. B. Du Bois, *The Souls of Black Folk* (Chicago: A. C. McClurg and Co., 1903; repr. (New York: Vintage Books/Library of America, 1990), 110. Subsequent quotations from this work are cited by page number in the text.

3. For a sampling of Weber's emphatic demand for scholarly neutrality, see his essays collected in *The Methodology of the Social Sciences*, ed. and trans. Edward A. Shils and Henry A. Finch (Glencoe, IL: Free Press, 1949).

4. As cited in Marianne Weber, *Max Weber: A Biography*, trans. and ed. Harry Zohn (New York: John Wiley & Sons, [1926] 1975), 296. Unfortunately, Marianne does not provide the whereabouts of these reflections.

5. Or, of course, of Hegel's discussion of the master and slave relationship in *The Phenomenology of Mind*. The reason I have opted to emphasize the influence of Plato on Du Bois's formulation of double consciousness rather than Hegel's is because the former seems more fitting to me if we include the opening of Du Bois's essay "The Souls of White Folk" as another instance of double consciousness, even if Du Bois did not label it as such there. About the souls of white folk he writes, "Of them I am singularly clairvoyant. I see in and through them. I view them from unusual points of vantage. Not as a foreigner do I come, for I am native, not foreign, bone of their thought and flesh of their language. Mine is not the knowledge of the traveler or the colonial composite of dear memories, words and wonder. Nor yet is my knowledge that which servants have of masters, or mass of class, or capitalist of artisan. Rather I see these souls undressed and from the back and side. I see the working of their entrails. I know their thoughts and they know that I know. This knowledge makes

them now embarrassed, now furious!" W. E. B. Du Bois, "The Souls of White Folk," in *Darkwater: Voices from Within the Veil* (Millwood, NY: Kraus-Thomson, [1921] 1975), 29. Du Bois's references to being able to see from "unusual points of vantage" and "from the back and side" lead me to believe that he was invoking Plato's parable of the cave more than portions of Hegel's *Phenomenology* in his conception of double consciousness.

6. David Fort Godshalk also suggests this interpretation when he notes that "by locating African Americans behind a veil, Du Bois was suggesting their access to insights and truths unavailable to others." *Veiled Visions: The 1906 Atlanta Race Riot and the Reshaping of American Race Relations* (Chapel Hill: University of North Carolina Press, 205), 62.

7. Max Weber, Introduction (1920) to *Gesammelte Aufsatze zur Religionssoziologie*, in *The Protestant Ethic and the Spirit of Capitalism* (London: Routledge, [1904–5] 2002), xxix.

8. Ibid.

9. See Max Weber, *General Economic History*, trans. Franklin H. Knight (Glencoe, IL: Free Press, [1927] 1950), 301.

10. Weber, *The Protestant Ethic*, 3.

11. W. E. B. Du Bois, "A Pageant in Seven Decades, 1878–1938," in *W. E. B. Du Bois Speaks: Speeches and Addresses, 1890–1919*, ed. Philip S. Foner (New York: Pathfinder Press, 2002), 24.

12. Weber, *The Protestant Ethic and the Spirit of Capitalism*, 19. Subsequent quotations from this work are cited by page number in the text.

13. In the opening chapter of his first sociological undertaking, *The Philadelphia Negro*, Du Bois states his belief and desire that his findings "possess on the whole enough reliable matter to serve as the scientific basis of further study, and of practical reform." W. E. B. Du Bois, *The Philadelphia Negro* (Philadelphia: University of Pennsylvania Press, [1899] 1996), 4. This was arguably Du Bois's goal in all his published work.

14. W. E. B. Du Bois, "The Conservation of Races," in Foner, *W. E. B. Du Bois Speaks*, 88.

15. I might note one of them, as it is quite significant. At one point in *The Protestant Ethic and the Spirit of Capitalism*, Weber writes, "As we shall see that at the beginning of modern times it was by no means the capitalistic entrepreneurs of the commercial aristocracy, who were either the sole or the predominant bearers of the attitude we have here called the spirit of capitalism. It was much more the rising strata of the lower industrial middle classes. Even in the nineteenth century its classical representatives were not the elegant gentlemen of Liverpool and Hamburg, with the commercial fortunes handed down for generations, but the self-made parvenus of Manchester and Westphalia,

who often rose from very modest circumstances." (28) As far as the two English cities are concerned, their rise cannot be separated from the slave trade and slave-cultivated cotton, a point that Du Bois underscored, as we shall see in the next chapter. For a thorough rendering of England's economic gains from Atlantic slavery, see Joseph Inikori's comprehensive work, *Africans and the Industrial Revolution in England: A Study in International Trade and Economic Development* (Cambridge: Cambridge University Press, 2002). It stood to reason, then, that some Liverpudlian slave merchants not only chose to invest in cotton manufacturing, but became manufacturers themselves; Samuel Touchet comes to mind. Thus neither the class nor the sectoral (commercial vs. manufacturing) distinctions that Weber draws between the cities he names is necessarily borne out in the facts.

16. As discussed further in chapter 3, Du Bois underscores some of these economic aspects of Atlantic slavery in his *The Suppression of the African Slave Trade to the United States, 1638–1870* (Millwood, NY: Kraus-Thomson, [1896] 1973), 27–29.

17. The adjective is Talcott Parsons's, and we would do well to bear in mind the whole passage as we attempt to come to terms with Weber's omissions: "Anyone who attempts to understand his sociological work in its completeness to any degree cannot fail to be impressed, and to a great extent bewildered, by the enormous mass of detailed historical material which Weber commanded. Indeed, so vast is the mass, and much of it so highly technical in the various fields from which it is drawn, that an ordinary human being is under very serious difficulties in any sort of critical analysis, since a real factual check on Weber's work as a whole would probably be well beyond the powers of any single living scholar. Weber's was, what is exceedingly rare in the modern age, an encyclopedic mind." *The Structure of Social Action* (Glencoe, IL: Free Press, [1937] 1949), 500.

18. Marshall Hodgson, *The Venture of Islam,* vol. 1: *The Classical Age of Islam* (Lahore: Vanguard Books, [1959] 2004), 28. Weber, of course, recognized the equivalent of "precommitments" in "presuppositions" (*Voraussetzungen*), which serve as the foundational tenets of any belief system, religious or secular. However, in his discussion of them, Weber stressed their use as bases more than as biases. See his "Science as a Vocation," in *From Max Weber: Essays in Sociology*, trans., ed., and introd. H. H. Gerth and C. Wright Mills (New York: Oxford University Press, 1946), 153–54.

19. The compilers of Weber's *General Economic History* included Du Bois's doctoral dissertation in the notes to the fifth chapter of the work, "Capitalistic Development of the Manor," 373.

20. Weber, *General Economic History*, 301.

21. W. E. B. Du Bois, "Die Neger Frage in den Vereinigten Staaten," in *Writings by W. E. B. Du Bois in Periodicals Edited by Others*, ed. Herbert Aptheker (Millwood, NY: Kraus-Thomson, 1982), 327.

TWO   Fields of Study

1. Sieglinde Lemke both questions and affirms Du Bois's recollections of his time in Germany: "Those Germans in Wilhelmian society who inter-acted with Du Bois saw him as a student, rather than a *black* student, and treated him with respect. At least this is what Du Bois wanted to believe. While it is hard to believe that Germany provided a racist-free environment for a black person at the turn of the century—at a time when 'imported' Afri-cans were exhibited at so called *Menschenschauen* at the Berlin Zoo—Du Bois affirms this impression again and again. . . . This boost in self-esteem and new worldview can hardly be overestimated." "Berlin and Boundaries: *sollen* vs. *geschehen*," *boundary 2* 27, no. 3 (Fall 2000): 50; emphasis in original.

2. W. E. B. Du Bois, *The Autobiography of W. E. B. Du Bois* (New York: International Publishers, [1968] 2007), 170–71.

3. See, e.g., Barkin's articles "'Berlin Days,' 1892–1894: W. E. B. Du Bois and German Political Economy," *boundary 2* 27, no. 3 (Fall 2000): 79–101; and "W. E. B. Du Bois' Love Affair with Imperial Germany," *German Studies Review* 28, no. 2 (2005): 285–302.

4. W. E. B. Du Bois, *Dusk of Dawn* (Millwood, NY: Kraus-Thomson, [1940] 1989), 27.

5. Jurgen Herbst, *The German Historical School in American Scholarship* (Ithaca, NY: Cornell University Press, 1965), 134. Axel Schafer also provides a good synopsis of the German historical school in his "W. E. B. Du Bois, German Social Thought, and the Racial Divide in American Progressivism, 1892–1909," *Journal of American History* 88, no. 3 (December 2001): 933–39.

6. Reinhard Bendix, *Max Weber: An Intellectual Portrait* (Garden City, NY: Doubleday, 1960), 38.

7. This was one of the tendencies against which he wanted the editorial board of the *Archiv für Sozialwissenschaft und Sozialpolitk* to guard, no less than submitters: "An empirical science cannot tell anyone what he *should* do—but rather what he *can* do—and under certain circumstances—what he wishes to do. It is true that in our sciences, personal value-judgments have tended to in-fluence scientific arguments without being explicitly admitted. They have brought about continual confusion and have caused various interpretations to be placed on scientific arguments even in the sphere of the determination of

simple causal interconnections among facts according to whether the results increased or decreased the chances of realizing one's personal ideals, i.e., the possibility of desiring a certain thing. . . . However, to *judge* the *validity* of such values is a matter of *faith*. It may perhaps be a task for the speculative interpretation of life and the universe in quest of their meaning. But it certainly does not fall within the province of an empirical science in the sense in which it is to be practiced here." Max Weber, "'Objectivity' in Social Science and Social Policy," in *Max Weber on the Methodology of the Social Sciences*, trans. and ed. Edward A. Shils and Henry A. Finch (Glencoe, IL: Free Press, 1949), 54–55; emphasis in original.

8. See Joseph A. Schumpeter, *History of Economic Analysis* (New York: Oxford University Press, 1954), 809–14.

9. "Statistik," in J. C. Bluntschli and K. Brater, eds., *Deutsches Staatswörterbuch*, X (1867): 464; as cited in Herbst, *German Historical School*, 138.

10. Schumpeter, *History of Economic Analysis*, 785.

11. As Woodruff D. Smith notes, "Indeed, by the middle of the [nineteenth] century, journalism had become a normal part of the early careers of even the most successful of academic social scientists." *Politics and the Sciences of Culture in Germany, 1840–1920* (New York: Oxford University Press, 1991), 17.

12. W. E. B. Du Bois, "Sociology Hesitant" (unpublished, 1905), repr. *boundary 2* 27, no. 3 (2000): 40.

13. Isaiah Berlin, *Karl Marx* (Oxford: Oxford University Press, [1939] 1996), 39.

14. Du Bois summed up this position in this way: "Man is not wholly a creature of unchanging law, he is in some degree a free agent and so outside the realm of scientific law." "Sociology Hesitant," 41.

15. These works are, respectively, Max Weber, "Capitalism and Rural Society in Germany," in *From Max Weber*, 363–85; W. E. B. Du Bois, "Die Neger Frage in Vereinigten Staaten" (The Negro Question in the United States), in *W. E. B. Du Bois: The Problem of the Color Line at the Turn of the Twentieth Century: The Essential Early Essays*, ed. Nahum Dimitri Chandler (New York: Fordham University Press, 2015), 285–330; and Max Weber, "Developmental Tendencies in the Situation of East Elbian Rural Labourers," in *Reading Weber*, ed. Keith Tribe (London: Routledge, 1989), 158–87.

16. Weber, "Capitalism and Rural Society in Germany," in *From Max Weber*, 374. Subsequent quotations from this work in this section and the next are cited by page number in the text.

17. Du Bois, "Die Neger Frage in Vereinigten Staaten," 287. Subsequent quotations from this work are cited by page number in the text.

18. Reiland Rabaka, *Against Epistemic Apartheid: W. E. B. Du Bois and the Disciplinary Decadence of Sociology* (Lanham, MD: Lexington Books, 2010), 53.

19. Chandler underscores this difference in Du Bois's and Weber's research methodologies: Nahum D. Chandler, "The Possible Form of an Interlocution: W. E. B. Du Bois and Max Weber in Correspondence, 1904–1905," *CR: The New Centennial Review* 7, no. 1 (2007): 246.

20. Weber noted in his summary of the Verein study of eastern German agricultural workers that the "data which [was] recorded . . . was collected from inquiries directed to *landowners*—considerations of cost prevented a direct approach to the workers. . . . The considerable amount of factual material that the investigation collected is therefore certainly one-sided and does not permit definitive conclusions on the actual situation of rural laborers to be drawn." "Developmental Tendencies in the Situation of East Elbian Labourers," 158; emphasis in original.

21. Du Bois admitted as much in his *Autobiography*: "First of all I became painfully aware that merely being born in a group, does not necessarily make one possessed of complete knowledge concerning it. I had learned far more from Philadelphia Negroes than I had taught them concerning the Negro Problem" (198).

22. Still, as Du Bois reports in his *Autobiography*, gaining the trust of black Philadelphians was no easy task: "The colored people of Philadelphia received me with no open arms. They had a natural dislike to being studied like a strange species. I met again and in different guise those curious crosscurrents and inner social whirlings. They set me to groping. I concluded that I did not know so much as I might about my own people" (198).

23. For some of these articles, see W. E. B. Du Bois, *Newspaper Columns by W. E. B. Du Bois*, vol. 1, *1883–1944*, ed. Herbert Aptheker (White Plains, NY: Kraus-Thomson, 1986), 1–23.

24. Du Bois, *Autobiography*, 108.

25. Ibid., 114.

26. Du Bois, *The Philadelphia Negro* (Philadelphia: University of Pennsylvania Press, [1899] 1996), 311.

27. W. E. B. Du Bois, "The Negroes of Farmville, Virginia: A Social Study" (1898), in *Contributions by W. E. B. Du Bois in Government Publications and Proceedings*, ed. Herbert Aptheker (Millwood, NY: Kraus-Thomson, 1980), 44.

28. Du Bois, *The Philadelphia Negro*, 310, 317.

29. Du Bois, "Die Neger Frage in Vereinigten Staaten," 329–30.

30. For the content and context of anti-immigrant or "nativist" sentiment in the United States, running from roughly the 1830s to the 1920s, see Roger

Daniels, *Coming to America: A History of Immigration and Ethnicity in American Life* (New York: HarperCollins, 1990), 265–84.

31. Shelley Baranowski, *Nazi Empire: German Colonialism and Imperialism from Bismarck to Hitler* (New York: Cambridge University Press, 2011), 22.

32. Ibid., 23. Moreover, as Volker R. Berghan notes, the "activities of the Settlement Commission had a somewhat paradoxical effect. In the twenty years after 1886 it used its funds of 250 mill. marks more for the purchase of German estates than Polish ones, raising the suspicion that heavily indebted German landowners were saved from bankruptcy under the guise of a 'Germanization' program which enabled them to sell land at vastly inflated prices." *Imperial Germany, 1871–1914: Economy, Society, Culture and Politics* (Providence, RI: Berghan Books, 1994), 116.

33. Chandler, "The Possible Form of an Interlocution," 222.

34. For a thorough discussion of the anti-Polish attitudes of German academics and politicians, and the policies they supported, see Sebastian Conrad, *Globalisation and the Nation in Imperial Germany* (Cambridge: Cambridge University Press, 2010), ch. 3.

35. He discussed them even earlier, and the testimonies of presumably Estreicher, in his address, "The Spirit of Modern Europe": "I have brought you thus abruptly to the eastern edge of Europe in order that we may first see the Culture of Europe in its lowest terms. Poland today is hardly a name and yet its spirit lives yonder within the carved portals of the old University where I once sat with a young Polish student: 20,000,000 souls he told me still beat with the one idea of making Poland again one of the great nations of Earth; he spoke of their literature, their language, their oppression and their unconquerable will—and finally as we walked by the Florian gate, the last relic of the ancient Polish fortifications, we looked northeast and he spoke of the rise of that mighty race of the east, and the day when the broad faced Slav, led by Russia, Poland and Hungary should lead down the world a new civilization that would eclipse the German as the Teuton overshadowed Rome. All this is not organization—Poland is not a State, but she represents the disembodied idea of statehood—of race ideal, of organized striving which some day must tell." W. E. B. Du Bois, "The Spirit of Modern Europe," in *The Problem of the Color Line*, 142.

36. Du Bois, *Autobiography*, 175.

37. Personal communication with the author, April 19, 2017.

38. Du Bois, "Die Neger Frage in den Vereinigten Staaten," 297.

39. Max Weber, *Economy and Society*, 3 vols., ed. Guenther Roth and Claus Wittich (New York: Bedminster Press, 1968), 1:391. The three-volume Bedminster Press edition is long out of print. In 1978, a decade after the

Bedminster printing, the University of California Press issued a two-volume edition that has been in print ever since.

40. Du Bois, "Die Neger Frage in den Vereinigten Staaten," 289, 288.

41. W. E. B. Du Bois, "My Evolving Program for Negro Freedom," in *Writings by W. E. B. Du Bois in Non-Periodical Literature Edited by Others,* comp. and ed. Herbert Aptheker (Millwood, NY: Kraus-Thomson, 1982), 224–25.

42. Fritz Ringer, *The Decline of the German Mandarins: The German Academic Community, 1890–1933* (Cambridge, MA: Harvard University Press, 1969), 85.

43. Weber, *Economy and Society,* 3:1179.

44. See Theodore Adorno's lecture, "The Nation and the Spirit of the People in Hegel," in *History and Freedom: Lectures, 1964–1965,* ed. Rolf Tiedeman (Cambridge: Polity Press, 2006).

45. Weber, *Economy and Society,* 2:614.

46. Max Weber, *General Economic History,* trans. Franklin H. Knight (Glencoe, IL: Free Press, [1927] 1950), 360.

47. W. E. B. Du Bois, "The Conservation of Races," in *W. E. B. Du Bois Speaks: Speeches and Addresses, 1890–1919,* ed. Philip S. Foner (New York: Pathfinder Press, 2002), 87, 88. Lemke underscores that "Du Bois's list reveals a bias for Herderian [i.e., Johann Gottfried Herder] thinking, as does his claim that each of these races has a particular message to contribute to the universal whole." "Berlin and Boundaries," 62.

48. Marshall Hodgson, *The Venture of Islam,* vol. 1: *The Classical Age of Islam* (Lahore: Vanguard Books, [1959] 2004), 82.

49. Du Bois, "The Conservation of Races," 91.

50. We are reminded here of Edward Said's words in *Orientalism* (New York: Vintage Books, 1979): "For such divisions are generalities whose use historically and actually has been to press the importance of the distinction between some men and other men, usually towards not especially admirable ends. When one uses categories like Oriental and Western as both the starting and the end points of analysis, research, [and] public policy . . . the result is usually to polarize the distinction—the Oriental becomes more Oriental, the Westerner more Western—and limit the human encounter between different cultures, traditions, and societies" (45–46).

51. See Chandler, "The Possible Form of an Interlocution," 253–55.

52. Weber, *Economy and Society,* 1:9. A few pages earlier, he defined it as how a particular entity would operate if it were free of the "irrational effects" of "anxiety, anger, ambition, envy, jealousy, love, enthusiasm, pride, vengefulness, loyalty, devotion, and appetites of all sorts" (6).

53. See Max Weber, "'Objectivity' in Social Science and Social Policy," 61, where he states that the "second fundamental imperative of scientific freedom is that . . . it should be constantly made clear to the readers (and—again we say it—above all to one's self!) exactly at which point the scientific investigator becomes silent and the evaluating and acting person begins to speak."

54. This conscious decision may well have been either catalyzed or encouraged by the findings of the 1911 First Universal Races Conference held in London at which Du Bois was a participant. Two of the Congress's findings, which Du Bois summarized in a *Crisis* article, were indicative of his new approach to culture: "(a) The deepest cause of misunderstanding between peoples is perhaps the tacit assumption that the present characteristics of a people are the expression of permanent qualities. (b) If this is so, anthropologists, sociologists and scientific thinkers as a class could powerfully assist the movement for a juster appreciation of peoples by persistently pointing out in their lectures and in their works the fundamental fallacy involved in taking a static instead of a dynamic, a momentary instead of a historic, a fixed instead of a comparative, point of view of peoples; (c) and such dynamic teaching could be conveniently introduced into schools, more especially in the geography and history lessons, also into colleges for the training of teachers, diplomats, Colonial administrators, preachers and missionaries." W. E. B. Du Bois, "Races," *Crisis* (August 1911), reprinted in *Writings in Periodicals Edited by W. E. B. Du Bois: Selections from the Crisis*, vol. 1: *1911–1925*, ed. Herbert Aptheker (Millwood, NY: Kraus-Thomson, 1983), 13–14.

55. Du Bois, *The Philadelphia Negro*, 5.

56. William James, *Pragmatism*, in *Writings, 1902–1910* (New York: Library of America, 1987), 510.

57. Du Bois, "My Evolving Program for Negro Freedom," 233.

58. Ibid.

59. Du Bois, "Sociology Hesitant," 43.

60. Ibid., 44.

61. Ibid., 43.

62. In his introduction to the Kraus-Thomson reprint of *Darkwater* (1975), Herbert Aptheker informs us (11) that parts of "The Souls of White Folk" chapter in that collection of essays were taken from two earlier ones: one with the same title that appeared in the *Independent* 69 (August 18, 1910): 339–42; and another titled "Of the Culture of White Folk" that appeared in *Journal of Race Development* 7 (April 1917): 434–37. Both are included in Meyer Weinberg, ed., *W. E. B. Du Bois: A Reader* (New York: Harper & Row, 1970).

63. Du Bois, *Darkwater*, 30.

64. Ibid.

65. For this reason, I strongly disagree with Schafer's contention that "Du Bois's abandonment of the belief in fixed racial attributes and his embrace of the notion that the true meaning of black culture would reveal itself only in the process of social interaction and participation were not the result of his disillusionment with German thought, but an integral part of the social ideas gleaned from his mentor Gustav Schmoller." Schafer, "W. E. B. Du Bois, Social Thought, and the Racial Divide in American Progressivism," 939.

66. Du Bois, *Darkwater*, 31.

67. Ibid., 35, 39. Du Bois reserved for Germany some of his harshest condemnations of European society at the time of World War I. In a 1914 *Crisis* editorial, he wrote:

> The triumph of Germany means the triumph of every force calculated to subordinate darker peoples. It would mean triumphant militarism, autocratic and centralized government and a studied theory of contempt for everything except Germany—'Germany above everything in the world.' The despair and humiliation of Germany in the eighteenth century has brought this extraordinary rebound of self-exaltation and disdain for mankind. The triumph of this idea would mean a crucifixion of darker peoples unparalleled in history.
>
> The writer speaks without anti-German bias: personally he has deep cause to love the German people. They made him believe in the essential humanity of white folk twenty years ago when he was near denying it. But even then the spell of militarism was in the air, and the Prussian strut had caught the nation's imagination. They were starting on the same road with the southern American whites toward a contempt toward human beings and a faith in their own utter superiority to all other breeds. This feeling had not then applied itself particularly to colored folk and has only begun to-day; but it is going by leaps and bounds. Germany needs but the role of world conquest to make her one of the most contemptible of 'Nigger' hating nations. Just as we go to press, the *Berliner Tageblatt* publishes a proclamation by 'German representatives of Science and Art to the World of Culture' in which men like Harnack, Bode, Hauptmann, Suderman, Roentgen, Humperdink, Wundt and others, insult hundreds of millions of human beings by openly sneering at 'Mongrels and Niggers.'

W. E. B. Du Bois, "World War and the Color Line," *Crisis* 9 (November 1914), in Aphtheker, *Writings in Periodicals Edited by W. E. B. Du Bois*, 1:84.

68. Weber, "Author's Introduction," in *The Protestant Ethic and the Spirit of Capitalism*.

69. Chandler, "The Possible Form of an Interlocution," 254.

70. Du Bois, *Darkwater*, 40.

THREE   The Fruits of Merchant's Capital

1. Isaiah Berlin, *Karl Marx* (Oxford: Oxford University Press, [1939] 1996), 116.

2. Save in "primitive" or communal societies in which the division of labor is often gender and age based but not class determined.

3. Karl Marx, Preface to *A Contribution to the Critique of Political Economy*, in *Selected Works*, vol. 1 (Moscow: Progress Publishers, 1969), 504.

4. Max Weber, Translation of "Zwischen zwei Gesetzen" ("Between Two Laws"), in *Die Frau: Monatschrift fur das gesamte Frauenleben unserer Zeit* (February 1916); reprinted in *Weber: Political Essays*, ed. Peter Lassman and Ronald Speirs (Cambridge: Cambridge University Press, 1994), 78.

5. Max Weber, *General Economic History*, trans. Franklin H. Knight (Glencoe, IL: Free Press, [1927] 1950), 277.

6. Max Weber, *Economy and Society: An Outline of Interpretive Sociology*, vol. 1, ed. Guenther Roth and Claus Wittich (New York: Bedminster Press, 1968), 163.

7. Karl Marx, *Capital*, vol. 1 (New York: International Publishers, [1867] 1967), 227.

8. Ibid., 188.

9. In describing the different forms of political capitalism in *General Economic History*, Weber remarked that "all these forms of capitalism relate to spoils, taxes, and the pickings of office or official usury, and finally to tribute and actual need" (334).

10. Karl Marx, *Capital*, vol. 3 (Moscow: Foreign Language Publishing House, [1894] 1962), 324. Subsequent quotations from this volume are cited by page number in the text.

11. Weber, *General Economic History*, 300.

12. Werner Sombart, *Der Moderne Kapitalismus* (Leipzig: Dunker & Humblot, 1902).

13. Werner Sombart, *The Jews and Modern Capitalism*, trans. M. Epstein (New Brunswick, NJ: Transaction Books, [1911] 1982).

14. Max Weber, *Ancient Judaism*, trans. and ed. Hans H. Gerth and Dan Martindale (Glencoe, IL: Free Press, [1917–20] 1952).

15. Werner Sombart, *Der Moderne Kapitalismus*, 2nd ed., 4 vols. (Munich: Dunker & Humblot, 1916).

16. Sombart, *Der Moderne Kapitalismus*, vol. 1, bk. 2, 896–919.

17. See Talcott Parsons, "Capitalism in Recent German Literature: Sombart and Weber," *Journal of Political Economy* 36 (1928): 641–44; 37 (1929): 31–51. Reprinted in Charles Camic, ed., *Talcott Parsons: The Early Essays* (Chicago: University of Chicago Press, 1991), 3–37.

18. Sombart, *The Jews and Modern Capitalism*, 110–11.

19. Ibid., 114. Du Bois had come to the same conclusion during his time in Germany: "It must be ever remembered that the great capitalists of Germany, the great leaders of industry are Jews; moreover, banded together by oppression in the past, they work for each other, and aided by the vast power of their wealth, and their great natural abilities, they have forced citadel after citadel, until now they practically control the stock market, own the press, fill the bar and bench, are crowding the professions,—indeed there seems to be no limit to the increase of their power. . . . All that Marx, Blanc, or Bellamy ever laid at the door of capitalism, is, by the German Antisemitic party, charged upon the Jew because the Jew happens to be the great capitalist of Germany." W. E. B. Du Bois, "The Present Condition of German Politics (1893)," *Central European History* 31, no. 3 (1998): 175.

20. W. O. Henderson, *The Rise of German Industrial Power, 1834–1914* (Berkeley: University of California Press, 1975), 51. See also Charles P. Kindleberger, "Germany's Overtaking of England, 1806 to 1914," in *Economic Response: Trade, Finance, and Growth* (Cambridge, MA: Harvard University Press, 1978).

21. Max Weber, "The Profession and Vocation of Politics," in *Weber: Political Writings*, ed. Peter Lassman and Ronald Speirs (Cambridge: Cambridge Unviersity Press, 1994), 356.

22. W. E. B. Du Bois, "The African Roots of War," in *W. E. B. Du Bois Speaks: Speeches and Addresses, 1890–1919*, ed. Philip S. Foner (New York: Pathfinder Press, 2002), 267–68.

23. Max Weber, *The Protestant Ethic and the Spirit of Capitalism* (London: Routledge, [1904–5] 2002), 30.

24. Guenther Roth, "Weber the Would-Be Englishman: Anglophilia and Family History," in *Weber's Protestant Ethic: Origins, Evidence, Contexts*, ed. Harmut Lehmann and Guenther Roth (Cambridge: Cambridge University Press, 1993), 103–4.

25. Ibid., 107.

26. The facts and figures about Corneille Souchay, not the speculation on why he settled in Cuba, are taken from Guenther Roth, *Max Webers deutsch-englische Familiengeschicte, 1800–1950: Mit Briefen und Dokumenten* (Tübingen: Mohr Siebeck, 2001), 658–59.

27. Weber, *The Protestant Ethic and the Spirit of Capitalism*, 21.

28. Ibid., 22.

29. Weber, *General Economic History*, 286.

30. The now-standard work in English on the Dutch economy is Jan de Vries and Ad van der Woude, *The First Modern Economy: Success, Failure, and Perseverance of the Dutch Economy, 1500–1815* (Cambridge: Cambridge University Press, 1997). Also indispensable is Jonathan Israel, *Dutch Primacy in World Trade, 1585–1740* (New York: Oxford University Press, 1989). Otherwise, for excellent overviews of the Dutch economy in its golden age, see the relevant chapters of Fernand Braudel, *Civilization and Capitalism, Fifteenth to Eighteenth Century*, vol. 3: *The Perspective of the World* (Berkeley: University of California Press, 1992); and Immanuel Wallerstein, *The Modern World System II: Mercantilism and the Consolidation of the European World-Economy, 1600–1750* (San Diego, CA: Academic Press, 1980).

31. See Andre Gunder Frank, *ReOrient: Global Economy in the Asian Age* (Berkeley: University of California Press, 1998).

32. Weber, *General Economic History*, 353.

33. Ibid., 303.

34. Ibid., 350.

35. Paul Mantoux, *The Industrial Revolution in the Eighteenth Century: An Outline of the Beginnings of the Modern Factory System in England* (London: Jonathan Cape, [1905] 1952), 208.

36. For details, see Chadra Mukerji, *From Graven Images: Patterns of Modern Materialism* (New York: Columbia University Press, 1983); Joseph E. Inikori, *Africans and the Industrial Revolution in England* (Cambridge: Cambridge University Press, 2012); Prasannan Parthasarathi, *Why Europe Grew Rich and Asia Did Not* (Cambridge: Cambridge University Press, 2011).

37. See Mantoux, *The Industrial Revolution in the Eighteenth Century*, 204–5; Mukerji, *From Graven Images*, 205–9.

38. This was Friedrich List's position. Referring to an earlier period in the history of the Low Countries, he remarked, "Flanders soon rose by her woolen manufactures to be the central point of the commerce of the North. . . . A policy of commercial restriction could not in their case be deemed necessary because as yet no competition had arisen against the manufacturing supremacy of Flanders." *National System of Political Economy*, vol. 1: *The History* (Roseville, CA: Dry Bones Press, [1841] 2000), 38. More recently, Liah Greenfield asserted, I think unfairly, "There was no national consciousness in the Dutch Republic, the identity of the Republican Dutch was not national, and the Republic was not a nation." *The Spirit of Capitalism: Nationalism and Economic Growth* (Cambridge, MA: Harvard University Press, 2001), 96. Fernand Braudel suggested as much in his *Civilization and Capitalism, 15th–18th*

Century, vol. 3 (New York: Harper & Row, 1984), 205–6. Yet the Dutch were nationalistically minded enough to have successfully revolted against Spanish rule.

39. List, *National System of Political Economy*, 38.

40. I have been surprised to find that in most of the "decline of the Netherlands" literature little or no mention is made of the Dutch choice not to protect the home market from the sale of imported goods and the negative impact that this decision had on potential industrialization. Perhaps the silence is because this is an awkward example of free trade not paying, which was precisely List's point contra Smith. If, in fact, free trade was the primary reason that the Dutch did not pave the way to industrialization, then it suggests that England's success was due in no small measure to its protectionist policies in the seventeenth and eighteenth centuries.

41. Max Weber, *The Religion of India: The Sociology of Hinduism and Buddhism*, trans. and ed. Hans H. Gerth and Don Martindale (Glencoe, IL: Free Press, [1921] 1958), 3–4.

42. Max Weber, *The Religion of China: Confucianism and Taoism*, trans. and ed. Hans H. Gerth (Glencoe, IL: Free Press, [1920] 1951), 242–43.

43. Ibid., 229.

44. Weber, *The Religion of India*, 336.

45. Ibid., 337.

46. Weber, *The Religion of China*, 231–32.

47. About the missionary sources, Weber remarked, "Regarding such traits [of the Chinese], the sociologist essentially depends upon the literature of the missionaries. This certainly varies in value but in the last analysis remains relatively the most authentic." *The Religion of China*, 231. Bhambra aptly describes Weber's error here: "By removing these texts from their context, and treating them in isolation of the conditions of their emergence, they are ascribed a neutrality that they do not possess. The bias of these texts . . . does not reside simply in the bias of their authors, but in the refusal of historians to *demonstrate* what appears to be obvious in them; the bias is in the failure to acknowledge the contestability of the archive and to regard it simply as a neutral repository of facts which can be pieced together to construct History without sustained examination." Germinder K. Bhambra, *Rethinking Modernity: Post-Colonialism and the Sociological Imagination* (Hampshire: Palgrave Macmillan, 2007), 26.

48. The works of those authors who take this perspective is vast. I list here some of the works that I have found particularly helpful: Samir Amin, *Unequal Development* (Sussex: Harvester Press, 1976); K. N. Chaudhuri, *Trade and Civilization in the Indian Ocean* (Cambridge: Cambridge University Press,

1985); Jack Goody, *The East in the West* (Cambridge: Cambridge University Press, 1996), and *The Theft of History* (Cambridge: Cambridge University Press, 2006); Frank, *ReOrient*; John M. Hobson, *The Eastern Origins of Western Civilization* (Cambridge: Cambridge University Press, 2004); Marshall Hodgson, *Rethinking World History*, ed. Edmund Burke III (Cambridge: Cambridge University Press, 1993); Marshall Hodgson, *The Venture of Islam*, 3 vols. (Lahore: Vanguard Books, [1974] 2004); Donald F. Lach, *Asia in the Making of Europe*, 9 vols. (Chicago: University of Chicago Press, 1965–93); William H. McNeill, *A World History*, 4th ed. (New York: Oxford University Press, 1999); L. S. Stavrianos, *Global Rift* (New York: William Morrow, 1981); Eric Wolf, *Europe and the People without History* (Berkeley: University of California Press, 1982).

49. About this literature, Donald Lach comments, "The missionary historians, mainly economic liberals and Protestants, tended in the nineteenth century to denigrate the work of their mercantilistic and Catholic predecessors. Out of these currents of historical writing a nineteenth-century view emerged in the West which emphasized the backwardness of Asia and its stubborn resistance to the spread of the Christian and Western way of life." *Asia in the Making of Europe*, vol. 1, bk. 1 (Chicago: University of Chicago Press, 1965), xiii–xiv. For an overview of nineteenth-century European writing on Africa and Asia, see Victor G. Kiernan, *The Lords of Human Kind: European Attitudes to Other Cultures in the Imperial Age* (London: Zed Books, [1969] 2015).

50. Marx, *Capital*, 1:226.

51. Ibid., 711.

52. Ibid., 166, 668.

53. Ibid., 668.

54. W. E. B. Du Bois, "Marxism and the Negro," in *Writings in Periodicals Edited by W. E. B. Du Bois: Selections from the Crisis*, vol. 2: *1926–1934*, ed. Herbert Aptheker (Millwood, NY: Kraus-Thomson, 1983), 698.

55. Ibid., 697.

56. Ibid., 699.

57. W. E. B. Du Bois, *The Suppression of the African Slave Trade to the United States of America, 1638–1870* (Millwood, NY: Kraus-Thomson, [1896] 1973), 27, 28, 29.

58. Eric Williams, *Capitalism and Slavery* (Chapel Hill: University of North Carolina Press, [1944] 1996), 51–52.

59. W. E. B. Du Bois, *The World and Africa* (Millwood, NY: Kraus-Thomson, [1946] 1976), 58.

60. W. E. B. Du Bois, *Black Folk: Then and Now* (Millwood, NY: Kraus-Thomson, [1939] 1975), 138.

202 Notes to Pages 95–109

61. Ibid., 142.

62. Andre Gunder Frank, *Capitalism and Underdevelopment in Latin America* (New York: Monthly Review Press, 1967), 9.

63. Du Bois maintained that the primary reasons that African societies "did not finally integrate into one great and unified culture, like that of Europe or of China, was the clear and logical result of its physical characteristics and of the slave trade." *Black Folk: Then and Now*, 219.

64. W. E. B. Du Bois, *The Negro* (Mineola, NY: Dover, [1915] 2001), 86.

65. For a thorough presentation of antiblack sentiments and practices in the United States in the late nineteenth and early twentieth century, see Rayford Logan, *The Betrayal of the Negro* (New York: Da Capo Press, [1954] 1997).

66. Du Bois, *The Negro*, 139–40.

67. W. E. B. Du Bois, *The Gift of Black Folk* (Millwood, NY: Kraus-Thomson, [1924] 1975), 52.

68. Moreover, skilled slaves frequently became wage earners during the "dead" season when their owners rented them out to fellow whites in need of their labor. Thus, some black workers were both enslaved and wage earners in the modern slave era.

69. Du Bois, *The Gift of Black Folk*, 257.

70. See Du Bois, "The African Roots of War."

71. Du Bois, *The Gift of Black Folk*, 254.

72. Ibid., 265.

73. Du Bois, *The World and Africa*, 246.

74. Ibid., 248.

75. Du Bois, *The Gift of Black Folk*, 312.

76. Sir Harry H. Johnston, *A History of the Colonization of Africa by Alien Races* (New York: Cooper Square Publishers, [1898] 1966), 162.

77. Ibid., 151.

78. W. E. B. Du Bois, "The Propaganda of History," in *Black Reconstruction in America, 1860–1880* (New York: Russell & Russell, 1935), 725. Subsequent quotations from this volume are cited by page number in the text.

FOUR   Leaders and the Led

1. Max Weber, "The Nation State and Economic Policy," in Max Weber, *Political Writings*, ed. Peter Lassman and Ronald Speirs (Cambridge: Cambridge University Press, 1994), 16; emphasis in original.

2. Max Weber, *Economy and Society: An Outline of Interpretive Sociology*, 3 vols., ed. Guenther Roth and Claus Wittich (New York: Bedminster Press, 1968), 2:917.

3. Ibid., 918.

4. Wolfgang J. Mommsen, *Max Weber and German Politics, 1890–1920*, repr. ed., trans. Michael S. Steinberg (Chicago: University of Chicago Press, 1984), 77.

5. Weber, "The Nation State and Economic Policy," 21; emphasis in original.

6. Ibid., 25.

7. Weber, *Economy and Society*, 2:919.

8. Hannah Arendt, *The Origins of Totalitarianism* (San Diego, CA: Harcourt Brace Jovanovich, 1951), 138.

9. See Mommsen, *Max Weber and German Politics*, 88.

10. Weber, *Economy and Society*, 2:920.

11. Ibid., 918.

12. Mommsen, *Max Weber and German Politics*, 78.

13. For details, see, among other studies, Helmut Bley, *Southwest Africa under German Rule*, trans. and ed. Hugh Ridley (Evanston, IL: Northwestern University Press, 1971); Isabel Hull, *Absolute Destruction: Military Culture and the Practices of War in Imperial Germany* (Ithaca, NY: Cornell University Press, 2005); John Iliffe, *Tanganyika under German Rule, 1905–1912* (Cambridge: Cambridge University Press, 1969); George Steinmetz, *The Devil's Handwriting: Precoloniality and the German Colonial State in Qingdao, Samoa, and Southwest Africa* (Chicago: University of Chicago Press, 2007).

14. Weber, "The Nation State and Economic Policy," 12.

15. Ibid., 16; emphasis in original.

16. Alfred A. Moss Jr., *The American Negro Academy* (Baton Rouge: Louisiana State University Press, 1981), 1.

17. W. E. B. Du Bois, "The Talented Tenth," in *Writings by W. E. B. Du Bois in Non-Periodical Literature Edited by Others*, ed. Herbert Aptheker (Millwood, NY: Kraus-Thomson, [1903] 1982), 20.

18. W. E. B. Du Bois, *The Souls of Black Folk* (Chicago: A. C. McClurg and Co., 1903; repr. (New York: Vintage Books/Library of America, 1990), 37.

19. Kevin J. Gaines, *Uplifting the Race* (Chapel Hill: University of North Carolina Press, 1996), 52.

20. Du Bois, "The Talented Tenth," 17.

21. Hazel Carby offers a related interpretation of Du Bois's denunciation of Washington's political stance, which gives a different meaning to my word choice above: "Not only is the reader [of *The Souls of Black Folk*] left in little doubt that Washington is not a man by Du Bois's measure of black masculinity, but his compromise with the dominant philosophy of his age is to be understood as a form of prostitution." Hazel Carby, "The Souls of Black Men," in

Next to the Color Line: Gender, Sexuality, and W. E. B. Du Bois, ed. Susan Gilman and Alys Eve Weinbaum (Minneapolis: University of Minnesota Press, 2007), 261. Thus, Du Bois virtually feminized Washington.

22. Du Bois, *The Souls of Black Folk*, 156.

23. See Wilson J. Moses, *The Golden Age of Black Nationalism, 1850–1925* (New York: Archon Books, 1978).

24. Alexander Crummell, "The Prime Need of the Negro Race," in *Civilization and Black Progress: Selected Writings of Alexander Crummell on the South*, ed. J. R. Oldfield (Charlottesville: University of Virginia Press, [1897] 1995), 201.

25. Ibid., 202.

26. Alexander Crummell, "Inaugural Address to the American Negro Academy," in *Civilization and Black Progress*, 198.

27. Alexander Crummell, "The Attitude of the American Mind toward the Negro Intellect," in *Civilization and Black Progress*, 210; emphasis in original.

28. Ibid.

29. Ibid.

30. When Du Bois attended the University of Berlin in the early 1890s, German women were still not permitted to attend the nation's universities, or even to audit classes, a right that they only won in 1895. As Barbel Maurer, Marianne Weber's biographer, notes, Germany was quite late in comparison to other western European countries and to the United States in opening its universities' doors to its young women. Barbel Maurer, *Marianne Weber: Leben und Werk* (Tübingen: Mohr Siebeck, 2010), 142, 147–48. On the general male attitudes toward and obstacles to the pursuit of higher education by German women, Gordon A. Craig remarked: "In a man's world the very idea of higher education for women seemed ludicrous, and there was strong resistance to any suggestion that women deserved the same right to professional training as men. In most of Germany no secondary schools comparable to the Gymnasien existed for women until the very eve of the First World War, and in Prussia it was not until 1896 that women were even permitted to take examinations for the Reifezeugnis, the certificate proving that they had the equivalent of a Gymnasium education. Not that this privilege helped them much, for until the turn of the century universities admitted no women students except those who came from abroad, and even after the barrier had fallen women in Prussian universities did not have the right to take the Staatsexamen or to qualify for higher degrees." Gordon A. Craig, *Germany, 1866–1945* (New York: Oxford University Press, 1978), 207.

31. Fritz Ringer, *The Decline of the German Mandarins: The German Academic Community, 1890–1933* (Cambridge, MA: Harvard University Press, 1969), 87.

32. Ibid., 104–5.

33. Reinhold Seeberg, "Hochschule und Weltanschauung," in *Das Akademische Deutschland*, III: *Die deutschen Hochschulen in ihren Beziehuungen zur Gegenwartskultur*, ed. Michael Doeberd, Otto Scheel et al. (Berlin: C. A. Weller, 1930), 166; as cited in Ringer, *The Decline of the German Mandarins*, 104.

34. W. E. B. Du Bois, "The Talented Tenth," 29.

35. For a thorough discussion of the impact of the 1906 Atlanta lynching on Du Bois, see Dominic J. Capeci and Jack C. Knight, "Reckoning with Violence: W. E. B. Du Bois and the 1906 Atlanta Race Riot," *Journal of Southern History* 62, no. 4 (November 1996): 727–66. A number of works provide the political context of the Atlanta lynching and discuss Du Bois's reaction to it. Among these are Mark Bauerlein, *Negrophobia: A Race Riot in Atlanta, 1906* (San Francisco: Encounter Books, 2001); David Fort Godshalk, *Veiled Visions: The 1906 Atlanta Race Riot and the Reshaping of American Race Relations* (Chapel Hill: University of North Carolina Press, 2005); Rebecca Burns, *Rage in the Gate City: The Storm of the 1906 Atlanta Race Riot* (Athens: University of Georgia Press, 2009).

36. Bill V. Mullen, *Un-American: W. E. B. Du Bois and the Century of World Revolution* (Philadelphia: Temple University Press, 2015), 58.

37. We will recall Lenin's remarks on the subject: "In this situation, the proletariat of Russia is faced with a two-fold or, rather, a two-sided task: to combat nationalism of every kind, above all, Great-Russian nationalism; to recognize, not only fully equal rights for all nations in general, but also equality of rights as regards polity, i.e., the right of nations to self-determination, to secession. And at the same time, it is their task, in the interests of a successful struggle against all and every kind of nationalism among all nations, to preserve the unity of the proletarian struggle and the proletarian organizations, amalgamating these organizations into a close-knit international association, despite bourgeois strivings for national exclusiveness." V. I. Lenin, *The Right of Nations to Self-Determination*, in *Selected Works in Three Volumes*, vol. 1 (Moscow: Progress Publishers, 1970), 646.

38. W. E. B. Du Bois, Preface to *Black Folk: Then and Now* (Millwood, NY: Kraus-Thomson, [1939] 1975), viii. In light of the importance of Boas's address to Du Bois, and how transformative I believe that it was to his intellectual and political outlooks, I include the larger framework into which Du Bois situated it here:

206 Notes to Pages 126–129

But we face a curious situation in the world attitude toward the Negro race today. On the one hand there is increasing curiosity as to the place of black men in future social development; in their relation to work, art and democracy; and judgment as to the future must depend upon the past. Yet this past lies shrouded not simply by widespread lack of knowledge but by a certain irritating silence. Few today are interested in Negro history because they feel the matter already settled: the Negro has no history.

This dictum seems neither reasonable nor probable. I remember my own rather sudden awakening from the paralysis of this judgment taught me in high school and in two of the world's great universities. Franz Boas came to Atlanta University where I was teaching history in 1906 and said to a graduating class: You need not be ashamed of your African past; and then he recounted the history of the black kingdoms south of the Sahara for a thousand years. I was too astonished to speak. All of this I had never heard and I came then and afterwards to realize how the silence and neglect of science can let truth utterly disappear or even be unconsciously distorted.

Du Bois included excerpts of Boas's Commencement Address in the 1906 Atlanta University study, "The Health and Physique of the Negro American." The same excerpt was included in the twentieth Atlanta University study, "Select Discussions of Race Problems." Moreover, from the 1906 study on, Du Bois always opened the Atlanta University studies he supervised with discussions of the African past. Reprints of these two and all of the Atlanta University studies have been collected in *Atlanta University Publications*, nos. 1, 2, 4, 8, 9, 11, 13–18 (New York: Arno Press and the New York Times, 1968); and *Atlanta University Publications*, nos. 3, 5, 6, 7, 10, 12, 19, 20 (New York: Arno Press and the New York Times, 1969). Curiously, as momentous as Du Bois claimed the impact of Boas's words were on him in the preface to *Black Folk: Then and Now*, he did not repeat that claim anywhere else.

39. W. E. B. Du Bois, *Darkwater: Voices from Within the Veil* (Millwood, NY: Kraus-Thomson, [1921] 1975), 43–44.

40. Du Bois, "The African Roots of War," in *W. E. B. Du Bois Speaks: Speeches and Addresses, 1890–1919*, ed. Philip S. Foner (New York: Pathfinder Press, 2002), 264.

41. Du Bois, *The Souls of Black Folk*, 60.

42. Isaiah Berlin, *Karl Marx* (Oxford: Oxford University Press, [1939] 1996), 56.

43. Max Weber, "Bourgeois Democracy in Russia," in *The Russian Revolutions*, trans. and ed. Gordon C. Wells and Peter Baehr (Ithaca, NY: Cornell University Press, 1995), 111.

44. Ibid.

45. From *Polnoe sobranie zakanov russkoi imperii* (St. Petersburg, 1911); as cited in Teodor Shanin, *Russia as a "Developing Society"* (New Haven, CT: Yale University Press, 1986), 18.

46. Teodor Shanin, *Russia, 1905–07: Revolution as a Moment of Truth* (New Haven, CT: Yale University Press, 1986), 42.

47. Weber, "Russia's Transition to Pseudo-constitutionalism," in *The Russian Revolutions*, 233.

48. Weber, "Bourgeois Democracy in Russia," 108.

49. Max Weber, "Russia's Transition to Pseudo-democracy," in *The Russian Revolutions*, 242.

50. Weber, "Bourgeois Democracy in Russia," 77.

51. Ibid.

52. Weber, "Russia's Transition to Pseudo-constitutionalism," 202.

53. Weber, "Bourgeois Democracy in Russia," 106.

54. Weber, "Russia's Transition to Pseudo-constitutionalism," 173–74; emphasis in original.

55. Weber, "Bourgeois Democracy in Russia," 69.

56. Ibid., 110.

57. W. E. B. Du Bois, "Russia and America: An Interpretation" (Unpublished manuscript, 1950), 40. Subsequent quotations in this section are taken from this volume and are cited by page number in the text.

In a number of instances in "Russia and America," Du Bois recycled passages from earlier writings. For example, this passage and the next one originally appeared in *Crisis* 33 (February 1927), reprinted in *Writings in Periodicals Edited by W. E. B. Du Bois: Selections from the Crisis*, vol 2: *1926–1934*, ed. Herbert Aptheker (Millwood, NY: Kraus-Thomson, 1983), 458.

58. One plausible and troubling one that draws on a point I made earlier is that Russian peasants were aware that the government was pocketing the price differential between what it offered them for their crops and what they sold for elsewhere and using that money to subsidize other projects, primarily the country's industrialization program. In other words, and we cannot imagine that Du Bois did not consider this, for the Soviet peasantry collectivization was state-sponsored serfdom, and the collectives themselves, state-owned estates. In the American idiom, we could liken it to a third slavery (in accordance with the "second serfdom" in eastern Europe beginning in the sixteenth and seventeenth centuries, as a number of scholars have referred to it) and a return to a plantation system like that which Du Bois maintained bankrolled and supplied English, continental European, and North American industrialization. Of course, to have raised or admitted this, Du Bois would also have been

forced to address the apparent parallels between the capitalist and communist paths to industrialization. To say the least, such an admission would have been fatal to his vision of communism, given that the vast majority of Africans, Americans (in the hemispheric meaning of the term), and Asians lived by agriculture in the mid-twentieth century. Better to remain silent on this, Du Bois may have thought to himself, then to abandon the socialist alternative to capitalism. In any event, the benefits of socialism outweighed peasant sacrifices, he may have further reasoned, even if those sacrifices made socialist benefits possible.

59. "Socialism," in Weber, *Political Writings*, 272–303.

60. Ibid., 298; emphasis in original.

61. Weber, *Economy and Society*, 3:957.

62. Weber, "Socialism," 291–92; emphasis in original.

63. Ibid., 279.

64. Ibid., 299.

65. Weber, *Economy and Society*, 3:974.

66. Ibid., 985.

67. Ibid.; emphasis in original.

68. Weber, "Socialism," 293; emphasis in original.

69. *Economy and Society*, 3:989.

70. See Alfred A. Moss Jr., *The American Negro Academy* (Baton Rouge: Louisiana State University Press, 1981); Patricia Sullivan, *Lift Every Voice: The NAACP and the Making of the Civil Rights Movement* (New York: New Press, 2009). Gerald Horne notes that in the brief period of Du Bois's return to the NAACP, after his professorship at Atlanta University had been abruptly terminated in 1944, Du Bois agreed with many in the organization who "felt that too much power was invested in the office of the executive secretary and the Administration Committee that he controlled . . . and emphasized that more local autonomy and decentralization were needed along with less heavy-handed rule from the top." Gerald Horne, *Black and Red: W. E. B. Du Bois and the Afro-American Response to the Cold War, 1944–1963* (Albany: State University of New York Press, 1986), 44–45. Unfortunately, Du Bois resigned from the NAACP before he and others could attempt to implement these structural changes in the organization.

71. Gerald Horne used the term in noting the continuity in Du Bois's sociopolitical orientation, when he moved from liberal elitism to socialism: "His concept of a 'Talented Tenth' leading the Black community was altered to the point where it resembled a Leninist vanguard." Horne, *Black and Red*, 7. In light of the parallels between black American uplift and socialist practice, I am inclined to believe that one of the facets of Soviet society that appealed to

Du Bois was precisely the fact that it was led by intellectuals who had assumed the roles of counselors and supervisors of the working class.

72. W. E. B. Du Bois, *In Battle for Peace* (Milwood, NY: Kraus-Thomson, [1952] 1976), 44.

73. Ibid.

74. Du Bois made that declaration in his famous essay, "Criteria of Negro Art": "Thus all Art is propaganda and ever must be, despite the wailing of the purists. I stand in utter shamelessness and say that whatever art I have for writing has been used always for propaganda for gaining the right of black folk to love and enjoy. I do not care a damn for any art that is not used for propaganda. But I do care when propaganda is confined to one side while the other is stripped and silent." *Crisis* (October 1926), reprinted in *W. E. B. Du Bois: A Reader*, ed. David Levering Lewis (New York: Henry Holt, 1995), 514.

75. Du Bois, "Russia and America," 203, 231, 222, 227, 235, 233, 236.

76. See John Patrick Diggins, *The Proud Decades: America in Peace and War* (New York: W. W. Norton, 1988), 110–17.

77. Max Weber, "The Profession and Vocation of Politics," in Weber, *Political Writings*, 367.

78. Ibid., 310–11; emphasis in original.

79. Ibid., 361; emphasis in original.

80. Ibid., 331.

81. Ibid., 369.

82. Ibid., 360.

83. Ibid.

84. Ibid.

85. Ibid., 353; emphasis in original.

86. Max Weber, "Parliament and Government in Germany under a New Political Order," in Weber, *Political Writings*, 182; emphasis in original.

87. David Beetham, *Max Weber and the Theory of Modern Politics* (London: George Allen & Unwin, 1974), 235.

88. Weber, "Parliament and Government in Germany under a New Political Order," 222.

89. Weber, "The Profession and Vocation of Politics," 354.

90. Weber, "Parliament and Government in Germany under a New Political Order," 231, 230.

91. Ibid., 230.

92. Ibid., 213.

93. Ibid., 182.

94. Mommsen, *Max Weber and German Politics*, 395.

95. Du Bois, "The Present Condition of German Politics," 187.

FIVE   Unequal Treatment

1. Curiously, it took twenty-five years for an English translation of Mommsen's work to appear.

2. Herbert Aptheker, "Editor's Preface," in W. E. B. Du Bois, *The Autobiography of W. E. B. Du Bois* (New York: International Publishers, [1968] 2007), 5.

3. For the proceedings, see *Verhandlungen des 15. Deutschen Soziologentages: Max Weber und die Sociologie heute*, ed. Otto Stammer (Tübingen: Mohr Siebeck, 1965). An abridged English translation appeared as *Max Weber and Sociology Today*, ed. Otto Stammer (New York: Harper & Row, 1971). My later references to the conference are drawn from the English edition.

4. Given the vastness of the work on Weber, such a claim is necessarily reductionist and appears to be an attack on the aims and direction of the greater portion of that body of work. However, this is not at all my intention. Rather, it is to point out that by comparison with the scholarship on Du Bois, Weber's legacy has had the advantage of the first two categories, which do not exist in interpretations of Du Bois's life and work.

5. Talcott Parsons, "Author's Introduction," in the reprint of "Evaluation and Objectivity in Social Science: An Interpretation of Max Weber's Contributions," in Talcott Parsons, *Sociological Theory and Modern Society* (New York: Free Press, 1967), 79.

6. Ibid., 80.

7. Ibid.

8. Talcott Parsons, Introduction to Max Weber, *The Theory of Social and Economic Organization*, trans. and ed. Talcott Parsons (New York: Oxford University Press, 1947), 5.

9. Originally published in *Review of Politics* 8 (1942): 66–71 (pt. I), 155–72 (pt. II), this article has been reprinted in a number of anthologies. This reprint is from Talcott Parsons, *Politics and Social Structure* (New York: Free Press, 1969), 17, 113.

10. Talcott Parsons, "Discussion on Value Freedom and Objectivity," in Stammer, *Max Weber and Sociology Today*, 78.

11. Principally Otto Stammer, then former president of the German Sociological Association; Talcott Parsons, professor of sociology at Harvard University; Rene Konig, editor of the *Kolner Zeitschrift fur Soziologie*; and Theodor Adorno, then president of the German Sociological Association.

12. Mommsen maintained that Stammer and Parsons presumably chose Aron to "refute once and for all the theses" that he advanced in *Max Weber and German Politics*. Wolfgang J. Mommsen, "Max Weber in Modern Social

Thought," in *The Political and Social Theory of Max Weber: Collected Essays* (Chicago: University of Chicago Press, 1989), 192. Mommsen's essay is also a good survey of the secondary literature on Weber from the time of his death to the years just after the centennial conference. For background to the Heidelberg conference, see Uta Gerhardt, "Die Rolle der Remigranten auf dem Heidelberger Soziologentag 1964 und die Interpretation des Werkes Max Webers," in *Zwischen den Stuhlen? Remigranten und Remigration in der deutschen Medienoffentlichkeit der Nachkriegszeit,* ed. Claus-Dieter Krohn und Axel Schildt (Hamburg: Hans Christians Verlag, 2002), 216–43; and Guenther Roth, "Reminiscences of the Weber Centenary 1964, Its Prehistory and Aftermath: Lessons in Academic Politics," in *Max Weber Matters: Interweaving Past and Present,* ed. David Chalcraft, Fanon Howell, Marisol Lopez Menendez, and Hector Vera (Surrey: Ashgate, 2008).

13. Raymond Aron, *German Sociology,* trans. Mary and Thomas Bottomore (Glencoe, IL: Free Press, [1936, 1950] 1964), 88.

14. Raymond Aron, "Max Weber and Power-Politics," in Stammer, *Max Weber and Sociology Today,* 98.

15. Ibid., 95.

16. Ibid., 99.

17. Herbert Marcuse, "Industrialization and Capitalism," in Stammer, *Max Weber and Sociology Today,* 149; emphasis in original.

18. Ibid., 145.

19. See Mommsen's discussion of these criticisms of his study in *Max Weber and German Politics,* 415–47.

20. Benjamin Nelson, "Discussion on Industrialization and Capitalism," in Stammer, *Max Weber and Sociology Today,* 167.

21. Georges Friedman, "Discussion on Industrialization and Capitalism," in Stammer, *Max Weber and Sociology Today,* 175.

22. Raymond Aron, *Main Currents in Sociological Thought,* vol. 2: *Durkheim, Pareto, Weber,* trans. Richard Howard and Helen Weaver (New York: Basic Books, 1967), 247.

23. Eduard Baumgarten, "Discussion on Max Weber and Power-Politics," in Stammer, *Max Weber and Sociology Today,* 123.

24. Reinhard Bendix, "Discussion on Industrialization and Capitalism," in Stammer, *Max Weber and Sociology Today,* 157.

25. Nelson, "Discussion on Industrialization and Capitalism," 168.

26. Ibid., 171.

27. Wolfgang J. Mommsen, *Max Weber and German Politics, 1890–1920,* repr. ed., trans. Michael S. Steinberg (Chicago: University of Chicago Press, 1984), 410. Mommsen explains in a footnote to the second edition of the work

(and on which the English translation is based) that at the suggestion of Ernst Nolte he changed the last part of this excerpt from what he had written in the first edition to this: "to make the German people receptive to support of a leader, and to that extent to Adolf Hitler." *Max Weber and German Politics,* 410 n. 73.

28. Mommsen was sure to note, "[Weber] never lived to see that the plebiscitary-charismatic rule by a leader would take the form not of a powerful democracy but of a totalitarian, fascist dictatorship. There can be no doubt about his own attitude to this form of charismatic rule. A policy that served the lowest instincts of the masses and nationalist emotions would have been anathema to him. His theory of the ethic of responsibility, which demanded of politicians that they account rationally for their ultimate motives and all possible consequences of their actions, was diametrically opposed to the brutal intolerance of fascist rule." *Max Weber and German Politics,* 409–10.

29. A short list of those notable works whose authors draw a clear dividing line between Weber's scholarship and politics would include Talcott Parsons, *The Structure of Social Action* (Glencoe, IL: Free Press, [1937] 1949); Reinhard Bendix, *Max Weber: An Intellectual Portrait* (Garden City, NY: Doubleday, 1960); Raymond Aron, *Main Currents in Sociological Thought,* 2 vols. (New York: Free Press, 1965, 1967); Randall Collins, *Weberian Sociological Theory* (Cambridge: Cambridge University Press, 1986); Wilhelm Hennis, *La problematique de Max Weber* (Paris: Presses Universitaires de France, 1987); Dirk Kasler, *Max Weber: An Introduction to His Life and Work,* trans. Philippa Hurd (Chicago: University of Chicago Press, 1988); Lawrence A. Scaff, *Fleeing the Iron Cage: Culture, Politics, and Modernity in the Thought of Max Weber* (Berkeley: University of California Press, 1989); Wolfgang Schlucter, *Rationalism, Religion, and Domination: A Weberian Perspective,* trans. Neil Solomon (Berkeley: University of California Press, 1989); John Patrick Diggins, *Max Weber: Politics and the Spirit of Tragedy* (New York: Basic Books, 1996); Richard Swedberg, *Max Weber and the Idea of Economic Sociology* (Princeton, NJ: Princeton University Press, 1998); Michael Sukale, *Max Weber—Leidenschaft und Disziplin: Leben, Werk, Zeitgenossen* (Tübingen: Mohr Siebeck, 2002); and Fritz Ringer, *Max Weber: An Intellectual Biography* (Chicago: University of Chicago Press, 2004). Of a monograph-length Marxist critique of Weber, I know of only Kieran Allen's, *Max Weber: A Critical Introduction* (London: Pluto Press, 2004). Otherwise, there is the brief chapter that Georg Lukacs devoted to Weber in his *Destruction of Reason* (Atlantic Highlands, NJ: Humanities Press, [1957] 1981). It should also be noted that the authors of studies of Weber's views on specific ethnic populations have also highlighted the overlap of his scholarship and politics. Noteworthy among these is Gary A. Abraham's *Max Weber and*

the Jewish Question: A Study of the Social Outlook of His Sociology (Urbana: University of Illinois Press, 1992).

30. Du Bois, *The Philadelphia Negro*, 3.

31. Du Bois, *Black Reconstruction in America*, 722.

32. Ibid.

33. Francis L. Broderick, *W. E. B. Du Bois: Negro Leader in a Time of Crisis* (Stanford, CA: Stanford University Press, 1959); Elliott M. Rudwick, *W. E. B. Du Bois: Propagandist of the Negro Protest* (Philadelphia: University of Pennsylvania Press, 1960).

34. Rudwick, *W. E. B. Du Bois*, 165.

35. Broderick, *W. E. B. Du Bois*, 227.

36. John Henrik Clarke, Esther Jackson, Ernest Kaiser, and J. H. O'Dell, eds., *Black Titan: W. E. B. Du Bois* (Boston: Beacon Press, 1970).

37. Henry Lee Moon, ed., *The Emerging Thought of W. E. B. Du Bois: Essays and Editorials from the Crisis* (New York: Simon & Schuster, 1970).

38. Shirley Graham Du Bois, *His Day Is Marching on: A Memoir of W. E. B. Du Bois* (Philadelphia: J. B. Lippincott, 1971).

39. Myron Weinberg, ed., *W. E. B. Du Bois: A Reader* (New York: Harper & Row, 1970)

40. Julius Lester, ed., *The Seventh Son: The Thought and Writings of W. E. B. Du Bois*, 2 vols. (New York: Random House, 1971).

41. Arnold Rampersad, *The Art and Imagination of W. E. B. Du Bois* (Cambridge, MA: Harvard University Press, 1976), 113.

42. Gerald Horne, *Black and Red: W. E. B. Du Bois and the Afro-American Response to the Cold War, 1944–1963* (Albany: State University of New York Press, 1986).

43. Manning Marable, *W. E. B. Du Bois: Black Radical Democrat* (Boston: Twayne Publishers, 1986), 215.

44. Adolph L. Reed Jr., *W. E. B. Du Bois and American Political Thought: Fabianism and the Color Line* (New York: Oxford University Press, 1997), 47.

45. Ibid., 54.

46. David Levering Lewis, *W. E. B. Du Bois: Biography of a Race, 1868–1919* (New York: Henry Holt, 1993); and *W. E. B. Du Bois: The Fight for Equality and the American Century, 1919–1963* (New York: Henry Holt, 2000).

47. Reiland Rabaka, *Against Epistemic Apartheid: W. E. B. Du Bois and the Disciplinary Decadence of Sociology* (Lanham, MD: Lexington Books, 2010); Aldon Morris, *The Scholar Denied: W. E. B. Du Bois and the Birth of Modern Sociology* (Berkeley: University of California Press, 2015) .

48. I have particularly in mind here Du Bois's *Black Folk: Then and Now*, to which he gave the subtitle, *An Essay in the History and Sociology of the Negro Race* (Milwood, NY: Kraus-Thomson, [1939] 1993.

INDEX

214

CHRISTOPHER A. MCAULEY is associate professor in the Department of Black Studies at the University of California, Santa Barbara. He is the author of *The Mind of Oliver C. Cox* (University of Notre Dame Press, 2004).

CPSIA information can be obtained
at www.ICGtesting.com
Printed in the USA
LVHW010040180723
752699LV00004B/101